ORGANIZATIONAL TRANSFORMATION

ORGANIZATIONAL TRANSFORMATION

How to Achieve It, One Person at a Time

BRUCE J. AVOLIO

STANFORD BUSINESS BOOKS
An Imprint of Stanford University Press
Stanford, California

Stanford University Press
Stanford, California

© 2018 by the Board of Trustees of the Leland Stanford Junior University. All rights reserved.

No part of this book may be reproduced or transmitted in any form or by any means, electronic or mechanical, including photocopying and recording, or in any information storage or retrieval system without the prior written permission of Stanford University Press.

Special discounts for bulk quantities of Stanford Business Books are available to corporations, professional associations, and other organizations. For details and discount information, contact the special sales department of Stanford University Press. Tel: (650) 725-0820, Fax: (650) 725-3457

Printed in the United States of America on acid-free, archival-quality paper

Library of Congress Cataloging-in-Publication Data

Names: Avolio, Bruce J., author.
Title: Organizational transformation : how to achieve it, one person at a time / Bruce J. Avolio.
Description: Stanford, California : Stanford Business Books, an imprint of Stanford University Press, 2018. | Includes bibliographical references and index.
Identifiers: LCCN 2017050479 (print) | LCCN 2017051763 (ebook) |
    ISBN 9781503605848 (electronic) | ISBN 9780804797931 (cloth : alk. paper)
Subjects: LCSH: Organizational change—Management.
Classification: LCC HD58.8 (ebook) | LCC HD58.8 .A93 2018 (print) | DDC 658.4/06—dc23
LC record available at https://lccn.loc.gov/2017050479

Typeset by Thompson Type in 10/13.5 Minion

Cover design by Tandem Creative

MY DEDICATION

Looking Back and Then Going Forward

A close friend and colleague of mine, Boas Shamir from the Hebrew University of Jerusalem, provided me with the inspiration for writing this book. As he has now passed from this life, he cannot say he didn't have this impact on me, which I know he would, so that remains in my sole discretion. When Boas passed away, I was asked by his colleagues at Hebrew University to speak at a conference (not a memorial as Boas requested) on Boas's lifework. For some time, I was unsure where to even start creating my presentation, so I sat down and organized by year every article and chapter that Boas had ever published. I then began to read and reflect on one article each morning, as an exercise in reflection and to help address my grief at the loss of a great friend and colleague. By the time I had finished all of his great works, it was blatantly obvious to me what I wanted to say at this conference. His body of work came back to the same core principle again and again, the idea that you understand, change, and develop people and the thing we call an organization, exactly *one self-concept at a time*. Everything he wrote about was tied to one's identities, and the "bucket" in which they are held called their self-concept. This epiphany that I shared with a large audience at Hebrew University was the inspiration for me to write this book on organizational transformation. Reading Boas's works, I realized one could never really change an organization, as that is just a label we use. In fact, one must change an organization one self-concept at a time. Consequently, I hope in writing this book that Boas continues to transform us all in terms of our thinking about what constitutes a better "organization," as he always did for me throughout our three decades of friendship.

Now dedicating forward, I want all individuals who take responsibility for changing our organizations to set as their goal to create the next best thing we call an organization, which will be far better than the ones I grew up with in my life and career. I want my daughters Casey and Sydney, and my son Jake, to engage in organizations over their respective life spans that treat them like owners and certainly organizations that encourage them to bring their brains to work every day. Finally, without the co-ownership I have had with my wife Beth over the last forty years, there would be no book, there would be no career of experiences to reflect on, and, most important, there would be no Casey, Jake, and Sydney to dedicate this book to going forward.

CONTENTS

ACKNOWLEDGMENTS

I have always been a firm believer that there is no such thing as a singly authored article or book. Why do I think that? So many people's ideas and efforts contribute to what we each write and produce that to think of any article or book as being the sole work of one person in my view is simply incorrect. Many people deserve credit for what is contained in these pages, and yet, I do believe that I am singularly responsible for its contents.

I will list in alphabetical order those I would like to acknowledge for their support, feedback and their lending a hand to this effort:

Margo Beth Fleming
Cristiano Guarana
Tom Kolditz
Ben Minicucci
Mike Manning
Lily Moriarity
Chelley Patterson
Peggy Willingham
Yong-Hsiang Frank Cheng

ORGANIZATIONAL TRANSFORMATION

PREAMBLE

If everyone is moving together, then success takes care of itself.
Henry Ford

It is hard to pick up a book, watch a Ted lecture, read a journal or magazine, and not hear someone emphasizing the importance of change: change or die; change or become irrelevant; change or lose your edge; change or change will pass you by—change, just change! We suspect that throughout human history, there has always been a message regarding the need to change as signified by the evolution of humankind, even though today it seems to be coming at all of us at a much faster pace.

For example, there were multiple human species on Earth for thousands if not millions of years, but for some reason *homo sapiens* survived, while others, such as the Neanderthals, disappeared from Earth.[1] Did the Incas need to change in the face of Spanish colonization? Did IBM need to change from a weights and measurement to a computer, technology, and now high-end services/consulting organization? Did Blockbuster need to change when video streaming came on the scene, representing a disruptive technology to their industry? How will health care organizations need to change with the advent of the Clustered Regularly Interspaced Short Palindromic Repeat, or CRISPR, which gives us the ability to reliably modify human genetics? Did the nascent U.S. government anticipate the need to change (given that there is the critical mechanism for using amendments included in its Constitution)? What signals necessitate change?

All of the preceding examples point to a very fundamental question: How do we actually know when we have to change? For example, is it really time to change the way we educate our children in primary, secondary, and high schools and college to remain competitive in global markets? How about how health care science and delivery will have to change in the future to foster patient-centered care and fostering healthy communities? Did we need to change after the first Russian cosmonaut was shot into space, considering that we had just opened the door a lot wider to being an interplanetary species? How did the great migrations and diaspora signal changes in terms of the cultural complexion of our world, including who won and lost wars, where great discoveries were made and missed? Did you ever wonder whether the Greeks or the Romans missed a specific window for change? How about the Ottoman Empire? Did Boeing really have to change after World War I ended, when all of its government contracts were canceled? In other words, did they really need to make wooden furniture to survive?

We must recognize that the signals for change and then change itself will occur either by choice, by necessity, by accident, or because we failed to do anything about changing. The question we can address in this book together is not necessarily about whether change is or is not occurring; it is, always has been, and always will be a force in shaping our very adaptations and existence. What we want to focus on in this book is examining how people and organizations recognize the signals for change and then organize themselves to successfully navigate through that change process to the next time change is needed.[2]

Our focus on organizing individuals to change reveals a core organizing principle that every scientist considers when defining his or her science, concepts, and methods of measurement—called the *unit of analysis*. The unit of analysis determines the lens through which we operationalize what we are attempting to study, describe, and understand. If you want to understand human genetics, an important unit of analysis is DNA. If you want to understand competition for limited resources, your unit of analysis will be at least two competing individuals. If you want to understand how a recession occurs, you focus on a nation's gross domestic product (GDP), interest rates, unemployment, individual purchasing patterns—or all of these levels of analysis are important.

In our case, the organizing principle for examining how organizations change in terms of our unit of the analysis is *each individual's self-concept*. Each individual's self-concept contains a narrative, which constitutes the story the individual has created concerning his or her relationships to entities like organizations, teams, movements, nations, professions, families, and schools.[3] This narrative comes to represent how we make sense of our world, as well as the challenges we face in changing ourselves and then our organization. To change, we need to help each person revise his or her narrative in line with how we want that individual to make sense of the emerging and impending organization. You simply cannot change an organization without changing the narrative associated with what it means to be a member of that organization. The term *organizational change* is actually oxymoronic in that each individual changes, and it is the combination of those changes that are what we then label organizational change. Organizational change must be represented in the minds of each individual and part of that person's evolving self-concept as well as identity.

We can refer to our narrative or story as being part of what constitutes our self-identity. Keep in mind that it is an open-ended story—one in which we as leaders, for example, can add new chapters to our story throughout life, through moments that matter. The portion of our overall identity that is active at any one time is called our "working self-concept." Our identity at any one point in time is not something we can recall, so we have our working or operating self-concept, which represents the knowledge we have about our self that we can access at any point in time, and it defines in that period of time, how we come across to others in a particular role or situation.[4]

Although there has certainly been a lot of good thinking that has gone into examining how we prepare to *change individuals to change something*, the unique contribution of this book is our focus on transforming the individual's self-concept as the key unit of analysis for change. We will use the self-concept as the mechanism that contains each individual's view or narrative of what is essential to his or her understanding of how "my organization" must change. The good news is that our self-concepts are elastic and can be stretched to incorporate what the change means for us. Consequently, when we set out to change an organization, we are essentially trying to change how the individual identifies and describes what constitutes his or her relationship to that organization.[5] The first step in exploring the process of change then is to understand what Snow and Anderson suggested in terms of their discussion regarding the development of the self-concept. This step involves understanding the "range of activities that individuals engage in to create, present and sustain personal identities, that are congruent with and supportive of the self-concept" (p. 1348).[6] The question you might consider is, which are the activities your organizational leaders should engage you in to change the organization? What activities should you choose to engage in to transform?

Consider that each individual in an organization authors his or her own narrative with input and advice from others—friends, union leaders, corporate leaders, peers, the external market, pundits, gurus, and a whole host of other characters. And to change, each employee's narrative and self-concept needs to be expanded by adding new information because the new information helps explain to each employee what constitutes "my organization" and how "my organization" is changing. It is the shift in narrative that is essential to sustaining organizational change and transformation. Why? The goal of any organizational change is to adjust, alter, or fundamentally transform how an organization organizes its people's work to accomplish its mission. This requires some change in the narrative or script that will guide how peoples' routines, responsibilities, and roles are organized. Although the change in script must occur at the individual unit of analysis, the employees and their collective narrative or story must also be aligned to sustain the complete spectrum of changes and transformation to call it organizational change.

A ROADMAP FOR NAVIGATING THROUGH ORGANIZATIONAL CHANGE

Each of the chapters in this book represents my narrative for how organizational change and transformation unfolds. Chapter 1 emphasizes the importance of changing each individual's narrative to be in alignment with the change the organization is moving toward. I start each chapter with a change readiness item from a survey we have developed that measures different aspects of what is the readiness of individuals and ultimately the organization to change and transform.

Chapter 2 focuses on what we call the first principle of change. In this chapter, we build on our preamble by discussing how the self-concept of each organizational member will eventually have to change for us to label that change indeed has occurred.

Chapter 3 provides a quick overview of the four states that comprise organizational change. States are not steps or stages but rather how we view where we are at that point in time, such as being in a very positive or pessimistic state about the future.

Chapter 4 introduces the idea of what constitutes the drivers of change as we move through the four states. The first driver of change is that we must be able to identify the signals that motivate us to consider changing our narrative and self-concept. Throughout human history, many if not most national or organizational leaders have missed identifying key signals in their markets, and without such recognition there is no motivation to change your narrative, so someone else will eventually do so, which has been a significant part of our evolution on this planet.

Chapter 5 moves you into the second state of change, which is more obvious than the first state in that you are initiating activities to foster the change in your organization. You might be "advertising" the need to change based on the signals identified, and you might also be entering into what you need to change in terms of routines, goals, processes, skills, and engagements.

Chapter 6 examines perhaps the most tenuous state, which is purposely labeled the Impending State. By impending, we mean that the change in the individual and collective self-concept is not yet firmly grounded, nor is the change in routines, goals, processes, skills, and engagements. In this state, there is often some slipping backward before moving forward occurs, or what researchers might call iterative change. In this state, people do not fully understand what the change means for them and are still working on making sense of it, as they experiment with different initiatives.

Chapter 7 represents the fourth state of change, which is called the Institutionalizing State of change. In effect, you now understand what the change means for you, and you also recognize as part of your narrative and self-concept how you do things differently and why. In this state, the organization can be labeled "changed," in that a new employee's narrative would represent only the way the "new" organization functions, as the old organization and its narrative are no longer evident to that employee.

Chapter 8 presents two different examples of organizations going through each of the four respective states. At this point, you might choose which example to read based on how well it relates to your own organization, as each case provides a similar narrative in different contexts about how organizations ultimately traverse change.

Chapter 9 closes off the discussion of narratives, self-concepts, identities, and change to bring together and make sense of the states of change you have reviewed in the previous chapters.

Chapter 10 offers you resources, tools, and guidance that could be helpful to your own change initiatives and those of your organization.

RESEARCH LINK: A DEEPER DIVE

Throughout this book, I will make a few important connections at the end of each chapter to relevant research that supports the main ideas that I've shared with you. In this preamble, the fundamental research link is to what constitutes each of our organizational identities and how that identity informs organizational change. Organizational identity represents how an individual creates, presents, and then sustains a personal identity that is in line with their self-concept.[7] To change an organization, our self-narratives comprising our self-concepts represent a transitional bridge spanning the gaps that evolve between new roles emerging as a consequence of change and the old ones, as we move to claim new aspects of our identities being promoted and granted by our organization. Our organizational identity encapsulates what we consider to be the necessary routines, skills, and decision-making processes that constitute how we do what we are supposed to do in "my organization." When organizations change what we do, it always involves some degree of change in each member's narrative, and the more significant the change, the more disruptive it is to our narrative. This premise is perhaps best captured in the quote by Henry David Thoreau (1854) from his classic book *Walden Pond*: "Things do not change, we change."

1   BUILDING THE NARRATIVE

I believe in the value of this change.

Oftentimes, we find that many people at the start, during, and even toward the end of a campaign for change in their organization will not say they believe in the changes being promoted by their leaders. The quote above came from an employee who was part of an organization that had successfully institutionalized a transformation in the way her organization did business. I will explore in this and subsequent chapters how such statements can be obtained from one's workforce and how important they are to sustain major changes and transformation that can benefit the future viability of an organization.

We encourage you to stop and consider what fundamentally changes when an organization transforms from one way of existing to something different or a more extreme transformation. Stop. Because we are only a few sentences into the first chapter of this book, let's consider if that is the right starting point for examining organizational transformation. Let's try another way of thinking about sustainable organizational transformation. First, assume that if an organization could speak, it might say to its founders, customers, or competitors, "I am not the organization you knew in the past; how I think, act, and perform is all fundamentally different and by different I mean _____" (now you can fill in the blank).

According to a 2008 survey[1] of 3,199 executives from a wide range of industries and regions worldwide, the objectives of transformational change attempts they'd witnessed and that could be reflected in the preceding fill-in-the-blank could include the following radical shifts (and analogs to personal transformations we experience in terms of our human existence):

- I now produce consistently great performance (36 percent) . . . like a person making the varsity team, graduating cum laude, or getting a well-deserved promotion.
- I'm no longer spending like crazy and have reduced costs (15 percent) . . . like a person trimming down after being overweight or figuring out how to be thrifty to afford her or his dream home.
- I have turned around a crisis situation; I'm a survivor (12 percent) . . . like a person coming back stronger or wiser after a severe illness or other personal tragedy.
- I have finished my merger and have integrated entities (12 percent) . . . like a person reporting a happy marriage long after the honeymoon is over.

Other transformation attempts in the survey might be reported by a personified organization as:

- I have expanded geographically; I'm global! (9 percent)
- I've been divested and am living successfully as a spin-off. Or I have divested a part of myself and am moving on with a more focused portfolio of personal human assets. (4 percent)
- I'm now privately owned. Or I've gone public! (2 percent)

Seven percent of the 2008 survey respondents were in an "other" category where we can imagine the need to adapt to radical shifts to an organization's existence—like implementation of large-scale technology or equipment changes, moving headquarters, or rapid growth.

An organization could speak in a first-person voice, similar to what we have portrayed in the preceding list, when it has only one employee. Where it gets difficult or decidedly more complex to personify the perspective of the organization is where there are two, or 20, or 200,000 employees, each of whom may think differently about what has or has not changed in terms of a narrative and how he or she might describe that change first to him- or herself and then to others. Rarely do we find even a few voices within the same organization saying the same thing about how an organization is transforming or has transformed in the early states of change, especially in unsuccessful change efforts. This is frequently the case when the organization is just entering into, is in the midst of, and even is years into the unfolding change process.

Examining the individual experiences to explain how successful change happens in complex organizational transformations is our focus and unique contribution to your change tool kit. As suggested in the preamble, you need to decide and then examine the *unit of analysis* to go beyond conventional change management methods and models. For example, in macroeconomics the unit of analysis is the nation's economy. The unit of analysis in business and financial markets is typically the firm. The unit of analysis in sociology is the group. In psychology, the starting point for the unit of analysis is oftentimes the individual. We are suggesting that leaders who achieve successful transformational organizational change will need to be flexible when examining initially and over the course of change the different units of analysis needed to foster and sustain a transformation. We recommend, as a starting point, that you zoom in and use the individual unit of analysis to address large-scale transformational change in your organization, in that such change is a function of individual-scale personal transformation in each organizational member.

Consequently, if our unit of analysis is the individual, then let's start by examining how an individual changes. Do you know anyone who has fundamentally changed or transformed his or her life—a friend, a family member, a co-worker, a famous figure, or perhaps yourself?[2] The person I have in mind is a leader whom I knew in my client network. Bill was an engineer who focused on numbers and technical systems as his basic principles for leading his organization. He was also a total workaholic, a hard-driving authoritarian leader who did not broker dissent. On one pivotal day, he had a massive heart attack at work and was rushed to the hospital. He survived and returned to work months later—a different and, in his words, "transformed" man.

Reflecting back on this pivotal time in his career years later, Bill described himself as being completely changed. How? You might imagine that Bill cut back on salt in his diet or exercised more—and you might be right. But Bill also thought very differently about his work relationships. He now really valued and listened to other points of view, encouraging not challenging or fearing dissenting views. He respected different opinions in a new and deeper way. He endorsed more of a work–life balance. He discovered that he enjoyed the people he worked with and would often say he really loved his employees and, in turn, how they loved him, rather than being fearful. We might then ask, did Bill fundamentally change, and was he a different man? Bill might fill in the blank as follows: "I am not the man you knew in the past; how I think, act, and perform is all fundamentally different, and by different I mean . . . What is important to me has changed, how I view myself has changed, how I interact with others and value them has changed, how they view themselves has changed, and what they want to accomplish has changed." Notice how this change in the leader's narrative cascades to other individual's narratives,

In the case of sustainable and planned organizational change, we see this sort of cascading of self-to-other change in every employee's narrative and self-concept. It is also worth noting in terms of what you can expect from this book; I am focusing on planned organizational change, meaning a choice the organizational leaders have made to do something different.

We see in Bill's example a person whose core self-concept changed, as this can be seen as an exemplar for organizational transformation. The self-concept is the vessel that contains the narrative we all create to describe ourselves, to "tell us" who we are to ourselves and to others. We might refer to this type of transformation as "breaking good" versus "breaking bad,"[3] in the sense that this leader went from someone who cared little about others who work for and with him to someone who was completely focused on the goodwill of his employees, while still striving to be a top performer.[4] Bill learned he didn't need to beat people down to be successful, but rather he could build people up instead. Moving to this new narrative, Bill created sustainable performance improvements in his organization over a period of years. It is this personal narrative in each individual within the organization that must change for an organization to create a sustainable transformation. Transformation sticks from the inside out—one person at a time.

Recall that my goal for this book is to demonstrate to you that the key unit of analysis for fully understanding organizational transformation is represented by how each individual in the organization organizes and adapts his or her self-concept in alignment with the organizational objectives for transformation. Prescriptive changes associated with an organizational transformation must align with a revision in the individual self-concepts and, by extension, the collective self-concepts of all employees in the organization.[5] You might be wondering why everyone's self-concept has to change to successfully transform an organization. Why is the self-concept the critical unit of analysis?

In our experience and research, it is not uncommon for organizational leaders to work very hard to get their employees to view the organization to which they belong as part of how they define themselves, who they are, or their self-concept and identity.[6] In combination, these perceptions ultimately influence how they choose to perform in that people who have a stronger sense of identity that is aligned with their organization will generally work harder for that organization to succeed and will be committed to staying the course.[7]

The same is true for every profession in that a profession is represented in an individual member's self-concept in terms of the way he or she defines being "a professional." For example, what does it mean to be a professional physician or nurse? What does it mean to be a marine, a minister, a lawyer, an accountant, or a teacher? Professions are defined by their mission, guiding principles, their boundaries of knowledge and practice, usually their core values, how you are selected in or out of the profession, and what you must do to maintain your professional status. In turn, a professional's self-concept is aligned with the beliefs of the profession. In combination, all of these facets become part of the individual's narrative script that he or she develops to become a professional, again from the inside out adhering to agreed-upon values, principles, and standards. We might then ask, what has to happen if a person's profession undergoes a fundamental shift? Must there be a corresponding fundamental shift in the self-concept of members of that profession? The answer is decidedly a yes.

Similar to professions, organizations are also defined by their missions, values, guiding principles, selection of members, and what is required when it is necessary to change or transform the organization. In health care today, organizations are being asked to extend their mandate and mission from focusing on healing to promoting healthy communities to avoid illnesses. Reflecting on this shift, and working with many health care practitioners, one knows that it represents a significant and transformative shift from dealing with health issues after the fact to the prevention of issues before they become a heartbreaking and expensive problem.[8] At the core of this narrative, this is a transformative shift in helping people who are sick to helping people stay healthy. Consider how this shift changes the physician's guiding ethos, "First do no harm to my patient." It seems to set the bar higher, especially in terms of focusing on prevention. What does that mean for the self-concept of all health care providers? We argue that to successfully transform health care organizations, for them to thrive and survive in their current and future reality, will require a significant change in the self-concept of organizational members and the profession that represent those members.[9]

Consider that one day your organizational leaders may realize the need to dramatically change and transform your organization. Will you be able to shift your own self-concept? Will you be able to address this at the level of the employee self-concept? What would that look like? At Microsoft, the current CEO, Satya Nadella, is trying to do just that. He is attempting to motivate his employees to consider a fundamentally different Microsoft by focusing on each employee's growth mind-set and to create a more collaborative culture.[10] Individuals who possess a growth mind-set (or learning orientation) believe their talents can be developed through hard work, trial and error, feedback from others, and other learning strategies at their disposal. These individuals are more likely to openly admit their talents are a work in progress and then to try something at which they might not initially succeed to experiment with and change. They are also more likely to engage with others to learn from them and collaborate.

In contrast, individuals who possess a fixed mind-set (or performance orientation) believe their talents are innate gifts that are set for life. These individuals are more likely to conceal gaps among their talents, experiences, and challenges, focusing on proving to others their competence by working only in their existing comfort zones. An organizational culture that nurtures a growth mind-set in employees will be notably different from one that fosters a fixed mind-set. A growth mind-set culture in each individual will exhibit a higher willingness in those individuals to explore and fail, whereas in a fixed mind-set culture taking such risks is not wired into the individual or collective self-concept.

Nadella's ability to successfully transform Microsoft is fundamentally tied to how each employee views him- or herself and how each has to personally change— from the inside out. What if everyone in Microsoft did have a growth mind-set— either through employee selection or development? If that were achieved, then the collective self-concept would transform Microsoft into a very different organization, one that is characterized by audacious experimentation, insatiable curiosity, and a culture driving toward relentless levels of innovation and collaboration, rather than one that has been known in the past for its stack-ranked performance system and "infamous for its toxic corporate culture, where individuals use politics to advance and groups are always fighting one another."[11]

Contrast Microsoft with another organizational icon of the Pacific Northwest— Alaska Airlines. Soon after the turn of the new millennium, Alaska Airlines was in deep financial trouble and on the brink of going bankrupt. All of the U.S. airlines and the travel industry writ large were suffering in the wake of September 11, 2001. Labor costs and fuel costs were adding to the roller-coaster ride being experienced by these airlines. During this time, the senior leadership realized that, although Alaska employees were unfailingly nice, they were not by any stretch efficient, and the reliability of its operations was in serious trouble.

Founded in 1932, Alaska had enjoyed a long history marked by unflappable passenger loyalty. By 2005, however, their formerly most loyal customers were opting to fly with other competitor airlines. Although they would still say, "We love you, Alaska," in regards to staff and their memories of the past, they were fed up with delays at the gate and their luggage not appearing at baggage claim. Certainly, being nice was ingrained in the self-concepts of the Alaska Airlines employees. Being efficient, reliable, cost effective, and lean were not even hinted at in their narratives back in 2005.

By 2008, Alaska Airlines had risen to be ranked highest in airline customer satisfaction in the J. D. Power North America Airline Satisfaction Study among traditional carriers—and they have continued to hit these high marks for the last nine years. In 2010, to understand the transformational turnaround they had demonstrated in what many would consider record time, we interviewed close to forty executives and directors in Alaska Airlines and reviewed a wide range of publicly available information including articles, blogs, and airline performance data. We have kept a close eye on how this transformation has been sustained in ensuing years and will now share what we learned from this and similar investigations about the key role of the employee self-concept in achieving this amazing organizational transformation.

Alaska Airlines executives were certainly aware of the political, economic, social, and technological (or PEST) factors of the external macroenvironment that were shifting their skyline. They set out to identify a laundry list of initiatives to enact in response to what they considered threats to their survival. However, what transformed the firm was the stunning realization that the shared self-concept of being an employee of Alaska Airlines meant being "nice," which was now running operational efficiency into the ground. Being nice was so central to the shared collective identity of members of this organization that it could not be abandoned as part of the ongoing organizational transformation. Instead, the meaning of "nice" in the minds, self-concepts, and narratives of employees from the runway to the boardroom had to be redefined.

As part of the change process, being "nice" was redefined in the new narrative in a way that protected the employees' collective self-worth while also accommodating the mandates of the strategic transformation that required radically changing operational procedures that didn't initially feel so "nice." For instance, under the old definition of nice, it was acceptable to delay a flight to wait for newlyweds who were running late from their wedding to board the plane for their honeymoon. Legendary stories that revealed defining narratives for Alaska about ways in which the ticketing, gate agents, and crew were "nice" to passengers had to be reexamined and reframed. A new set of nice behaviors had to be proposed and adopted to integrate them with efficiency and effectiveness. The "new nice" norms included pulling away from the gate on time, so that all passengers on board got to their destinations as expected—doing the least harm to the most people. Of course, Alaska agents would arrange as best they could for late-arriving newlyweds to take a later flight. This meant thinking about nice differently—not abandoning nice as a core part of the airline's collective self-concept. Changing the narrative allowed them to "break better" and become a more reliable organization.

Over the course of several very challenging and intentional years of change, Alaska Airlines engineered a dramatic turnaround in operating efficiency, which can be sourced to astutely identifying the crux of the collective self-concept that needed to be addressed.[12] They then gently, but relentlessly, reworked the self-concept through numerous town hall meetings, online "water cooler" discussions on the company intranet, and face-to-face interactions between the top executive leadership and *every single employee*. The employees became passionate about optimizing this organization's performance and results while retaining and reshaping their niceness. In fact, this may be one of the most successful organizational transformations in the last fifty years, and one perhaps you've never heard of before.

In the process of changing, Alaska Airlines and its employees expanded their collective self-concept to include the idea of operational literacy as a means to being faster, better—and "nicer." The self-concepts of employees became more complex in terms of efficiency, as well as generative, to enable this organization to incorporate a new way of *doing things around here*, to turn a failing enterprise into one of the most profitable and highly regarded U.S. carriers year after year. As of this writing, they are now the fifth-largest airline in the United States with the recent acquisition of Virgin America.

In this book, we will consider the change discussed in the previous pages as being *fundamental* or *transformational* versus representing *incremental* change. We center our focus on how employees change the way they view themselves and their roles and how those narratives change to become aligned with the planned or prescribed transformations in the organization. Accidental events (like the heart attack Bill survived that reframed his self-concept and leadership) certainly will happen in organizations and can create a pivot, which becomes part of the "story" of organizational transformation that we will share in this book. Yet we primarily focus on what you can intentionally control to promote successful and planned organizational change.[13]

Profound radical change occurs when organizational members understand why they should or need to change and what this means in the context of defining themselves and their individual and collective identities. Profound and radical change occurs when there is alignment with what the organization needs to do in the future to organize to effectively, efficiently, and consistently execute its vision, culture, mission, goals, and processes. Consequently, the focus of this book can be stated very simply: *This is a book about how each individual's self-view or concept changes and how those changes align with a new narrative and, in turn, organizational change and transformation.*

To be clear, my principle goal is to help each reader navigate through the transformation process bringing into focus how you and others change your self-concepts in line with the changing narrative in your organization. To repeat, *you can't change an organization by starting with the organization as your unit of analysis*. Indeed, an organization is simply a convenient label we use to refer to a collection of people working on a common mission that strives to do things each day and be successful. To change an organization, you must change the self-concept of people who represent what it means when they say to themselves or others, "my organization."

Through each chapter, I will discuss the components of key states of change and the corresponding steps that are needed to successfully transform the self-concepts into the collective self-concept of an organization. At times, this discussion will no doubt appear sloppier than most books on organizational change, in that how people change will vary, even within the same individual over time, let alone across organizations. There is some legitimate messiness in change, so please suspend judgment until all of the arguments, examples, and narratives have been presented. However, I am confident that, by going through this step-by-step process, you will learn a finite set of truths about what triggers and sustains organizational change and transformation, starting with identifying the appropriate unit of analysis as a starting point—the individual self-concept. For most readers, this likely represents a new and different view of a time-worn topic.

HOW DID THIS BOOK AND ITS NARRATIVE EMERGE?

In my study of organizational change, I reviewed the primary literature on organizational change and transformation, including theories that are "deep in the weeds" through to the most practical books on the topic of organizational change.[14] My primary goal was to build on the prior body of knowledge and practice that identifies the fundamental principles that you need to learn to transform an organization. In that regard, I want to join the legion of prior authors who have grappled with answering the question, *how do organizations change*?

To be completely transparent, I had a major "aha!" experience when I came to realize that any significant transformation of an organization has to be fundamentally rooted in each individual in the firm. Similar to our approach to democratic elections, we need to assume that every vote for change matters. Running for election means that you have to understand who the voter is and what she or he wants to change, as well as what that voter wants to not change, to win an election. Also, your self-concept is what forms how you view who you are and who you need to become to change. Your self-concept contains your unique identities, which are ostensibly distinct from everyone else, except when we want you to be connected to something like a profession or an organization. Indeed, the ideal of many organizations is to have employees see themselves as being identified by the organization they belong to such as the following: I am a NASA engineer, I am an Amazonian, I am a Mayo Clinic provider, I am a Costco associate, I am a Valve game designer, and I am on the University of Washington faculty.[15]

A transformative change in an organization must ultimately change your self-concept regarding how you identify with your organization and what meaning that has for you relative to the multiple identities you house in your self-concept. For example, a woman who worked for AT&T for over three decades once said about her job and career that "I am AT&T." However, after the court ordered the breakup of this massive organization, she had a difficult time saying, "I guess I'm Lucent," adding, "whatever that means." When any organization goes through such an externally driven fundamental change, it invariably is linked to how each employee comes to describe who she is and why she is that way. To repeat, successful organizational transformations occur in the workforce, *one self-concept at a time.*

In addition to walking through four fundamental states (not stages) of change, this book also covers the type of leadership and ownership required to move through these states of change. Including the concepts of leadership and ownership helps us to understand and explain how we can build a reliable, repeatable practice of engaging with employees differently as the organization moves from one state of change to the next. Toward the end of each state, we will also detail the predominant leadership and ownership orientations that we have witnessed during planned organizational change.[16]

We begin the next chapter by further exploring why the self-concept is fundamentally important to initiating and sustaining organizational transformation. In subsequent chapters, we will break down the transformation process to provide a clear line of sight or arc of change on what you need to do to initiate, execute, and sustain fundamental change.

Some questions for you to reflect on as you move into the first principle of change:

- Consider an organization that you worked with that attempted to change, but whose approach did not affect the way you viewed yourself. What do you feel failed in your organization's efforts to change you and then itself?

- Look back to an earlier period in your life, perhaps before you started your career. Can you recall a time when you were trying to describe to someone what comprised the career you aspired to enter? How is the narrative you used then different than the one you use today to describe that career?

- Have you worked for a leader who fundamentally changed the way he or she saw him- or herself and what impact that had on the leadership style you observed, as well have experienced? What caused that leader to change his or her self-concept, and how did that impact the leadership style you observed?

- Most fundamentally, think about something you changed in terms of your behavior, and then consider how the narrative that guided that change also was transformed. This change can relate to any aspect of your life both in and out of work.

The type of statements that typically represent the awareness that change was imminent included the following:

Prototypical Comments in the Identifying State: A Transportation Company

- "We have a miserable reputation with our customers."
- "We had fallen to the bottom of the pack in on-time service; we had fallen to 20 out of 20."
- "Customers would say if you can't fix this in four months we are switching."

Protoypical Comments in the Identifying State: A Health Care Organization

- "It wasn't a specific event, although there were several big events that have occurred that now we look at as serious safety events. It was the confluence of events and the leadership."
- "The federal change in pay-for-performance has definitely been a driver."
- "Equally motivating is the expectation of our general public, our patients, and our consumers for transparency. There are websites, health grades; there are all kinds of places where you can go online and see what we're doing well and what we're not."

RESEARCH LINK: A DEEPER DIVE

As noted earlier, there are dramatic signals in the space of health care that are causing many professionals in our health care system to consider the need to change.

One such signal in the Canadian health care system indicated a need for physicians to change from the sole contributor model to being part of an integrated team model.[17] In the case of transformative change ongoing in the Canadian health care organizations, researchers showed that these organizations had to change the set of institutional logics that comprised the narratives and self-concepts of physicians. By examining microwork processes, the researchers were able to show that, by changing these processes, the organizational leaders could create challenges with the existing logic of how an individual's work gets done, which led to challenging the dominant logic associated with being a physician to move them from describing themselves as autonomous experts to valued members of a patient care team. By reembedding this new logic into the individual and collective self-concepts of physicians, the organizations demonstrated how challenging the dominant logic changes individuals and organizations.

2 FIRST PRINCIPLE:

CHANGING THE SELF-CONCEPT

The nature of my work has changed.

In this chapter, I will cover what I refer to as the *first principle* for organizational transformation. To prime you about this first principle, I'll use an example that represents a transformative change in an organization that has unfolded over the past three decades. Many readers will know of the Mayo Clinic and its outstanding brand in the market for health care research and service. The Mayo brothers and their father founded this clinic in Rochester, Minnesota, a century ago, based on the principle that the best health care is delivered collaboratively. However, we wonder if many of our readers will know of the Cleveland Clinic's story, as well as its less than stellar history.[1]

Back in the 1970s, the Cleveland Clinic was not on anyone's benchmark list of organizations to aspire to be like in health care. This clinic was considered subpar, unsafe, and not a leader in any aspect of health care. Over the last thirty years, the Cleveland Clinic for many health care providers has become an aspirational organization for changes they seek in their own health care organization. A nurse who worked for the Cleveland Clinic during its past and present said that she would never have recommended a family member or close friend to the clinic, that in her own words it was a "butcher shop." Now, thirty years later, this same nurse describes the Cleveland clinic as being one of the best cardiac care centers in the world. This same nurse went from disparagement and disdain to being a raving fan, proud to be part of this health care enterprise. We suspect a lot of self-concepts and narratives changed to produce what we now view as the Cleveland Clinic—same name or label, but fundamentally a different organization.

WHY A FIRST PRINCIPLE

The *first principle* idea comes from physics and represents what physicists strive for in their quest to understand "how things work" at their most rudimentary level. In physics, it is the most basic or foundational law, concept, or rule available to explain how the universe works or, applied to our universe, how fundamental change unfolds in organizations. Thus, *first principles* thinking involves the following: "a mode of inquiry that relentlessly pursues the foundations of a problem."[2]

This type of thinking is represented by one of the most iconic leaders in corporate America today, Elon Musk. With respect to first principles thinking, Musk stated,

> I think it's important to reason from first principles rather than by analogy. The normal way we conduct our lives is we reason by analogy. [With analogy] we are doing this because it's like something else that was done, or it is like what other people are doing. [With first principles] you boil things down to the most fundamental truths . . . and then reason up from there. (Elon Musk 2013)[3]

I have found that a lot of interesting literature on organizational change is guided by analogies, including one of the most frequently cited change models in the research literature, which describes three phases of change: *freezing-unfreezing-refreezing.*[4] I find the same use of analogies in other models whereby their authors focus on melting icebergs,[5] burning platforms,[6] and the rider-elephant-path.[7] Please understand, I also like metaphors and analogies as a means of communicating what change looks like, but I also suggest that reasoning by way of analogy can shortcut systematic inquiry and root cause analysis of change. Instead, by using *first principles* thinking, I am motivated to break problems down that are associated with explaining organizational change into their fundamental and most basic rules and components. This approach then allows us to ask formative questions about what needs to change and how that change originates, where, and its impact. Rest assured, I won't completely abandon rhetoric, but we will use it sparingly to model a more disciplined focus on explaining organizational change as clearly as possible, with the goal being that you can do it in your own organization, whether it's a team of two or 200,000.

You will see when you examine the four-state model that my goal was to plainly describe the end-to-end states of change between early identification and awareness where change becomes essential to one's narrative, to the institutionalization of the transformation based on what I have learned in terms of how change unfolds. To get there I have asked myself the following questions:

- Which signals raised an awareness of the need for change amid all of the noise for complacency or sticking to your norms?
- What is (was) actually going on and emerging in the proximal and distal organizational environment that signaled change, which you noticed?
- What drove or caused the change to be seen in the first place and by whom?
- What hindered how the change was interpreted and unfolded?
- How did the change alter the way you saw yourself and what you owned in terms of considering what constituted "my organization"?

My goal is to help you anticipate or engage with the change to fully understand the basic founding principles that explain how change occurs, rather than just thinking about analogs and abstractions that may suggest or reflect what is going on but don't clearly explain *why*—and, more important, *how* the change impacts each individual and then, ultimately, the larger collective of individuals we label "the organization."

Using first principles thinking, I have looked first at what actually changes and, using the terms I introduced in the preamble, defined the unit of analysis as being the individual's self-concept.

FIRST PRINCIPLE: YOU MUST CHANGE THE SELF-CONCEPT TO CHANGE WHAT YOU MEAN BY "MY ORGANIZATION"

The self-concept is the cognitive container in which we each hold our identities—images of who we believe we are and what we describe to others when asked, "tell me about yourself." And we all possess multiple identities in this cognitive container, such as parent, engineer, community organizer, Catholic, and so on.[8]

For example, we know that as we go through life we have certain identities that are quite stable, such as being a supporter of democratic values in countries like Sweden or the United States, yet we are still subject to change as life within and outside our organizational experiences changes. For instance, we might start out with an identity such as "I am a girl, a daughter, a sister, a student, a dancer, a Canadian, a Caucasian with a Norwegian last name and sense of heritage" or "I am a boy, a son, a brother, a paperboy, a New Zealander, a Caucasian with an Italian last name and a Jewish mother." As life goes along that identity changes or perhaps expands to include, "I am a spouse, a parent, a teacher, a scientist," and so on. All of these identities are contained in one's self-concept and narrative and *by design* or *serendipitously* will no doubt change over time, more or less for different individuals.

The self-concept is formed and developed over the course of our lives.[9] At the source of our self-concepts are the experiences we have with our followers, peers, leaders, culture, families, society, education, and so forth. For example, when people born in the United States describe what it means to be a U.S. citizen, they often describe that using terms such as having liberty, independence, and freedom. These are terms that are ingrained in the self-concepts of most U.S.-born citizens and those who settle here and become part of how we all view ourselves and in turn others in our country. We know these ideas are part of our self-concept; when they are violated, we seek to defend them in our arguments, debates, and courts. But individuals who come to the United States as adults from countries led by despots and dictators are often startled by how "chaotic" it is to live in the United States because they have formed a self-concept based on controls, compliance, and a prevention focus versus being able to exercise independence or liberty.[10]

People do change their self-concept as they become more immersed in a different way of doing things. We suspect you have experienced this sort of change in the way you view yourself, if you have traveled and spent time in a different national culture from your own. With such travel, one can quickly see how differently people behave in terms of work, leisure, family, and community, in contrast to one's own cultural experiences. It is reasonable to assume that the scripts for how people behave or should behave were written by very different authors, and that is largely true as one transforms over time.

The same is true for individuals who move from one organization to another and discover that some organizations are loosely structured, highly empowering, and open to trying new things, whereas others are characterized by being locked down, preserving the past, and making sure all of the rules are always followed—always. Try talking to individuals who have worked for these two very different organizations for their entire careers, and we suspect you will see a very different interpretation when asked, "Can you tell me a little about what you do at work?" These different interpretations by each individual are, in part, rooted in the individual's self-concept and work identity, and someone who comes in to change either of these organizations will quickly discover how ingrained these self-concepts and identities are in each individual.

THE SELF-CONCEPT'S ROLE IN CHANGE
AND TRANSFORMATION

By studying successful, unsuccessful, and somewhere in between transformations in organizations, I've learned that fundamental organizational change occurs when there is a change in the knowledge structures and scripts that people use to understand and explain their experiences with each other and with their customers and other stakeholders. Starting with leadership and extending over time throughout the organization's transformation, one or more very stable, centrally defining attributes (essentially, the organization's identity) gets redefined, and this opens up new possibilities, unlocks new behaviors, and redefines constraints into opportunities that have an impact on each individual's self-concept.[11]

To represent how this type of change occurs, let's consider an organization that produces very intricate chrome parts for large industrial manufacturers like Harley-Davidson. The founder's son and CEO of the company emphasized to his employees that they should behave just as owners do in this organization, and the culture that was created empowered and rewarded them to do the right thing for advancing their organization's mission.[12] The CEO encouraged his employees to "step up" if something wasn't working right in *their* business by giving awards for this kind of thinking. These "step up" awards were very common and often suggested by peers recognizing other peers.

For one award, a peer nominated a fellow worker for noticing that a visiting U.S. senator, who was walking across the manufacturing floor, had been twirling his safety glasses while making a point to the senior leadership team. Safety was the top priority for this workforce day in and day out, given the extremely dangerous conditions on the shop floor. The employee who received the award turned his machine off, walked over to the senator, and reminded him that he was in a safety zone, so he needed to wear his safety glasses to assure a safe visit to their facility. According to the CEO, who hadn't noticed the senator had removed his safety glasses on the tour, this type of ownership behavior and recognition of it by peers was very common among this workforce. If you listened to employees describing "my organization," you would hear them describe the ownership they assume for being safe, taking care of each other, and making safety an operating goal for their success. Employees expressed a great deal of confidence in having their own voice and being able to challenge others in any position, including their CEO, to follow the guiding principle for creating and sustaining a safe work environment. When new employees entered the organization, they quickly learned this narrative, and within more or less a couple of months into working there you heard them speak in the same way about "my organization." Here we see how the culture of an organization helps employees to make sense of how they are supposed to behave.

THE COLLECTIVE SELF-CONCEPT AND ORGANIZATIONAL NARRATIVE

How then can an organization made up of scores, hundreds, or thousands of individual self-concepts achieve a collective identity? In the Microsoft example, the CEO is attempting to shift employee's self-concept from an organization that worked to put a PC on every desk to an organization with a broader mission that continues to innovate beyond writing code for PCs to building new technologies, connecting individuals in fundamentally different ways to solve problems, and advancing the world we will engage in, such as through virtual or mixed reality technology.

The question I encourage you to consider now is: how can what we know about individual identity formation and change be applied to organizational identities and change? In 1985, Stuart Albert and David Whetten[13] proposed that, just as individuals have unique identities that include a stable self-concept, so do organizations have a collective identity. Individual self-concepts help each of us make sense of and navigate through our world. Similarly, collective identities in organizations are based on organizational members' shared experiences based on their consensus about what makes sense regarding how employees work in and for the organization. The organization's identity is different from its image, brand, or reputation—the impression that it hopes to make or actually makes on outsiders. Rather, it is a shared set of perceptions and beliefs among *insiders* with regard to the central, enduring, and distinctive attributes of an organization and what matters to "its workforce."[14] If you are going to change an organization, you must change these shared sets of perceptions—one individual at a time.

A good example of an organization with a strong emerging identity is Amazon. Amazon's founder, Jeff Bezos, works diligently to ingrain the now fourteen core principles of their business into every employee from orientation to evaluation. For example, one founding principle is called Day One, which means each and every day is like day one, so innovate! It is such an important principle that Bezos had two buildings named after it, Day One North and Day One South.[15]

Understanding how this shared organizational identity works and can be changed is at the very heart of the work covered in the remainder of this book. Consequently, for you to fully understand how organizational change actually works, we look to how the individual identity and self-concept are constructed, operate, and then ultimately are formed into a collective identity that characterizes the organizational identity.[16]

A few years back, I worked with a cable manufacturing facility that had previously been part of the AT&T organization. Since its founding in 1895, AT&T had gone through many transitions, including bankruptcy, acquisitions, and divestitures. In 1996, the AT&T Technologies business unit was divested and became Lucent Technologies. At one of its town hall meetings, following the third or fourth major change in as many years, senior leaders were describing the new ownership and asking for questions from the crowd. Ray, the CEO of this business division, knew almost every employee out of the 2,000 who worked in his facility, and knew one employee very well, who rose to her feet to speak at this company forum. The employee had started working at this facility when it was an AT&T plant roughly fifty years earlier. The woman's comments began with an expression of appreciation for Ray's description of what was going to happen with the company's new owners, including his transparent statement regarding the high probability they had to significantly downsize the workforce. She went on to express how she had lost a part of who she was through the ongoing change process:

> When I was a young woman, I could go into any place in this town, and if someone asked me what I did, I simply had to say, AT&T. That's it. That told them everything about who I was and what I did. My job was to do something amazing that connected people to people through technology—at that time, a phone. But today, I could spend an hour trying to describe my organization, and I still wouldn't convey what it is I do because I don't know anymore. Now, I am just biding my time until I get out or am let go.

Ray addressed the entire town hall audience asking how many felt the same as this woman felt. A thunderous response represented the embodiment of the collective identity crisis.

Many organizational leaders work to create a coherent identity and self-concept: "I am a Starbucks barista; I am a Doctor Without Borders; I am a Seattle Seahawks football player; I am a 'twelfth person' (Seahawks fan), I am a member of the Geek Squad or the Second City Improv Group." Many leaders work for years to build this collective identity and work hard at authentically wiring a core identity into the self-concepts of each of their employees with a vision of the organization's future. Then, one day, the company merges or is acquired; it changes its name with oftentimes an implicit expectation that a new identity must form in the employee's self-concept. Imagine two rival high schools merging and the outcome having just one identity—one mascot and one fight song. The challenge of merging two high schools is not all that different than two firms merging and their failure rates at trying to do so.[17]

Social psychologists studying the nature of the self-concept originally saw it as a singular thing—a person's sense of unique identity making one different from others. In the past twenty-five years, however, these self-concept theorists have realized that one's identity consists of multiple levels of self-concepts, including the individual level, and also two other levels that are critical in understanding how member identities can form into an organizational identity—these are relational and collective identities that comprise the self-concept.[18]

The self-concept is a label we use for those cognitive structures that include specific content, that is, rules, attitudes, and value judgments that are employed by the individual to make sense of his or her world, goals, and basic worth[19]— essentially containing all information related to the sense of self.[20] You might think about the individual, relational, and collective self-concepts as different files containing different types of information about the self that we can refer to as needed to help understand our self in different situations. This especially occurs when we are trying to figure out how a change conflicts with one of our central identities, that is, being a physician who heals sick people as compared to being a physician who promotes healthy communities.

The *individual-level* self-concept "folder" is where people define themselves in terms of being a separate, unique, and valuable entity based on the perceived similarities and differences compared to other individuals (see Figure 2.1). Here, behavior is driven by self-interest and preservation and promotion of self-worth. We use this information, in broad terms, to answer the question, "Who am I?"

Next, the *relational-level* self-concept "folder" is where people define themselves in terms of connections, interactions, and role relationships with valued others. Here, behavior is driven by the welfare of the valued others and one's self-worth, based on enacting the appropriate role behavior directed toward a valued other. We use this information when working one-on-one with another person to manage the interaction and of course relationship. This could also extend to thinking about "how to be" in small groups.

The relational identity script connects a person to other individuals who have certain signature characteristics with which the person wants to vicariously be associated and that enrich and complete the "who am I?" picture or narrative.

The *collective-level* self-concept "folder" is where people define themselves in terms of membership in social groups, including the organizations where they are employed and professions we used earlier. Here, behavior is driven by an

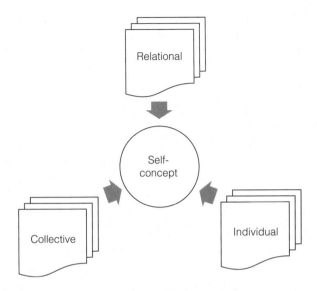

Figure 2.1   Figure of core identities.

orientation to sustain if not protect the welfare of these groups in which one belongs and from which one derives a sense of self-worth based on favorable intergroup comparisons. The degree of one's belonging includes the extent to which an individual internalizes the norms and attributes of a valued reference group and forms more of a "we–based" self-identity.

These collective self-concept data are what gets integrated across organizational members forming a sense of "we" as in "founder" or "owner" mentality among the employees of the facility supplying Harley-Davidson with chrome parts. It is also what gets threatened when organizations attempt transformation where employees are not properly readied for change, in that change may be viewed as an attack on their individual and collective self-concept.[21]

Returning to Microsoft, many in its Windows software division saw themselves as "the Microsoft," the ones who ensured a PC on every desk. As Microsoft's core businesses shifted into such things as "cloud computing" or building products like the surface tablet or Xbox, it was difficult for many in this division to change. Indeed, often other Microsoft workers would lament that the Windows folks would do anything to keep them from advancing, and we might assume that the changes being proposed threatened their narrative about what constituted their self-concept of "my organization."

Interestingly, what unfolded at Microsoft under Steve Ballmer's previous leadership and continues to unfold under Satya Nadella's mirrors what happened at IBM beginning in the 1980s and over a period of several decades. At IBM, the mainframe division was analogous to Microsoft's Windows division. These folks could not understand how a little box on someone's desk would alter computing as they knew it in their narratives. They fought vigorously to keep the PC from taking over, not recognizing that IBM had to change what it was doing to survive and reach being a 100 plus year old company. As we know from history, IBM changed, not only from a mainframe company to a PC company but to a global services company under Lou Gerstner's leadership. This may have contributed to Lou Gerstner's comment in 2016, long after he retired from IBM, stating, "In anything other than a protected industry, longevity is the capacity to change, not to stay with what you got."

Perhaps it is fortunate that the founder of IBM, Thomas Watson Sr., engrained in the self-concepts of IBM employees going back to the second decade of the last century that they should be *owners*, who actually *think* rather than just do their jobs. In line with this promotion on thinking, IBM remains one of the most thinking-based organizations on Earth, with year over year having the largest number of new discoveries, as represented by its total number of patents.

When collective identities are activated, the most prominent features of the self-concept become those that are shared with other members. If ideas, meanings, attitudes, and value judgments are shifting, for a time they may no longer be shared, and that will have a causal impact on one's collective identity. If the collective identity of one person in a 2,000 strong employee organization becomes "blurred," or no longer clear and resonant, the impact would be minimal. If all 2,000 identities, as in the AT&T, Lucent, and what became the Connectivity company after it was acquired, are becoming blurred, the impact on the organization's efforts to transform will be difficult if not disastrous. Why? You have to change the self-concepts of each employee, but you also have to realign those self-concepts around the emerging, new narrative and collective self-concept.[22] To do so requires a bit of elasticity in the self-concept and identity to stretch into a new area of understanding.[23]

As you can imagine, when organizational leaders embark on a transformation, this can trigger changes in all three levels of one's self-concept—the "Who am I?" as well as the "With whom am I connected and associated?" and, most obviously, the "Who are we and what do we do that's meaningful to me and my organization?" These changes can evoke emotional and sometimes irrational acts of self-protection to defend one's identity. An understanding of this fundamental truth—this is the first principle of organizational transformation.

A simple but profound example of the self-preservation capacity of the self-concept as a first principle occurred when an attempt was made to get rid of the green beret and have all U.S. Army Special Forces wear a black beret, just like the rest of the U.S. Army troops, with an admirable goal of denoting unanimity and cohesion across the various forces constituting the Army—being, as the motto stated back then, "An Army of One!"

This seemed like a rather simple change on the surface. Just change the color of your beret! What's the big deal? Well, the big deal was that the color of the beret was more than a fashion statement. Since 1954, when the first green caps were commissioned for the 10th and 77th Special Forces Groups to visually set them apart, that green beret had become a symbol of membership in a unique and very meaningful organization. The beret took on even more significance when, in 1961, JFK designated it as the exclusive headdress of the Army Special Forces and called the cap "a symbol of excellence, a badge of courage, a mark of distinction in the fight for freedom."[24] This collective identity, tied to an act of presidential leadership, makes the "green beret" a symbol of a shared, collective self-concept worth fighting to retain. It touches all three levels of identity, including who am I, with whom do I want to be associated, and who are "we" that together do something meaningful and important for our nation.

At a workshop with some health care providers, I used the example of the green beret in a discussion of what it means to be a psychological owner in terms of one's collective identity. A physician, who was also a U.S. Army veteran, came up during a break and said that the change in beret went to the very heart and soul of his identity. For him, it was not about the color of the beret but the connection to his community and people who, he said, died to save his life and to protect our freedoms. You don't just rip out a symbol of fundamental importance to a group's identity and expect people to go quietly forward with some new sense of who they are and what they represent. As in this individual's case and the case of organizational change, you must understand how the self-concept will change to appreciate what it takes to transform an organization's collective self-concept. In some cases, I realize that you might not know how it will change, so in those cases we suggest you experiment and do some tryouts first. We see this occurring when a leader develops a very different orientation toward his or her leadership when that leader has accumulated different experiences across domains of challenges he or she had not experienced that shift the leader's thinking about what constitutes effective leadership.[25]

All leaders, especially those at the top of organizations, need to analyze their individual, relational, and, ultimately, collective self-concepts first to determine what content, attitudes, and value judgments might need to be addressed by abandoning, redefining, or expanding these features of an organization's identity. They need to ask themselves the question, "How I am I going to write this narrative and exemplify the arc of change in a way that others will be motivated to try to make sense out of and then adopt?" This certainly will be more challenging for those leaders who are new to the organization or leaders acquiring another organization, who haven't yet assimilated the sense of who the employees are in terms of their identity. To accomplish this sort of change requires a lot of dialogue around the existing shared self-concept and the desired one being developed that will transform all three levels—individual, relational, and collective self-concepts—of organizational members. This dialogue will serve to uncover what is central to the collective identity of organizational members, such as Alaska being nice, and what is peripheral and perhaps easier to change.[26]

The idea that shared self-concepts based on organizational membership is as much an expression of the self as one's individual identity has been demonstrated in research on collective identities that feature prominently in people's spontaneous self-descriptions preceding references to the personal self.[27] Consequently, the commonly recognized "resistance to change" can be better understood and managed by simply recognizing the fundamental issue that transformational change is identity altering for every member of the organization.

Consider that the range of future possibilities that organizations can pursue in terms of transformation is, in part, linked to the self-concepts of each individual. Indeed, "the essence of transformational leadership is to develop a collective rather than individual identity in followers, which makes group-oriented visions meaningful."[28] Leaders have to therefore work on transforming their own self-concepts and identities and behave in alignment with those identities to move organizations forward toward transformative change. To the degree that there is a great deal of variance across one's workforce and its leadership, the challenges of changing an organization to a new way of "doing things" is that much more difficult, if not impossible. You can't wish away this variance or anchoring in identities. You must come to understand it, work with it, and mold people's self-concept into a new collective focus. The same is true with quality, if we didn't address variance, we would not have a chance of achieving high-quality processes and products.

Corresponding to first principles thinking, there are fundamental leadership processes that are present prior to, during, and following the change process. It suffices to say that leadership is, at its core, a positive social influence process, whereby some individual or collection of individuals motivates others to think and act in a way that achieves organizational goals. I say "positive" here, in that I am going to focus on positive styles of leadership that are associated with the different states of change. For example, I will discuss how instrumental and transactional leadership help to clarify goals and expectations as one enters into the change process. I will also address the importance of authentic leadership in terms of building sufficient goodwill to sustain changes when they hit some rough spots. I will discuss transformational leadership in terms of its focus on developing followers to lead and own the change process, along with inspiring them to do so for all of the right reasons and values. In terms of ownership, I will define it as a possession of sorts.[29] Ownership can be related to an object or something a bit less tangible. The discussion of ownership will include five levels: territorial, accountable, confident, identified or sense of belonging, and collective ethos.

We can say ownership means that it's mine *not* yours. From there, as instrumental leaders set expectations for change and goals, people become accountable for engaging in and contributing to the change process. Once they have shown they can succeed in changing, they start to feel confident that the change is reliable and will be repeatable. From there we see that individuals come to identify with the change in a way that alters their identity and self-concept. If everyone comes on board, the collective self-concept of the organization will drive the creation of a new narrative associated with change processes and the direction the organization intends to pursue into the future.[30]

In this chapter, I have invested a lot of time to ensure that we have anchored the *first principle* in your logic, regarding how to interpret organizational transformation. In Chapter 3, we will provide a high-level overview of the four states of organizational transformation and will then build on the first principle to understand how organizational transformation emerges and unfolds.

As I close this chapter, I ask you to reflect on the following questions because, as you see from the following Confucius quote, it is perhaps the best driver of personal change:

By *three* methods we may learn wisdom: *First*, by reflection, which is noblest; *Second*, by imitation, which is easiest; *Third* by experience, which is the bitterest.

- Do you currently work in a profession or an organization that is fundamentally linked to your self-concept and identity?
- If so, can you think about the time before you were a member and how you described yourself to someone you had just met?

- How was your description of yourself different than what you would now describe?

- Can you recall a time where your identity was challenged, if not threatened? If so, did you defend your identity or did you change it?

- Have you been a part of an organization that has tried to go through transformative change? If so, what did the leaders do to facilitate the change in individual, relational, and collective identities tied to the organization, and how did their efforts work?

- What aspects of leadership and ownership shaped the success of that change effort?

RESEARCH LINK: A DEEPER DIVE

There has been some research and discussion on the elasticity associated with our identities. And we perhaps observed the lack of elasticity, when discussing a very central identity for some U.S. Army soldiers in the example about the green beret. Nevertheless, to change one's identity requires that there is some degree of tension that motivates at least some negotiation of what does and does not constitute an extension to my identity. In other words, how far can I stretch myself, in terms of my definition of who I am and am not? In doing so, I have to consider: What do I gain and what do I lose when changing how I define myself? This internal dialogue with myself, perhaps triggered by my leader, will create some messiness until it gets resolved. Unfortunately, with many organizational changes, it just stays messy, and that frequently changes neither the individual nor the organization.[31]

3 THE FOUR-STATE MODEL

I have a significant influence over what happens in my organization.

My goal in this chapter is to provide you with a summary review of the change model that I will then use to examine how organizations organize themselves to trigger change, guide and support the corresponding shift in members' self-concepts, and ultimately institutionalize the desired changes in the form of a shared organizational self-concept. After I have provided you with a complete picture of this model, we will go into more detail on how each state unfolds in subsequent chapters.

HOW THE MODEL WAS BUILT

In tracking transformative changes in organizations that span many months, or more typically years, I and other authors have found distinct developmental states that happen in the same sequence from one organization to the next and with respect to one change after another. Based on this work, I would conclude that these states represent normative states that all organizations go through as they start, move through, and complete a strategic organizational transformation.[1] I've identified four such states and have labeled them *Identifying, Initiating, Impending,* and *Institutionalizing.* Figure 3.1 is a graphic illustration of the components of each state that lead to a successful strategic change initiative.

As I go through this very high-level overview of the four states of change in this chapter, I want to develop a picture in your mind of the overall flow for states of change. I will then build out the details in each state expanding on what constitutes the narrative of the change process and outcomes. I will highlight how change unfolds over time, what gets embedded in each of the states of change, and how

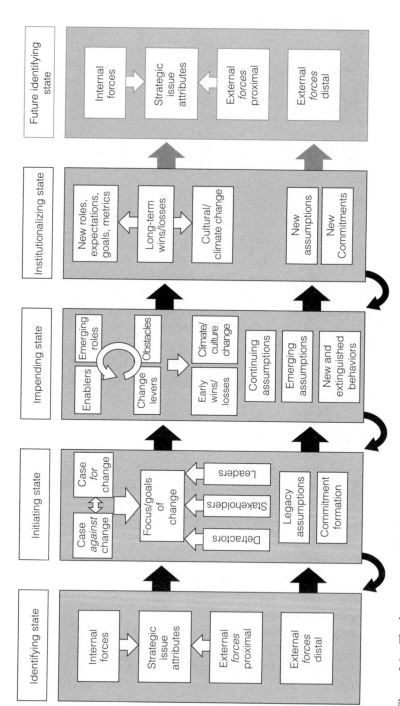

Figure 3.1 The four-state model of organizational transformation.

one's individual and collective self-concept changes in line with the overall change narrative. The unfolding of the change narrative is a huge step into the change process where most organizations, unfortunately, falter and fail. One very important reason why organizations fail during initiating and implementing the impending change, and ultimately institutionalizing change, is that people have different stories representing the narrative for change.[2] The differences among these interpretations can be so dramatic that different people and units are literally working off pursuing different scripts or narratives about why the change is needed, what it means, how it can and should unfold, and where they will end up when it is institutionalized.[3] When this occurs, we know members of the leadership in the organization at some if not all levels are working from different scripts or narratives in guiding the change process.

THE IDENTIFYING STATE

Our leaders made a case for the urgency of this change prior to implementation.

Every transformative change begins with the Identifying State, during which a focal issue demanding a change in strategic direction flashes on the organization's "messy" radar screen. I intentionally use the term *state* here, in that a state is a transitory condition. As individuals, we can move from one state to the next over time. A state is not fixed; it is just a temporary condition you are experiencing until you experience or enter into the next state of being or, in our case here, change.

Focusing on the individual unit of analysis, states include being excited, positive, challenged, depressed, hopeful, resilient, optimistic, or reflective. In terms of an organizational unit of analysis, the collective state can also include being excited, challenged, depressed, hopeful and reflective, optimistic, resilient, and confident. I am sure you have been challenged in your work, and you have also been on a team that has felt challenged to accomplish a goal. Entire organizations can share a positive or negative state of feeling challenged. These states can apply across units of analysis.[4] For example, a leader who is a champion for innovation gets very excited about the possibilities she sees emerging on the horizon for her organization. This leader then talks to her peers and direct reports and conveys the ideas and excitement she is experiencing, such that the state of excitement is transferred to them; this is typically referred to as being a contagion effect. As this effect unfolds, individuals come to identify with the need for change, which reaches a collective level, when all are aligned with this prospective change process and outcome(s). Ultimately, the excitement can become so contagious that it unfolds and emerges across the entire organization, whereupon we witness a number of very exciting initiatives unfolding, which may or may not compete for attention. This new state then represents a change where discipline and direction become important to sustainable transformation.

Going back to identifying, when a major or persistent "blip" grabs the attention of an organization's leader or some other individual with the potential to voice the need for change, the forces that generated the strategic issue then become the focal point for attention as this individual or these individuals work to recognize, identify, and make sense out of what is happening and what to do next, while a new future course and narrative for that organization is being determined. It is essential that the "signal" be picked up before any change is possible. Without the signal being recognized, there is no recognized need for change, at least internally. This does not mean that change is not needed, just that it is not recognized as yet.[5]

Analysis of this Identifying State involves examining both internal organizational signals and trends, as well as external signals, trends, and key events. The Identifying State provides the "backstory" or narrative that builds on the history through which the organization has evolved, as well as the emotions of the starting cast of characters, who will become prominent in the change process narrative. At this point in the unfolding of the change process, a clear transformative plan has not been crafted, but the nature of the strategic issue or signal that will begin to define the transformation is being clarified.

Some examples of these signals could be the shift in consumer preferences for online shopping that arrived when the Internet began; the move toward designing and deploying clean energy methods; the emergence of rap in American culture; 24/7 news channels with constant breaking news; the need to efficiently search the massive amounts of data that we're accumulating on the web; the need to address nontraditional college students via private universities; the shift to purchasing music services versus owning the actual album; and some emerging today, including the moves toward patient-centered health care, becoming an interplanetary species, and virtual, augmented, or mixed reality.

An example of one of these signals with respect to management science and practice is Kaplan and Norton's balanced scorecard approach, which was introduced into the management literature in 1992 in a very popular article and then in a subsequent 1993 book by these authors.[6] Essentially, the balanced score card was a strategic management tool that aided managers in keeping track of what their people were doing, based on the actions taken by their leadership. The balanced part was to get organizational leaders and their employees to consider four key aspects that influence how an organization performs and, in our context here, how one might use this approach to analyze attributes of a strategic threat or opportunity recognized during the Identifying State. The four perspectives or categories advocated in the balanced scorecard approach included:

- *Financial.* Is there something about how we obtain, account for, allocate, or think about our financial resources that should change (do less, more, better, faster, or differently)?

- *Customer.* Is there something about our vision or approach to the market or our customers that should change?

- *Operational,* To satisfy our customers, employees, shareholders, regulators, and so on, what business processes must we excel at? Are there technologies, methods, capital, or natural resources involved?

- *Learning and growth,* To achieve our vision, how will we attract, manage, train, and develop our human capital resources to increase or sustain our ability to change?

To identify and be aware means that a signal or set of signals has been recognized that are relevant to your organization, but they are not necessarily fully interpreted or understood, such that one knows whether they are in fact meaningful or important. In the field of psychology, there is a classic theory known as signal detection theory.[7] According to this theory, a signal must stand out from the background noise for one to be aware that it exists. For example, have you ever been in a noisy crowd and heard someone mention your name? If you turned your head to see if they were referring to you, that was a signal amid all of the noise that you were experiencing in that crowd, and at that moment, that you had become aware of your name. Signals that are meaningful or relevant to you are more likely to be detected. However, there is no guarantee that a signal relevant to your organization's survival will be detected—that takes discipline and being open to new experiences and ideas.

Turning to organizations, signals can come from the outside in their markets indicating, if recognized, that something might be happening to cause a need for that organization to change. For example, returning to Microsoft, University of Washington researchers working with collaborators in Microsoft's research division have been experimenting with how to use DNA to store information. Just one strand of DNA has an enormous capacity for storing the zeros and ones that make up information coded into an entire server farm. This research team has already shown that they can translate the zeros and ones into the four-letter genetic code, while then storing that information similar to the way the human body works. Such DNA strands could last intact for literally a thousand years with unheard-of storage capacity. However, the challenge now is to be able to quickly gain access to these data as any server does almost instantaneously when a program or search is enacted. Once that challenge is addressed, the way we store information may go through a radical shift, which overnight could eliminate the need for large server farms in Iowa, Nebraska, or northern Sweden, for that matter.[8]

If you were in the business of building large server farms today, would this signal rise above all of the other noise that is out there regarding how to improve the efficiencies of our data processing servers and centers? This work may or may not be relevant to either the survival or growth of your business, but in the next ten years we will all know whether it was an important signal or not and perhaps one worthy of being at least identified if not contemplated and reflected on before discounting.

On December 30, 2016, there was a story in the *Wall Street Journal* about Amazon's floating procurement centers in the sky. Amazon is proposing to put procurement centers in the sky and then deliver something you ordered via a drone to your house or work or at a sporting event. Is that a signal that is getting someone's attention in their industry, such as retail stores in malls? Now it is January, 6, 2018, and those Amazon procurement centers in the sky still don't exist, but is it a signal that other competitors of Amazon should keep in terms of their focus on the future?

In the 1980s, there was a signal appearing in the computer applications and technology market. This signal indicated that the little "toy boxes" called personal computers, or PCs, might someday supplant mainframe systems. As one IBM engineer stated, "These toy boxes will never replace the computing power of the mainframe," and, in his opinion, it was just a blip in the long arc of computing technology transformation. I would agree that it was a blip, and certainly something worth identifying, but would anyone say that it fell off the arc of change in computing? Indeed, it was a huge driver in that arc of change, along with the DNA being experimented with for information storage, which could end up being much more than just a blip. Certainly a company called Digital Equipment Corporation, or DEC, didn't see this PC blip on the screen as being important to their survival, and that company went from 100,000 plus employees to zero by the end of the 1990s, along with an acquisition by Compaq, which by the way is also now gone, with both landing on the large heap of former organizations.

In the first phase of organizational transformation, being aware of something and identifying it means it happens first in at least one individual, who could be at any organizational level. If the signal persists, it then enters into the awareness state of a collection of individuals, which may then provide sufficient momentum and a starting point for change to begin to unfold. For example, in an organization that I worked with over several years, the COO had started a strategic change initiative, actually the second iteration of the same change, which hadn't worked the first time. The change was meant to transform the organization from a holding company to an operational one. This organization had gone on an acquisition spree for ten years and kept adding other companies into the larger holding company. After a while, it became obvious that the holding company was not designed to leverage all of the diverse resources that had been acquired. This led to several leaders identifying the need to transform the company from a holding to a lean and more tightly integrated operating company.

At one all-hands-on-deck meeting of 500 leaders, the COO, who was a champion for the change process, was discussing the strategic change and citing two articles he had written that were sent to all of those in attendance. These articles covered why they needed to change and what that change meant in terms of their current and future work together. These articles were his translation of the signals he had seen in the organization's global market that required immediate attention in their organization requiring the need to change and transform.

The facilitator for this session asked everyone, including the COO, to write down the date they thought this current strategic change initiative began. The COO responded first indicating the official campaign for this change had started exactly eighteen months ago. Then when the facilitator went around the room, randomly selecting attendees, some leaders read out that it started exactly three months ago, nine months ago, two years ago, five years ago, and some ten years or more ago. One manager said he thought the initiative was something they had always done, so he was unsure anything new had actually started!

Without even an awareness or identification of when the change started, amid all of the typical noise in this large, complex, and geographically distributed organization, how could one expect to actually move this change effort toward the next phase, called Initiating? By the way, this organization and its leaders tried to do so through brute force, and their efforts failed multiple times before the massive layoffs began, including the COO, who simply did not identify the source of the problem. Specifically, the change narrative that he understood and believed in was not the change narrative that existed in even his closest leaders' narratives and certainly not their self-concepts.

In the following list, I have summarized the typical comments that are expressed during the identifying state. These comments come from two very different organizations, which I have investigated with my colleagues, which were undergoing transformation change. I will use these two respective organizations to provide comments for each state.

Prototypical Comments in the Identifying State: An Airline

- "We have a miserable reputation with our customers."
- "We have fallen to bottom of the pack in on-time service; we have fallen to twenty out of twenty."
- "Customers would say, if you can't fix this in four months we are switching."

Prototypical Comments in the Identifying State: A Health Care Company

- "It wasn't a specific event, although there were several big events that have occurred that we look at now as serious safety events. It was the confluence of events and the leadership."
- "The federal changes in pay-for-performance have definitely been a driver."
- "Equally motivating is the expectation of our general public, our patients, our consumers for transparency. There are websites, health grades; there are all kinds of where you can go online and see what we're doing well and what we're not."

THE INITIATING STATE

Our leaders built a broad coalition up front to support the change.

Throughout the Initiating State, specific goals for strategic change are articulated and adapted as it unfolds over time. Typically, someone in leadership puts a stake in the ground and says, "Here, this is where we should focus—this is the direction to pursue," and "This is how it differs from what we have been doing." Many leaders will use the term *starting a new chapter*, in the sense that I have been describing in terms of their narrative for change.[9]

Discussion and even debate around the need for a change in the direction now being scripted precedes and follows these pronouncements. Hopefully, as individual self-concepts change to embrace the emerging narrative, there is a greater acceptance of it being a legitimate course of action that employees will embrace and align around. With Alaska Airlines, discussed earlier, the arguments in favor of the change became so critical as to be considered a "burning platform," or "melting iceberg," suggesting a logical but very difficult route to the survival of their organization.

Usually, subsidiary or nested goals are formed around this major "stake in the ground" that represents the initial steps toward achieving the desired goal. The choices made in line with the new narrative can become either a tragic ending to the organization's story or the beginnings of a new revival. Because only a few companies actually live as long as the human lifespan, we suggest that the endings of these narratives are more common than new beginnings. Whether an organization dies or not is not necessarily a bad thing; an economist by the name of Schumpeter called it "creative destruction."[10] Simply put, like evolution, we have to destroy those organizations that are no longer adapting to move on to building the more adaptive ones. We will just say at this point, *maybe.*

During this initiating state, traditional or "legacy" assumptions and "typical ways of operating in terms of the workforce narrative" are beginning to be seriously challenged and defended, while new positive attitudes and deepening commitments form to foster the change. Impacts on stakeholder groups are identified and included in the initiating plan or not, as the case may be, a topic I will focus on later in this chapter. Ignoring, overlooking, or ineffectively identifying key stakeholders can keep an organization stuck in the Initiating State, whereas they can create more obstacles when entering into the following Impending State.[11]

Some individuals and groups may remain privately or openly opposed to the change and detract from the distribution of clear and compelling "why, how, and when" messages. All the while, where successful change is unfolding there are a growing number of key individuals and groups who continue to understand, advocate, and lead a change in the narrative script and subsequent actions that foster change. It is evident during this state that how conflicts emerge and are resolved can be adaptive or maladaptive, which with respect to the latter can derail the change effort. People may become so embedded in conflict that the conflict becomes the main source of attention as opposed to the change that is required to help the organization adapt. When conflict is adaptive, it is sometimes no less frustrating or messy, but, as individuals move through the conflict, they actually create insights and ways of behaving that become part of the new narrative.[12]

What we also know about this state of change is that, if you are going to initiate change, you need a very clear starting point to launch what is nothing short of your campaign for changing the organization. You will need to consider how you first want to signal your employees regarding the reason you need to change and what specific and demonstrable signals you have picked up that suggest such change is necessary amid all of the noise. If you go past this point without assuring a significant number of employees "get it," expect that more ambiguity and confusion will result, as you begin to invest in new and often expensive impending initiatives that promote, operationalize, and work toward embedding the change process in the new narrative.[13]

Most successful campaigns may need to go longer than leaders are typically willing to invest in with their time and energy. However, if you fail to provide a clear, consistent, and redundant signal to your employees, the variance in interpretations will likely doom the change process before it lifts off the ground, as already noted with the organization trying to go from a holding to an operational company. The amount of time for the campaign will also be affected by how employees view what constitutes "my organization," how much they trust your leadership, how instrumental they see the change as being needed to continue to be successful for themselves, how much the leadership consistently models the need for change, and how much time and how many resources they will need to have to make it all work to the point where it is a reliable, repeatable practice. Yes, it's complicated, but doable.

Based on the in-depth research that we have done again in the airline case, as well as in health care organizations, we provide some prototypical comments one is likely to hear in the initiating state.

Prototypical Comments in the Initiating State: An Airline

- "We're not trying to fix something that just happened recently. We're really trying to fix something that is culturally who we are in an industry that is actually expecting more."

- "Our company initiative was, 'We're going to fix [the hub].' That was our mantra—that's what we were doing."

- "We were not good at operational literacy [and we need to fix that]."

Prototypical Comments in the Initiating State: A Health Care Company

- "The purpose of the Culture of Safety initiative is to change the way people understand safety, understand safety behaviors, and thereby improve safety for patients."

- "Produce a common language and framework for which we can work on these across the system and be able to talk about."

- "We need to improve in terms of many of the core metrics, in terms of a measured outcome, and then preventable injuries in the hospital will dramatically drop."

THE IMPENDING STATE

Our leaders listen to new ideas.

In the Impending State, implementation of the specific tactical goals for change advance as more resources are dedicated to support the change effort. During this phase, work roles often shift, and temporary "task force" or "special project" as-signments, as well as new job titles, emerge to align human capital with the strategic change initiative and process. These changes may have an impact on not only the individuals' self-concepts but also their central identity, as shown earlier with the shift from green berets and the change at AT&T after its breakup by the U.S. government.[14]

New or different investments in capital, including human capital, production-related resources, and processes are common in this state and are used to enable strategic change and transformation to proceed along the arc of the new narrative. For example, as health care moves toward a patient-centered model, how does that affect what gets measured in terms of performance and what is rewarded in terms of health care services? These changes are having a fundamental impact on what it means to be a health care provider in terms of one's identity as a physician, nurse, or specialist.[15] As this impending state unfolds, different ways to leverage and fine-tune the flow of change are discovered as early wins and losses are noticed and analyzed. Revisions to the practice are made and adjusted given the assumption the organization's leadership is serious about staying the course and investing their time and resources in navigating the arc of the change process. Obstacles to change are encountered and worked through or around if the change actually proceeds forward versus sliding backward.

What most characterizes this phase is that it is not fixed but rather evolving and emerging. This is why I suggest that this state may be the most precarious and challenging for organizations, and indeed, based on research, most organizations never succeed in moving through this state to where the leadership can declare victory and say the change has actually been institutionalized.

In a health care organization I worked with for several years, the leadership initiated a strategic change initiative to take the organization from having a physician-centric culture, policies, procedures, incentives, and evaluation to being patient centric. In a physician-centric organization, the world revolved around the physician in terms of decision authority, schedules, demands, resources provided, tolerance for mistakes, support, rewards, and so on. In the desired patient-centric organization, everything was geared toward making the patient the center of this organization's universe. Schedules would be designed that met each patient's needs. Physicians and others would be challenged if the best care were not provided to each and every patient, which was rigorously measured from the time the patient entered the facility till the time he or she was back home and fully recovered. This was a radical shift in the self-concepts of the physicians and for that matter everyone else, including the patient, insurance providers. and family members.

The CEO of this organization had a reputation for being somewhat autocratic. She initiated the campaign several times, without a great deal of success in signaling its importance to her workforce, as well as signaling why the physicians had to change their narrative and ultimately their identity. One challenge she may have had was the fact that she was a nurse by training, not a physician. Consequently, one would hear from key physicians that this was a nurse's narrative about health care and it was not a physician's, who actually knew better what would be best for his or her patient. Of course, the CEO could have just as well been a MBA executive, and then the reaction might have been, "She is just a bean counter who doesn't care about the quality of care, just the money."

A year into the process, this CEO hired a consulting firm—founded by a physician—that was well known in health care circles for rigidly driving change initiatives following a very prescribed step-by-step process—usually into the ground, by the way. The formula required a very specific rollout and protocol for changing health care organizations that was so formulaic it was stifling, such as the verbatim greeting that had to be used with all patients. The consulting firm's promise, or I would call it a "hook," was that they would not charge this health care organization until there were positive results from the change process, and I might add: or else. This consulting firm was also well known for firing clients who did not adhere to their protocol to protect their brand in the market. This was actually a methodology for ensnaring health care organizational leaders, who certainly did not want to tell their peers at conferences they had been fired by this so-called prestigious consulting firm. Pride clearly got in the way of the logical need and narrative for change in this health care system.

I should say that their bringing large groups together of 500 to 600 health care providers at a time and at great expense is one way to launch the campaign. Using this strategy in this complex organizational system comprised of over 30,000 employees did promote a sufficient level of awareness regarding the necessity for change. This consulting firm had also made it very clear what needed to be done to be more patient centric during the initiating phase, including handing out cards to employees on the steps one goes through to greet a patient. The plans and steps were so detailed that for each employee engaging with a patient there was list of statements that employees must use when starting the engagement process, for example, acknowledge the patient's presence, refer next to his or her name, make sure you have pronounced the name correctly, now tell the patient your name, tell the patient what your role is, confirm why he or she is here, and so on.

There was nothing inherently wrong with the checklist protocol that each employee had to follow. Indeed, a lot of the safety problems in health care that are causing hundreds of thousands of deaths annually in the United States are due to not having a clear step-by-step repeatable process that everyone follows whether he or she is in one surgical suite versus another in a different hospital. Don't be surprised when I tell you the protocols across different hospitals in the same health care system are actually different.

Many protocols like this and tracking mechanisms were initiated in this health care system at the same time, and, for the first couple of years, there were varying levels of resistance and dissatisfaction with the rollout process, as well as pockets of success. Interestingly, one pocket of success was in radiology, a unit in this health care system with a $300 million budget. The success, in part, was due to the director, who learned the consulting firm's narrative and then interpreted that narrative for his employees to accommodate how it fit into the new directions for change that he and his leadership were setting for his unit. These leaders literally edited the scripts, made them more relevant to the employees in that unit, and it worked for them—better than for most other units in the same health care system. This leader worked on the basis of introducing a commitment versus a compliance model, so employees would own the change process.

One of the biggest reasons for resistance to the overall change process throughout this health care system was being told what to do as opposed to building a sense of identity and ownership around a patient-centric world. Many employees told me they felt these protocols were inauthentic and didn't fit their style of interaction with patients going back decades, which they felt was already patient centric in terms of their own historical narrative. Some joked about how silly this whole initiation process was and that it kept them from genuinely focusing on their patients in a way that was "patient centric." The story or narrative they were being asked to buy into was not part of what is called one's authentic self.[16] This approach can actually be a good disruption if the narrative for the authentic self doesn't make sense to change, but in this case it did and was largely ignored. In the end, many of the health care providers didn't commit or comply with the change.

To be fair to the organizational leaders described earlier, on some hospital metrics that should have changed there was incremental improvement, but it was also easy to see what was not emerging, and that was a deep commitment to impending changes required in the collective self-concept of this workforce. The CEO has now gone to another health care system, and the consulting firm is being released at the end of the current contract with some minor incremental improvements in this organization—nothing that actually justifies the amount of investment of time and resources in their services. Interestingly, this same consulting firm repeatedly fails in these change processes, and yet because of their name brand, they pop up somewhere else either in the United States or as far away as Dubai with yet another failed script for change.

There are some clear lessons to be learned in the Impending State, but the simplest one for now is that you cannot force a change in someone's self-concept from the outside in, if it does not make sense to that individual and, worse, the larger collective. To change a self-concept, you have to build a sense of understanding and ownership in what you are trying to change from the inside out, not the outside in, which this health care consulting firm clearly does not understand.

Often, as these change processes unfold, I find that things tend to get worse before they will get better, whereby we witness a loss of confidence in the wisdom of leadership and change goals are shaken. The culture (shared values, beliefs, and assumptions about the way things are done around here) and the climate (perceptions, attitudes, and feelings that characterize life in the organization) will begin to change if employees develop a greater level of trust in the process and the organization's leadership while also seeing it as being instrumental to their success. This was largely not the case in the example described in the preceding paragraphs, even though the CEO was respected for her hard work but not her authoritarian style in initiating and implementing the change process.

Just as members of the organization begin to scrutinize and test legacy assumptions, beliefs, and values in the Initiating State, in the Impending State useful assumptions continue to take root while new assumptions emerge to replace the legacy assumptions that no longer serve the organization's mission and purpose. Likewise, some new ways of behaving and performing the work of the organization will emerge, whereas others cease and become extinct. In this health care organization, there still are many legacy assumptions that have not emerged into new ways of thinking about what "my organization" and "my work" mean to all of the 30,000 employees.

Based on our research into this Impending State, we have found that some of the common statements about this state of change in the airline and health care organization are reflected in the following comments:

Prototypical Comments in the Impending State: An Airline

- "[The Mad Dog Task Force] probably created a culture of communication that was nonexistent, so from that sense we had a good by-product. It set up the foundation [for the change initiative]; I believe that was the task force."

- "We gave the employees a tool kit; before then they had very limited ability to solve a customer's problems on the spot."

- "One of the biggest things that helped us with this whole initiative was that it started with [the CEO] at the top. It had a lot of visibility."

Prototypical Comments in the Impending State: A Health Care Company

- "So, quantitatively, we can measure it. We have a serious safety event rate; we can measure that."

- "The organization . . . especially it's something that has to do with safety and quality because it's something that's so deep in the walls of the organization. This type of initiative, the organization really rallies around it."

- "We're pretty integrated. I feel as if we have changed the culture, and we're getting into that phase where we're really trying to reboot and do Culture 2.0. So we did the 1.0 and the 1.5, and now it's 2.0."

THE INSTITUTIONALIZING STATE

When someone praises my organization, it feels like a personal compliment.

In the Institutionalizing State, roles, expectations, behaviors, goals, and methods for evaluation take root and become part of the standard operating procedures and "ways of thinking" about themselves for employees in the organization. They are no longer seen as short-term or experimental fixes to a problem, nor mandates from above, but rather as tried-and-tested methods and processes that make sense in terms of how individuals view "my work" and "my organization," resulting in what I have referred to as a repeatable and reliable practice.

New employees entering the organization will work in ways that are fundamentally different than previous employees, who were embedded in the change process; for them, it is "the way the organization does business now." The way things used to be is relegated to history, and the new regime and protocols are clearly evident throughout the organization. To the extent the change is reinforced with a steady progression of substantial wins, the strategic change becomes anchored in the way people routinely think and behave about themselves and their interactions with each other and their clients, which become part of the collective self-concept represented in the organization.

In this state, watch for signs that the "storm" or "swirl" of change has subsided and a new equilibrium or comfort zone has been attained. Be mindful of how strategic leadership has distributed itself across multiperson units, or potentially all organizational members, in concerted action influencing—sustaining, reinforcing, strengthening—the strategic direction of the organization. This could show up in a unified representation of the system to the outside world; it has an impact on the way people collaborate and make decisions spontaneously; it reflects a shared intuitive understanding among colleagues and even vendors, customers, and other stakeholders about the organization's strategy and ways of delivering results; and it influences the structure and distribution of resources that normalize strategic actions so that they are no longer driven, for example, from the top on down.

As you might surmise, once you get to this state of change, you may already be entering a new state of identifying and looking for the next set of signals to interpret whether they are relevant to your organization. Indeed, the process is never ending, so you don't get to the ultimate, as they say in U.S. football, spiking the ball in the end zone.

To summarize, in this chapter our goal was to provide a relatively quick overview of the entire four-state model that I have proposed to encompass the complete cycle of organizational transformation. I understand, at this point, that I need to go into more detail for you to fully understand each of the mechanisms within each state and how one state evolves into the other, sometimes not as cleanly or in sync as one would prefer. Before going forward, however, please reflect. Stop and think about these following questions:

- Are there any signals right now, that you are aware of, that indicate a need to consider changing what you do as an organization? How about as an individual?

- How have you and/or your leadership worked to make others aware of these signals?

- What has been your experience in terms of making others aware?

- Have you seen, in the model described in the preceding pages, connections made between the awareness of these signals and what people are being asked to initiate?

- Do people understand when the change actually started and why?

- What have you seen emerge in the change processes? Has it been resistance, compliance, acceptance, identification, or ownership?

- Have you ever experienced the institutionalization of change in your career, and, if so, what impact did it have on your self-concept and that of those around you?

I am providing some prototypical comments in the following list for just the airline case study. You may then conclude that the health care organization did not make it to the Institutionalizing State.

Prototypical Behaviors in the Institutionalizing State: An Airline

- "The Executive Committee [now] understands how important process is for sustainability. You just can't do it on people's love for the company; there has to be some structure that holds it together and the processes."

- "Our performance has never been as good in the twenty-eight years I've been here; people get great paychecks and performance bonuses, and we've changed culture."

- "We are now to a point of maturity and kind of we're on the hill; it feels good. We would be afraid to give up whatever got us to the part that feels good. And so there wouldn't be this sense of wanting to let it roll back."

RESEARCH LINK: A DEEPER DIVE

As you think about and examine these four states of change and transformation, realize that time is a critical factor to keep in mind. Research on strategic change has shown, however, that time is not always associated with one's clock time, especially as we traverse different cultures around the globe. Beyond clock time, we also know that time may be assessed in terms of events both internal and external to the organization. For example, it is not uncommon for employees to discuss how the course direction of their organization was changed by the Great Recession, the loss of a key leader, or the introduction of some new process and/or technology.

The third aspect of time is referred to as cycles, and those cycles may vary in terms of the type of industry the organization operates within. Some organizations are in industries that turn over new ideas and methods for engaging with one's customers very rapidly, whereas in other industries the cycles are stretched out more and the number of transformative changes are fewer and farther between. Consequently, time matters to understanding organizational states of transformation, but which time criterion you use does depend on different factors. Whether time is explicitly recognized in terms of examining and understanding the unfolding of strategic change and transformation, it's important.[17]

4 THE IDENTIFYING STATE:
THE SIGNAL FOR CHANGE

It is not good to question the way things are done, because those who have developed the routines are likely to take it personally.

In any given state of change, there are specific mechanisms and drivers of the processes, events, and activities within that state. What I mean here is that these are the means used to drive the transformation process forward. In each state of change, the drivers are unique to the particular goals for that state.[1]

IDENTIFYING STATE: A QUICK REVIEW

Recall that every transformative organizational change begins with the Identifying State, when some members of the organization realize there is an issue or opportunity demanding a change in strategic direction, referred to as a signal. During this state, leaders recognize and then come to understand what is happening out there and what to do next if the signal is strong enough while beginning to formulate a new future course and narrative. Analysis of this state involves examining internal organizational patterns or trends, as well as external trends and key events.

This state provides the backstory that sets the historical context, mood, and starting cast of characters in the change process narrative. At this point in the change process, a clear transformative plan has not been crafted, nor is it necessarily considered relevant or needed. This type of planning does not occur until the nature of the strategic issue or challenge that begins to define the transformation is better understood, interpreted, and translated repeatedly for others in the organization to consider as being relevant or not.

There are quite a few different activities an organization might go through on an annual or routine basis to evaluate the significance of changes happening in the political, economic, social, and technological realms that could signal the need for transformation. Corporate boards and investors might also be on the lookout for such changes and could bring these to the attention of the senior leadership in an organization, as well as consultants or university experts.[2] Many leaders are normally part of different forums in their industries or engaged in think tank discussions that motivate them to actively scan their external environment for signs of things changing or that their current decision making and operational assumptions are shifting in their respective industry.[3]

SIGNAL DETECTION

In our overview of the Identifying State in Chapter 3, I introduced signal detection theory as a way of thinking about how organizational leaders identify the need for strategic transformation amid the myriad of messages they filter day in and day out. Each moment of every day, there are potentially thousands of signals that could be relevant to how your organization evolves over time, as well as how you, as an organizational member, evolve in terms of your self-concept and narrative. For example, for companies like Uber, Lyft, Zipcar, or car2go, the founders received a set of signals that consumers around the globe were ready for a transportation company that provides a service that was more customer and driver centric versus the traditional taxi and rental car business models. This signal motivated these founders to create different ways of getting riders from one location to another.[4]

Let's look at Uber, which is currently the largest taxi service on Earth, yet doesn't own one vehicle. An on-demand car service accessible via a mobile app represents an enormous shift from what taxi and limo companies have traditionally used as their business model to Uber's model. Why did these traditional service companies fail to see or act on the initial signals emerging in the transportation market that were detected by Garrett Camp and Travis Kalanick in 2009? More important, once these companies identified what ventures like Uber or Lyft were up to, why didn't they initiate changes in how they operated to compete more successfully with these new start-ups? Perhaps the same can be asked about why Borders did not see Amazon's on-line business model as a threat.

For reasons we may never fully understand, these established organizations did not do well in identifying signals that were indicating shifting markets and preferences. These organizations were caught off guard. In the case of Uber and Lyft, the taxi and limo services' first strategy was to block these new competitors from picking up passengers from certain locations, such as airports. Appealing to various regulatory bodies and staging protests, taxi and limousine companies and their drivers took the stance that Uber drivers were not following the same rules, treating drivers as employees, paying the same employment costs, and paying the same licensing fees required in many jurisdictions—thus creating an unfair advantage. However, when Uber drivers started to buy business licenses, the taxi services appeared to have no backup plan for change, leaving the competitive landscape wide open for Uber and Lyft, among others, to rapidly expand. The jury is still out as to whether the app enables price fixing in violation of antitrust laws,[5] but meanwhile a traditional industry has been disrupted with little warning or, perhaps for some, not a sufficient level of warning to do something about these changes.

Similarly, we see the same pattern emerging when Amazon first came on the scene to sell books. The large bookstores didn't detect the signals for change in consumer preferences that Amazon's founder Jeff Bezos apparently recognized. They didn't adjust their business models, and many went out of business. By 2014, Amazon had a 41 percent market share of all new book purchases, 65 percent of online print and digital book sales, and 67 percent of the e-book market.[6] Today Amazon is one of the largest retail organizations on Earth hitting $500 billion, moving toward becoming the "everything store" from being just the "on-line book store." Repeatedly, as Amazon has moved from one business sector to another, its competitors have not seen them as competition and failed to recognize the signals triggering changes in markets—now global ones.

As mentioned in Chapter 2, the self-concept addresses the identity-shaping questions:

- "Who am I?"
- "With whom am I connected and associated?"
- "Who are we and what do we do that's meaningful to me and my organization?"

When comfortable answers to these questions are challenged, emotional and even irrational acts of self-protection to defend the organizational identity are evoked. For instance, taxi companies that see themselves as the owners of the fleet and are not able to shift their self-concept to a driver-owned model cannot transform. Book retailers that see themselves as brick and mortar stores, who are not able to shift their self-concept to an on-line model, cannot transform their business model and organization. Their existing and strong individual self-concept and shared self-concept is resistant to change and often jams the signal detection process that should be the harbinger of the need to transform.

THE TIPPING POINT FOR CHANGE

Malcolm Gladwell defined a tipping point as "the moment of critical mass, the threshold, the boiling point."[7] A key success factor for achieving organizational transformation—a fundamental shift in the individual's self-concept to a shared self-concept among a critical mass of organizational members—is the recognition that change will be considered and ultimately will need to happen. For example, back in the 1980s, financial service organizations were discussing what a remote banking process might look like, prior to the advent of the Internet and on-line banking emerging on the world scene. There were some signals that suggested to them that, as technology evolved, people might shift from coming to the physical brick and mortar bank location to doing their business over the phone. This sort of transformative shift would require a very different way of thinking about what it meant to be a banker, bank, and indeed financial service provider. Some leaders started to ask whether their banks should continue to erect new buildings, or would they simply become empty vessels? Would younger customers move toward this new service platform quicker, while older, less technology-savvy customers would still prefer to walk into the bank to do their business, with those numbers inevitably declining in the future?

As we have seen, it has taken several decades for these early signals to take hold; even today, there are banks like Umpqua Bank in the Northwest United States that are still building more brick and mortar facilities with the goal of making them gathering places that are more like community centers in the same vein as Starbucks, thus mimicking a very successful strategy that Howard Schultz and his team pursued to transform the coffee business. For Umpqua Bank, the goal is to make the physical place sticky, in the sense that people will want to hang out and meet their friends at their local bank or use the bank's meeting room for community activities—making the bank both a social and a transactional place to engage with people and products/services.

We propose that there often isn't one absolute landmark starting point for a change, nor does one necessarily typically receive a very strong signal to move in a dramatically new direction. Although there are some transformations that we can trace back to a specific pivot point or a particular event, such as the bursting of the dotcom bubble or the passage of the Affordable Care Act, or even to a specific date such as September 11, 2001, most transformations involve the intersection of different and sometimes subtle political, economic, social, and technological (PEST) signals and trends spanning time, geographic regions, and industries. There is the rapid pivot change and the slow churn or burn, as we noted in the last chapter in terms of different pacing or time clocks for different industries. Thus, the starting point is often in the eye of the beholder, which then translates into data being collected showing that people now know about the change that will eventually have an impact on their organization and are in the process of determining whether it is a threat or opportunity. The trigger event(s) also relate to when something was started, as well as when changing or transforming the organization became an important blip on the radar screen. Try asking a group of key leaders within an organization that are in the midst of a strategic transformation the question the facilitator asked 500 attendees from a large health care organization: When did the current transformational change initiative begin?

I've quickly discovered in both my research and practice that you are likely to hear lots of different responses to this question—including some that may indicate a total lack of awareness of the strategic change initiative that is being considered as relevant, if not urgent. Asking this question and considering the range of responses within an organization—in terms of the timing and triggers of the change process—can be one way to determine the extent to which your organization has collectively moved into the Identifying Phase.[8]

It is also not uncommon for individuals to think they have heard about the change but not know for sure when it started or why, particularly in organizations where trust and transparency are low.[9] Alternatively, there are others in the organization who may be deeply aware of the change and wondering why their colleagues have not heard about it or understand what it means for them or their organization. And unless there is a critical mass of awareness that some sort of transformation is needed, the organization may remain stuck in this state for a considerable period of time, if not until the organization goes over the brink into oblivion.

GETTING STUCK

Another example of the variation we've found in different views about the starting point for an organization's change effort that resulted in getting stuck in the Identifying State occurred in another hospital system we worked with, which was part of a multistate health care system that we'll call Coastal Health. In 2012, we interviewed the entire top management team—over a dozen executives in one of the regional hospitals—regarding their history and the current status of a planned culture change that was focused on how the overall hospital system approached implementing their so-called patient experience. This change was one of three key strategic initiatives that we were told by the hospital CEO were absolutely essential to surviving the changes the organization was facing as a result of ongoing health care reform in the United States.

For Coastal Health, like all U.S. health care organizations, and for that matter many around the globe, the landscape of health care reform began to change in a way that favored consolidating individual health care entities (like this regional hospital) into more integrated systems of care that could encompass the needs of various patients and potentially fully customizing its services. Through such consolidations, these larger health care systems could leverage their economies of scale. Although Coastal Health already had a growing system of hospitals in place, these hospitals were largely independent both in operations and definitely in terms of their cultures.

To integrate these individual entities into a seamless system of health care delivery, Coastal Health created a new five-pillar strategic plan intended to integrate the various entities operating across a number of states. Later on into the arc of their change, and as part of the strategic planning process, it was determined by the senior leadership that the particular hospital I investigated was underperforming in the area of patient satisfaction and would be a good place to pilot a transformational change that might later be cascaded throughout the total multistate health care system. At that time, they anticipated that federal reimbursements would soon be tied to scores on patient satisfaction surveys, which ultimately resulted in the hospital's CEO launching a patient experience initiative to get ahead of the changing regulations curve. However, at the time I started working within this health care system, there were concerns that this transformation lacked traction, which was based on interviews with the CEO and some of the key leaders who directly and indirectly reported to that CEO.

Indeed, in terms of the first principle regarding the employees' self-concepts, I frankly didn't see a lot of change in this organization at the start of the strategic change intervention. There was little evidence in the narratives that reflected a change in the top leaders' self-concepts, all the way on down across subsequent levels of management, regarding their interpretation of what constituted a transformative patient experience. As far as I could discern, there was a great deal of ambiguity regarding what the patient experience should be and whether this "strategic" initiative involved a change at all—let alone a transformation in the way the organization and every individual in it would think about themselves, their work, and what constituted "my organization." Some had heard about the strategic initiative but felt it was just reinforcing what they already were doing, whereas others were trying to determine how it would change the delivery of health care in their units and were asking why it was necessary. These individuals apparently had not seen or perhaps understood the signals others had that prompted the strategic change.

Entering into this project, I examined where Coastal was in terms of the four states of organizational transformation shown in Figure 4.1, including Identifying, Initiation, Impending, and Institutionalization. (I will start simple here with the initial version of Figure 4,1, with just the four columns representing these states, but over the course of the next few chapters I will begin to fill in this framework with more details that represent the mechanisms that trigger change, as well as how leadership and ownership factor into the change process.)

At the outset of this phase, I was interested in where the top leaders in this health care organization were in recognizing these signals and the need to transform the way they thought of the patient experience. These were the individuals who interacted with the CEO on a day-to-day basis, and I wondered, specifically, to what extent were they seeing in their own and each other's self-concepts the enactment of a transformation in how the patient's experience was being operationalized.

We started the interviews of senior leaders by using a statement created by the CEO that described the patient experience change initiative, and then we asked the question about that statement, "And when did this change initiative start?" Some leaders said the initiative had always been a part of the mission and culture of Coastal, and they didn't see it as a change in the way they delivered health care or in how they viewed their roles as leaders. This was clearly not the way the CEO viewed this change effort and its start, and she was considered by many of the employees at Coastal as being very charismatic, authoritative with a touch of authoritarian leadership that would help to successfully drive this change. Here are some representative comments regarding the start of this change initiative:

> *Patient Care Director:* "The concept of the patient's experience had been around actually before I got here . . . eight and a half years ago . . . my goodness, it would be nine years coming July . . . so early 2000s."
>
> *VP Strategy:* "I can tell you we identified it five years ago, 2008, as a key driver for us to achieve success in our overarching strategic vision in becoming a regional network of care and that unless we had a fabulous patient experience, we could have all the best doctors in the world and people may not choose to use us, or come to work here, or send their families here."
>
> *CEO:* "I want to say two to three years ago "
>
> *Director of Nursing Administration:* "In November of 2011, we had what we called a Patient Experience Summit, where all the hospitals came together, and that's where it was kicked off."

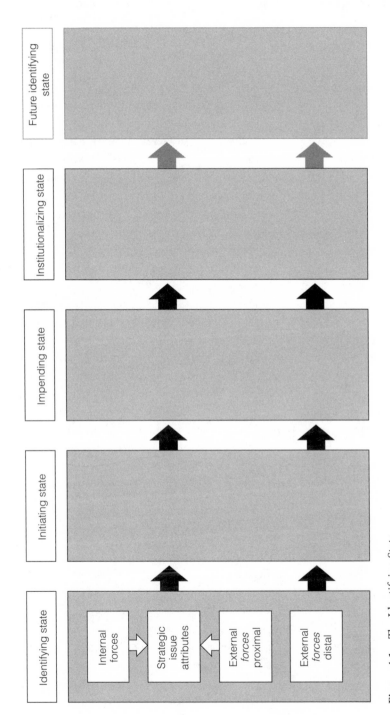

Figure 4.1 The Identifying State.

So in this health care organization, although almost all of the people I spoke with in the interviews and subsequently in small to large forums said that improving the patient experience was important, there was no consistent narrative or script around each individual's awareness of when, how, or why the transformation was triggered—or what the transformation entailed. Most important, in terms of the first principle regarding each employee's self-concept, the lack of consistency regarding the history of the initiative and what success of this initiative would look like meant there was no way to coherently shape how people would define and embrace needing to do "their business" or "their work" differently in this health care system. Many employees simply didn't know what "different" meant for them and what constituted "my work" with the patient experience supposedly requiring any significant changes. Their link between their individual identity as health care providers and the patient experience was not clear or consistently shared at the collective or organizational level, including among the top leadership. They were clearly reading from different narrative scripts.

The lack of a shared self-concept at Coastal related to the patient experience led to a diffusion of progress throughout the entire Identifying State that was characterized by many jam ups in the change process, including lots of false starts and frustration expressed by these leaders regarding the promotion and support for this strategic change. It is not that these providers were necessarily against improving the patient experience. Rather, it was that they simply did not know what that meant or why it was being promoted. Those pages of script in their narratives had yet to be written and certainly were not widely understood.

Also, with respect to the wide variation in individual perspectives regarding this proposed change effort, by the time I began the interviews with the leaders in Coastal, there were signs that some leaders had even moved from the Identifying State (where people begin to recognize internal and external forces impacting the organization that signal the need for change) into the Initiating State of change (where goals start to form and cases for and against change are prevalent, which in part can be driven by differences in what the change actually means for each individual). Even though we want to focus just on the Identifying State, we typically see across the organization and its different units that people enter these states at different times, if at all. Worse yet, there were also signs that a few leaders were ready to launch into the Impending State (where the parts of the organization had created a variety of ways to motivate the rollout of the change process, such as creating new roles and processes to support the change initiative, along with resources). This scattered and disjointed progress across the Coastal enterprise created a misalignment in the transformation process that would essentially leave the organization as a whole stuck with one foot in the Identifying State, dragging many groups backward as it unfolded over time through various initiatives.

With respect to the first principle associated with each employee's self-concept, to transform an individual's self-concept, that person has to first be able to connect the aim of the change initiative with one or more of the individual, relational, or collective levels of his or her self-concept in terms of the following sequence of development:

- "Who am I?"
- "With whom am I connected and associated?"
- "Who are we, and what do we do that's meaningful to me?"
- "What do I do now, and how does that reflect the essence of what I do and describe in my narrative?"

If the change has no coherent connection to the employee's self-concept, then a shared self-concept within the organization cannot form and take hold to change, thereby aligning the employees' behavior when they are interacting with one another. Within the Coastal nursing staff, which seemed to be a step or maybe two ahead of other parts of the organization in embracing this change, there was a clearer connection between the patient experience initiative and the employees' self-concepts. The nursing leaders, including the chief nurses and their staff, had embraced the need for change, in part because they have more frequent interactions with patients, day in and day out. The nurses were able to articulate how the change was being interpreted and exhibited in terms of their own work, and they could see that the patients and family members, as well as some external groups such as insurers, contract physicians, and specialists were all asking for a different experience.

The narrative that was emerging in nursing had a much clearer focus on what this change meant for nursing care in Coastal. Indeed, the nurses had created specific goals to implement three best practices and were more than six months into initiating these goals while most others in the organization were still trying to identify the need for change and what change meant to their self-concept and, importantly, how they delivered patient services. Meanwhile other senior leaders were sketchy about the details of the patient experience initiative, including again whether it was a "real" initiative or not. I would argue that for these employees the connection was a weak signal between the concept of the patient experience being advocated by the CEO and their personal self-concepts. For instance, the director of cardiology, a physician, said this about the initiative, suggesting that it did not have a "who am I?" or "who are we?" connection:

> So it is one of our core initiatives around here, the patient experience, and about the experience from the time they enter the door to the time they leave the facility, so that's about as much as I know about it other than you hear bits and pieces about it. I've never seen anything that gives a formal overview of what the whole goal and objective of the patient experience is.

In contrast, this statement by the director of quality indicates a different sense of ownership and personally meaningful outcomes—suggesting a connection to his self-concept:

> The patient experience initiative has finally gotten some traction and is bound for success. It had a false start a year or so ago, and I think it's fabulous. We now, I think, have a clear focus around it as a key initiative for the organization. And I think we've got some great plans in place to move forward to actually move the numbers.

Going one step further, the director of rehabilitation medicine indicated that, for behavioral health practitioners, there was a very low awareness of the current need for change because this group had already (or believed they had) institutionalized the philosophy of patient care, and so nothing really needed to be changed. Although this may at first glance be discouraging with regard to readiness to transform an organization, the statement suggests a strong (albeit currently nontransformational) connection between the initiative and this person's self-concept:

> I'm kind of in a unique place, I think, because especially in behavioral health (in psychiatry), the primary treatment modality is to understand the patient experience. That's how we do our interventions on a day-to-day basis. So when we talk about the patient experience initiative for the hospital, that's my career. That's not something that's unique; it's not an initiative; it is the way that we operate, the way that I operate.

I would suggest that this is a person who now needs to alter his view of the patient experience to be something that is not merely the unique purview of those in the behavioral health field but for employees in every part of the Coastal system. So we can start to see that transforming the organization around a new way of defining the patient experience involves looking at how it does or does not connect to each individual's self-concept and ways the individual goes about doing his or her work. If we don't, it will no doubt fail to sustain, and the arc will go south in terms of the success of the change process.

So while the CEO was still working on making leaders at multiple organizational levels aware of the initiative, the fact that this initiative had varying degrees of connection to people's self-concepts was totally overlooked. Although she was forceful and even inspirational with her message, she wasn't very good at listening to or observing the signals from her own leaders. In interviews, observations, and casual conversations, I could see that employees had very different ideas about whether creating an optimal patient experience defined who they were as individuals, whom they related to as professionals, and what constituted what they viewed as meaningful work. It was clear that what constituted an optimal health care experience had not been operationalized for them. Given these facts, we know for sure there is not a shared self-concept regarding this single, but profoundly complex, change narrative.

I now realize through the accumulation of a lot of extensive research and experience with organizational transformations like the one that Coastal was trying to go through that it is not uncommon for different leaders and others within the targeted organization to initially become aware of the need for transformative change at very different points in time, depending on their roles and relationships, familiarity with the mission and vision, and their individual beliefs about the "state of the organization" and the "state of the industry," as it applies to the change initiative.[10] This goes back to the arc of change often being rather messy. For example, an individual could see herself as serving customers to the best of her ability and coming to work every day with that being central to her self-concept. This self-view would include specific targets on what it meant to take care of the needs of her customers, and that would be the starting point in terms of changing her narrative. Handing this person a new script without any background or justification will not change her self-concept, at least not easily.

OWNERSHIP

One day, the organizational leaders might suggest that serving customers means partnering with them in terms of the creation of new products and services, which might be different compared to the way the organization operated previously. For example, at lululemon, when Christine Day assumed the role of CEO, the organization was stagnating under the direction of its founder Chip Wilson. Christine felt, based on her years of experience working at Starbucks, that she needed to develop her employees and customers to think about working together as co-owners of the lululemon clothing brand, to create a unique experience for its customers and each other. She wanted the store employees to feel their customers were "theirs," as if it were their own store in terms of ownership—not unlike being a Starbucks barista. She frequently said that potentially all of their customers and employees could offer the company fantastic ideas about improvements to lululemon's products, and that together they could coinvent innovations in product design and delivery. Lululemon's employees were not aware of this initiative and therefore it was not part of their self-concepts as employees.

To develop a sense of accountable ownership, which moves organizations and their employees from the Identification State by supplanting territorial ownership (for example, as reflected in the founder knowing what was best for product design and his company), Christine knew she had to develop employees to feel as if they were owners in terms of their self-concepts and to do so with at least a significant cadre of customers. What that meant to Christine was that they should be able to influence how lululemon works, feeling as if they were truly owners of the store.

To reinforce this self-concept identity transformation, Christine promoted ownership by having employees decide on the design of their respective stores, which varied by region and sometimes within the same city. With customers, she started an initiative to recognize those customers who contributed great ideas to advancing or innovating product designs, who were called lulu Ambassadors. These individuals had their pictures prominently hung on a recognition wall in each respective store to very publicly recognize their contributions to lululemon.

In an executive retreat comprised of other senior leaders across different industries, now well into the ownership initiative at lululemon, Christine was describing the ownership employees at her company were taking for managing each store in terms of its design, layout, and engagement with customers. She indicated that employees were very aware of the ownership initiative and knew it was their job to choose the color schemes for stores, arrangement of furniture, and how they advertised products to make the story and narrative "my store." This was also evident from other data collected from the employees throughout the organization. Christine encouraged employees to e-mail her directly if they needed any help but told the group that it was very uncommon for her employees to send an e-mail to her because they felt they owned the problems or changes needed in their store. What they typically would send is an example of taking ownership instead of asking for permission to do so.

Christine emphasized that, in her view or self-identity, the best employees thought of themselves as being owners in terms of how they defined themselves.

Another CEO who was present at this retreat could not understand how Christine could promote and reward such inconsistency across stores in terms of their look and design. This strategy, in his mind, would lead to chaos and a complete destruction of a brand's coherence. He also was clearly uncomfortable about not having his employees follow a specific script in terms of how they did their work day in and day out, like the hospital CEO I described earlier, who had hired the consulting firm to force change. This latter example was change that was not centered on employee ownership. For this bank CEO, reinforcing uniformity was very much part of how he viewed the role he played as a senior leader in his organization, in terms of making sure employees complied with the edicts of top management, and how he himself conducted his business in terms of his leader identity and self-concept.

Christine was clearly working toward building a commitment versus compliance narrative for employees; to do so, she had to develop her employees', and indeed customers', self-concepts about lululemon's focus on "taking ownership," which she did repeatedly in company forums, store visits, and when exchanging calls and e-mails with managers and store employees. Christine focused squarely on rewriting the script that defined the company's ownership narrative.

I don't necessarily use these examples regarding different conceptualizations of ownership to point to one being better than the other. Rather, I will let the reader make that determination and come back to these examples later on, as we move through all of the different states of transformation. What I want you to consider is how different the leaders' self-concepts were and how those differences manifested in the way they behaved and what they expected from others in terms of their individual and collective identities and the behaviors associated with employee and customer ownership. In part, a leader's job is to transfer that narrative and to cascade it through the organization in a way that creates a new alignment around the collective self-concept of an organization. This also becomes the job of all leaders at all levels and the teams in which they operate.

Regardless of which concept you use for "how work is supposed to be done," for now my point is that it can be very challenging to precisely mark the start of the Identifying State. We saw that Christine Day would start a dialogue among her leaders in corporate headquarters and at the store level, to examine the need for change, repeatedly discussing its necessity and what it would mean for them to take ownership at work, over and over again. For the bank CEO in the preceding paragraphs, we suspect that a change initiative would roll out more as an edict than a dialogue, which might have an impact on how his employees at least initially understood and interpreted what constitutes the change, let alone what to take ownership for in terms of the change initiative. And we are not suggesting that sometimes you do not need an edict to initiate change, but one cannot direct identifying the change; that is, it is something each individual must accomplish from the inside out in terms of a change in his or her self-concept.[11]

In organizations that move more consistently and successfully through the Identification State, we all can witness leaders taking the time that is necessary to assure that their employees understand what it means to change in terms of what they do at work and, more important, why they do it. In these respective organizations, we see clearer and more consistent narratives or scripts about the need for change forming as a result of activities undertaken by the leadership during the Identification State.

IDENTITY

Based on how abstract the change is or how different it is from what people are used to doing, this may require more time to systematically work through this Identification State to assure that people understand what the change means for their self-concept and identity, including when it started. In fairness to our previous health care leader at Coastal, thinking about what constitutes the patient experience versus taking ownership for serving customers coming in for a new yoga outfit, is decidedly more complex, given the range of services/products required in the health care organization and the risk. Moreover, health care organizations operate with many different professions as part of the larger enterprise, and each of those professional groups may have a different view of what constitutes the best patient experience based on their respective collective self-concepts and identities formed over decades.

Whether we are talking about health care or apparel, however, what we need to observe in the Identification State are the early signs of active exploration in terms of seeking out how to change how one understands work and then the collective self-concept within and between leadership levels near the end of this state. To successfully navigate through the Identifying State requires that individuals understand the need for a transformative shift in their own self-concept of what is needed to remain successful in terms of the way each employee executes his or her work. And one must keep in mind that some may have very strong opinions on what is the right way to do business, based on what they've learned and how they have previously performed in their roles within their organization and/or profession.

The level of awareness concerning a need to shift mind-sets for an organization to transform itself may not happen in earnest until the next phase (Initiation), particularly if the leaders identifying the need for change are newer and less entrenched in the organization's identity than are the rest of its employees. Moreover, some leaders may already possess a more complex set of ideas, meanings, attitudes, and value judgments in their self-concept that are related to the proposed strategic change, and they may be ahead, even too far, of others in seeing what is required to transform the organization.

Every transformative change must begin with a collective experience that marks the entry into the Identification State, during which a focal issue demanding a change in strategic direction flashes on the leadership's radar screen (and this could be at many levels of the organization). When such a major or persistent blip grabs the attention of the organization's leadership, the forces that generated the strategic issue also become a focal point for leaders to identify and understand what to do next while a new future course is being plotted. This state involves examining internal as well as external trends and the key events that shape the need for change in each individual's self-concept.

With lululemon, Christine Day could see there was a niche for her company that could differentiate her from larger competitors, such as Dick's Sporting Goods, which did not provide the type of customer experience through employee ownership that she had seen contributing to Starbucks' rapid growth and success. The absence of this type of customized experience, where customers could even see the lululemon products evolve based on their feedback to lululemon, was a clear signal to Christine that her strategic initiative to build owners in her workforce had significant merit.

Also, during the identification phase, there is a need to confirm the start, trajectory, and direction of change, while the bulk of the internal and external environmental scanning is also focused on understanding the core need for change. This state generates the "backstory" that sets the historical context, mood, and starting cast of characters within the change process script that becomes input into transforming the collective identity and self-concept of the workforce.

As I illustrated with the Coastal Healthcare system, a consistent and compelling script is an essential element to creating a collective sense of awareness. If the script is absent, the sense of awareness regarding the need for change can be lost, resulting in a misalignment around what it means to change, typically followed by frustration, misdirection, conflict, and loss of motivation. At this point in the change process, a clear strategic change initiative has probably not yet been determined, but the nature of the strategic issue should be clarified in terms of what constitutes the options for change.

This state is also characterized by exploration[12] and other preplanning activities, including preliminary data gathering and diagnosis, eventually resulting in a decision to develop a plan and commit resources to a strategic change. Successfully moving out of the Identification State requires a critical mass of individual and then collective awareness—with many employees telling and hearing the same story, one that touches the individual and collective self-concept of organizational members, shaping it to how one will interpret the change and its impact on how work gets done.

Recall that the state model is intended to help leaders and key change agents navigate the sequence of four states an organization must go through as they recognize the need for, start, and complete a strategic transformation. This involves recognizing when your organization has entered a new state, what is happening during this state that should be getting your attention, and the conditions that ideally should be met before moving fully into the next state.

Please consider that these states are by definition fluid and bound to overlap. Also, realistically, some members of the organization will have one foot in a current state and another foot in the next state, and not everyone will always be in the same state at the same time—or likely ever. The ultimate goal here is to decide if your employees are ready to move forward or whether there is more work to do in the current state to make sure there is a collective understanding of what needs to be done and why. Successfully moving through the Identification State means organizational members have detected the signal that highlights the need for change, and they are then preparing to proactively move forward in operationally defining it. Activities in this state produce data that can be used to create a case for change that will be tested in the Initiating State.

If the leaders driving the strategic change have begun to consider its ramifications with regard to their own self-concepts and the shared organizational identity at this state of the change process, they can also begin to craft a script that contains past, present, and future elements, which address what needs to be protected in terms of the values, culture, and ultimately the welfare of their organization.

At this point, it is essential to understand how the first principle regarding the self-concept works—how it both defines members' sense of inclusion and motivates behavior aimed at protection of the welfare of the organization (even if that motivation is ill informed, shortsighted, or, worse, defensive) and how it also affects each individual's self-worth in terms of what favorably differentiates this organization from its rivals. A script that touches on these elements will be a very powerful tool to aid in making the necessary changes to the content, attitudes, and value judgments in the shared collective self-concept of all employees. Specifically, how you see yourself becoming is part of how organizational members will see themselves becoming over time.

For all of these reasons, the organization's leadership cannot expect the change to occur in the way that it occurred at Coastal Healthcare, by executive fiat or mandate. People do not sustainably change their self-concept based on mandates from others; this merely represents adopting a compliance rather than an identity or commitment-based model.

Failure to enter and move through the Identification State means the organization either has failed to detect the signal promoting the need for change, has ignored important signals, has failed to fully explore the signals, and/or is therefore not ready to move forward with the strategic change. Unfortunately, many leaders in organizations who have a grasp of what the change means for them and their organization may not be aware of the fact that those who report to them have not fully understood or embraced the need for change, nor what change means for them in terms of how they do their work or organize their self-concepts. This was clearly the case for the first health care organization I reviewed with you, where many employees said they already were patient centric in terms of the care they provided to patients.

As mentioned at the outset of this chapter, in any given state of change, there are specific mechanisms that drive and moderate the key processes and activities within that state. By activities in terms of organizational change, we mean attempts by individuals to convert one form of information into energy directed at changing the self-concepts of employees in the organization to incorporate the required change in strategic purpose and direction.

During the Identification State, organizational leaders must also keep an eye on internal and external progress that works to shape the strategic direction the leadership is planning to pursue over time. For example, the organizational leaders could track such things as how their most valuable customers view the organization's services, as with Alaska Airlines, whose most loyal customers loved them but would no longer fly them due to their inefficiencies. Also, in the case of lululemon, Christine was taking a successful customer engagement model from another industry and thinking how it could shape the sport/retail industry.

In my experience, it is rare that someone isn't already doing what you think might serve your organization or industry better, frequently in a different industry, that can be replicated or at least borrowed in part for your industry. Clearly, hotels have been moving toward a customer-centric view that is not all that different from what we are now seeing emerge in health care organizations, including such things as upgrades in food services, facilities, providing valet service, a concierge to manage the patients' flow through the health care system, 24/7 personalized services, and so on.

Organizations that are successful in moving through the Identification State of a transformational change will pay heed to signals from one or more of these sources and also engage these triggers in arriving at a decision to develop a preliminary plan of action that requires an investment of resources to begin to move into the Initiation State. Yet, the leaders must also realize that prior research has shown that transformational change in organizational operations decreases efficiency and increases failure rates, at least in the short term, as resources and attention are diverted from normal routinized operating functions to processes involving reorientation and adaptation. An organization's competitive capabilities are typically enhanced only after working through this initial disruption, as it takes time for employees to learn and become proficient at using their new script and narrative.

Thus, the key drivers in the Initiating State are bound to be near the top of the organization; therefore decisions to invest in transformative change will involve top leadership. This is not to say that other leaders will not be aware of the necessity for change, but, without the senior leadership being fully aware, such change is likely to derail the change process due to a lack of investment of time and energy from the top leaders.[13]

What I also wanted to convey in this first state in the change process is that it takes a lot of discipline to make others aware of the need for change and what the first steps are that should be taken. This means that leaders have to repeat themselves a lot; they have to consistently model what they expect in others; most important, they need to be willing to be challenged when their employees don't understand why the specific change is needed, what it entails, and whether it is even a new initiative. The less trust and goodwill there are in the senior leaders at the outset, the more likely the Identification State will take longer to move through successfully.[14] In an environment where distrust is high and transparency is low, there will have to be a lot of narratives addressed until one becomes the organizing script or focus for the strategic change.

The predominant leadership styles in the Identifying State are associated with being able to recognize signals that point to the future direction or trends that could have an impact on your industry. Being transformational and visionary helps, as does providing an environment where your employees feel they can safely speak up, challenge assumptions, question future directions, and experiment. Because not much is being done in terms of initiating changes, we don't expect that instrumental leadership would be as evident as authentic and transformational.[15] This is not to say that there may not be goals set for employees to continue to look for new ways of operating and competing, which could fall under transactional leadership.

Please review this summary of some key points and things you should reflect on in the first state:

- In this chapter, we introduced the importance of building consistency in the awareness individuals have regarding the need for change and the changes that must also occur in the self and collective self-concept.
- We provided a more in-depth analysis of what constitutes making people aware and the tactics and strategies for doing so.
- We reintroduced the idea of key drivers to explain how organizations move within the awareness phase.

Now please reflect on the following questions:

- Think about something that you first noticed that signaled a need for you to change. What was that signal, and how did you notice it was there?
- Have you seen other signals as being a consequence of noticing that first signal?
- In what situations have you seen a signal that turned out to be premature or, worse yet, false?
- How have you or others attempted to make people aware of these signals? What has been most successful for you in doing so?

Right now in your organization, are you aware of a change initiative that is just starting or started? How has that change initiative been unfolding in terms of making others aware of what is needed in terms of how they define "my work"?

RESEARCH LINK: A DEEPER DIVE

I have used the terms *narrative* or *scripts* throughout this and previous chapters. I have done so because it is pivotal to how people make claims regarding their identity. The individual's and collective's identity is built from these narratives and scripts that are experienced, made sense of, and then incorporated into what is then claimed.[16] For example, McAdams noted with regards to how stories and scripts influence our identities that "the internalized and evolving story that results from a person's selective appropriations of past, present and future" (1999: 486).[17]

For example, when a new story comes along it can challenge if not rupture the way one sees him- or herself; by telling and then leaving the story, the self then emerges to a new possible self-identity. These changes in self-narratives are a means that form the bridge between the old roles and self-concept and the new ones that are forming.

In some cases these stories can even be recovered from an old narrative or script that was lost. This occurred with the Nike track town at the University of Oregon and its famous Hayward Field. The track at the university was considered at one point very sacred ground for runners. The narrative surrounding the track and the town had been built by individuals such as Bill Bowerman, Bill Hayward, and Bill Dellinger, who were beloved track coaches at the university in Eugene, as well as great runners such as Steve Prefontaine, Mac Wilkins, and even Phil Knight. You may also know that it was Phil Knight and Bill Bowerman who started Nike, and it was Bill who made the first Nike sneaker using a waffle iron. Over time Nike and Eugene would become synonymous with being the runners' mecca.

Unfortunately, these mythical stories about Eugene had been lost over time with respect to the town and university being the Mount Olympus of track. Then, in 2005, the university hired Coach Lananna, and by 2008 Track Town was hosting the Olympic trials at Hayward Field. Coach Lananna realized there was a dormant narrative that needed to be reactivated such that the individual and collective self-concepts of the community would again be aligned around being the track town.[18]

A similar narrative reemerged at Ford Motor Company. When Alan Mulally left Boeing and was hired by Henry Ford's great-grandson, he realized after a short period of time in the role of CEO that something was missing at Ford. He recalled that in his first meeting with one of the union presidents, he asked him whether he still wanted to build world-class quality cars. The union president had become very cynical about the leadership at Ford and didn't answer the question directly but indicated he would think about it and get back to Mr. Mulally. It wasn't long afterwards that Mr. Mulally received a call from that union president early one morning, when he gave his reply to the question: he was ready to build world-class cars again, reactivating a narrative that had been lost for many years at Ford. This preceded a transformative turnaround at the company.

5 THE INITIATING STATE: BEGINNING THE LAUNCH

Work groups in the unit cooperate to get the work done.

In contrast with the Identifying State, in the Initiating State there are a lot more activities that are being started with added investments and expenses. In this chapter, I examine the type of focus you need to take once you have decided which signals that you have received in the Identifying State are legitimate and relevant to motivating a change in your and your employees' self-concepts and narratives. Also, in terms of a spoiler alert, as we begin to discuss changes in the Initiating State, you will no doubt see that the unit of analysis or focus will not be just on the individual but on groups or teams, larger units such as divisions, and hopefully at some point the entire organization. Yet, at the epicenter of change and transformation, the unit of analysis remains the change in an individual's self-concept and narrative.

In Figure 5.1, we provide a simplified panel of this second state of organizing change in organizations.

SETTING UP "EXPERIMENTS"

An experiment is something a colleague of ours once referred to as "a succession of tryouts." Each and every day, there is some organization out there trying to roll out an experiment focusing on some change. They may even be transparent about the proposed change and call it an experiment, although such a change is typically referred to as an initiative or something akin to change management. What we want to emphasize here is that thinking like an experimenter as opposed to worrying about what the initiative is labeled is really what's most important. I will describe the rigor of thinking that goes into creating an experiment and why it is important to this Initiating State of organization change.

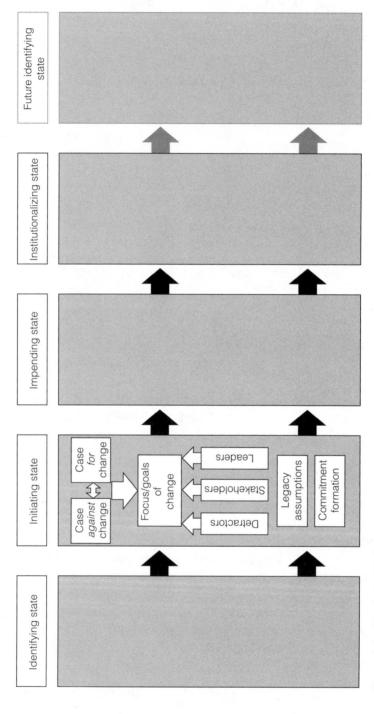

Figure 5.1 The Initiating State.

In its simplest form, a true field experiment, often considered the gold standard in organizational research, includes several components that make it an experiment.[1] First, you need to systematically manipulate or change something that you feel will have an impact on something else that you desire to change. Then you need to randomly assign people based on your unit of analysis to an intervention and comparison or control condition; let's say "individuals," to be consistent with our organizing theme and first principles thinking. The intervention condition should be designed to have a measurable impact on specific and desired outcomes you expect to change. Third, you need to compare that intervention condition to either a control condition, where the individuals don't receive the intervention, or to a comparison condition similar to pharmaceutical research where you compare the best new drug—your intervention—to the previous best drug. For the drug experiment to yield any meaningful findings and obtain FDA approval, the experimental condition to which individuals were randomly assigned must yield significantly better results than the previous best drug. That's pretty much it, and now you can call yourself a budding organizational experimenter.

I want you to consider change initiatives as *tryouts* and *experiments*, so that you can systematically assess the effects of a proposed initiative with a subsample of employees randomly assigned to the intervention versus the control or comparison condition. By doing so, you are now able to do a series of pilot experiments to try out what you are attempting to change in your organization at a substantially lower cost. How? Instead of doing a full system rollout, you can test the effects of your change intervention with a subset of your organization and its employees. This strategy was represented in part by the Alaska Airlines leaders focusing on what they called the "fix Seattle" initiative. This type of intervention would be classified as a quasi-experimental intervention, in that they didn't use randomization of people or location in this first intervention, but it was an intervention compared to a comparison group in terms of other locations for this airline, for example, Los Angeles or LAX airport.

In this chapter, I am going to examine different "field" experiments to demonstrate how you can initiate and test your own organizational change initiative. All of those discussed represent attempts at real changes in an organization. Many of the examples are not true experiments, except one that I will share based on my own research with the Israeli Defense Force. The key message here is that being rigorous in your thinking, methods, and interventions in no way compromises the interventions' relevance with respect to affecting organizational change. Indeed, if done properly, the employees involved should not even notice that it is an experiment. Rather, your employees will experience it as a well-designed and executed change initiative.

I should add one other piece looking back to the Identifying State—the reason for conducting the initiative in the first place. In this state, a signal or signals are picked up and then acted on. If we consider that each of us has a theory or narrative regarding how organizations should function, and one day there is a signal that prompts you to experiment with something different, then the nature of your theory or narrative is an important consideration in terms of not only what you choose to initiate but also how the initiative is designed and measured in terms of its impact on relevant outcomes.

Let me share a practical example of what I've already discussed here. Microsoft has gone through a lot of changes over its forty-one-year history, especially under its current CEO's leadership. Satya Nadella recently initiated a quasi-experiment at Microsoft, among many experiments he and his leadership team have been trying out over the past two years. In this quasi-experiment, he invited outsiders to Microsoft's annual retreat. In the minds of many of Microsoft's top 180 leaders, and based on past history, these outsiders were not usually invited to this exclusive event for Microsoft. In this meeting, the individuals Nadella selected to come were not chosen using the old operational definition of a "top" Microsoft leader that had started with Bill Gates and then continued on with his successor Steve Ballmer. Some of these outside leaders came from companies that Microsoft had acquired, such as LinkedIn. As reported in the *Wall Street Journal*, "Some Microsoft senior leaders complained to Mr. Nadella, saying the new hands didn't have the titles or tenure to attend the two-day event at Suncadia Resort, a mountain getaway 80 miles east of Seattle."[2] In their view, Satya Nadella's actions were a breach of their culture and narrative.[3]

Why did Nadella invite these so-called outsiders to this elite leadership meeting? One might consider that he was trying to experiment with bringing in new perspectives and ideas into the mix, to ostensibly challenge Microsoft's deep cultural belief and concern about preventing anything not invented by Microsoft getting into their business ecosystem. It seems there is an old Microsoft culture in juxtaposition to a potentially new emerging culture—each clashing with the other. Some might say that Nadella's initiative was squarely focused on promoting a different way of thinking in Microsoft with respect to the source of good ideas.[4]

In Nadella's quasi-experimental condition, he had outsiders coming from companies that have been acquired that were not randomly assigned but chosen for the retreat. The comparison group might be groups of other senior leaders, who have not invited outsiders to their retreats. Nadella could test his idea with the top

180 leaders, as a pilot intervention that could then be systematically rolled out throughout the organization with more control and comparison groups built into his experimental design. For example, he could randomly select two divisions and their units in Microsoft, one of which receives an outsider contingent and the other a comparative learning experience but with no outsiders present. The outcomes measured could include new ideas, initiatives, processes, and procedures that are generated in each group.

Nadella has argued in favor of his implementing his experiment based on the idea that if Microsoft's culture regarding not accepting ideas from outsiders was correct, then why has Microsoft missed so many important trends in computing over the years? His theory and narrative of what constitutes an adaptive organization is linked to what is called a growth mind-set. A growth mind-set culture will promote learning from a diversity of sources, including outsiders, who are more likely to bring new ideas into their interactions.[5]

Microsoft has done thirty-six major acquisitions since Nadella has taken over as CEO. Clearly, we can consider this strategy as being part of a larger narrative, which is to populate Microsoft with so many outsiders that it will have a continual stream of new and different ideas that are not homegrown or, worse, inbred. His quasi-experiment is currently unfolding in the sense that it is not a true field experiment with randomization of interventions but a number of quasi-experimental tryouts that are going on in Microsoft at the same time. Now, we will have to wait and see the yield on these initiatives over time.

One of the big challenges for Microsoft and its leaders going forward is not just bringing in these new ideas but making sure they are vetted and seriously considered before being discarded. Many companies do a lot of acquisitions, but they also do a terrible job of mining the ideas they bring in based on the premise of "not invented here," so those ideas get discarded or end up as new startups.

In our next section, we emphasize the importance of launching what we call "the campaign" for planned organization change. In terms of using that word, *campaign*, we believe it is essential for organizations to be cognizant of the nature of the campaign and who is responsible for rolling it out throughout the organization when initiating strategic change.[6]

LAUNCHING THE CAMPAIGN FOR CHANGE

In many change efforts, we have found that a great deal of time and energy is invested in determining what to change and how to do it, whereas much less attention and resources are invested in explaining *why* the change is happening, *where* it should be started, *when* it should be started, *how* exactly should it be rolled out, *who* will be responsible, *why* should they be responsible, and *what* are the costs, benefits, and risks associated with the change versus remaining with the status quo. For all of these reasons, we view the initiative of any change effort as a campaign process.

Like all good campaigns, you need a clear platform for change; champions, people who are your surrogates to carry the message forward that support the initiative; sufficient resources to sustain the campaign, especially into the third state in our model called *Impending*, where change is in flux and emerging; and some inspiration and ownership for the change process along with a dose of resiliency, which will be required to help to sustain it. Let's first review two different attempts at organizational change, one that was totally unsuccessful and the other where change has been sustained now over five plus years.

HEALTH CARE DIS-INTEGRATION

The first case is the health care organization that we mentioned where the COO completely underestimated the need for presenting and reinforcing the case for change. In other words, it lacked a sustainable campaign, along with numerous other problems. This strategic change largely involved the health care organization transforming itself from being a holding to an operating company. In a holding company, there is not necessarily the need for high levels of integration and synergy. These attributes are nice to have but not "must haves" to be efficient and productive. In an operating company, the purpose is to create economies of scale while also optimizing the levels of integration necessary to produce the best products and services at the least cost and highest quality. Recall that when a facilitator working with this health care organization asked a room of 500 senior leaders when the campaign for change started, there were widely different estimates, with some unaware that it had actually started at all.

Prior to that event held with the 500 leaders, I met with the COO of this health care organization and his corporate communications officer in what appeared to be the early stages of the Initiating State toward change. Certainly the COO had identified change as being absolutely necessary for his organization to go from a holding to an operational company and to remain competitive. The purpose of the meeting was to discuss how leadership development already underway within this health care organization could be used to facilitate the case for versus against this change. The expressed goal for these training programs was to help bring on board the current and next generation of key leaders to support the change process. Clearly, the proposed organizational changes would have an impact on every leader's unit and jobs. For example, many of these leaders had run their own hospitals in the role of CEO and were given a lot of independence as an operating unit within the larger holding company. As the change process unfolded, their reporting structure would change, with a growing corporate entity taking greater responsibility for decisions. Resource allocations would also change, budgeting would change, and how IT was purchased would change. Indeed, almost overnight the titles of these CEOs would change from being CEOs to presidents. In many leaders' narratives, the change in title alone was a demotion.

During this meeting, the COO was very clear that the change in this health care organization had already begun. He used as evidence an article he had written and distributed to all of the leaders on what this transformative change process entailed, as well as the goals that were formulated to foster change. Leveraging the upcoming management retreat was meant to reinforce the message of change—not to introduce it for the first time. The communications officer confirmed that this was indeed the purpose of the upcoming retreat and indicated that she was also working on a presentation that would help explain the changes being initiated, when and why this course of action was being taken, and each leader's role in the change process.

During most of this meeting, the COO pontificated on what he felt was the right thing to do, and what he and his leaders were going to do, to make this century-old health care organization succeed. He had already formed a very strong commitment to the strategy for change and was going to see it implemented by his direct reports and their direct reports. Throughout the meeting, the communications officer simply agreed with most of what the COO said. In a separate conversation later on, she tried to explain how his colleagues needed to work with the COO to help him understand the impact these changes would have on leaders to be successful in promoting and sustaining change. The COO had a very technical view of the change process that was logical and clearly laid out but neglected to consider that the change required people to actually come on board and be positively energized by the change. He completely underestimated the changing of hearts and minds that would be required to sustain this change initiative among his employees—even his direct reports.

In subsequent meetings with this COO, he never seemed to miss an opportunity to show everyone that he was the smartest person in the room and that they just needed to follow his plan to all be successful. Telling people they must change their narrative is usually not a strategy for winning the hearts and minds of your stakeholders and constituents. It's a starting point, but it is not a continuing or finishing strategy.[7]

At the all-hands-on-deck leadership retreat in Las Vegas, the COO spoke to the leadership audience with a strong sense of conviction. Not surprisingly, his message was very mechanistic, emphasizing that the change he would be discussing that day was already underway, and so it was time for everyone to simply get onboard. His presentation referred to the articles he had sent to them on the change process. In my separate conversations with the leaders in attendance, most admitted they had received the articles but had not read or discussed them with their colleagues or the COO. Few, if any, could cite any of the specific key points raised in the article that were supposedly pivotal to the change process in this health care organization.

After the COO had spoken, the CIO addressed the group with a review of so many IT initiatives that were tied to the proposed change initiative that it seemed as though he was talking about five or ten health care organizations versus just one large, complex operation. He kept throwing out dates associated with major change initiatives such as, "We will have that system fully implemented in three months, and another system in five months that will be completed on such and such a date, to the new system that will be deployed successfully organization-wide in less than one year," and so on and so on. He presented a dizzying array of initiatives and dependencies.

Ironically, as I discovered later, most members of the audience had gone through one IT implementation failure after another under this same CIO's leadership. It would be a huge understatement to say that he was not positively adding to the case for change and had not built sufficient goodwill with these leaders. He did not appear to have any credibility with this group, and his detractors were not seeing any of his goals and dates as realistic. The more he spoke it seemed the worse things got in terms of his believability—heralding a rather rough road ahead on the campaign.

To this day, as far as I know, none of those IT initiatives has been successfully implemented in that health care system. In fairness to the CIO, and as part of the legacy assumptions in this workforce regarding the outcomes of IT implementations, most IT change initiatives are received with a great deal of skepticism, and often the key question in people's minds is just how long it will take to fail. The best strategy for the retreat might have been to omit the CIO's talk. If he felt compelled to speak, he might have limited his talk to focus on one achievable IT initiative rather than ten dubious ones.

I was invited to address the group of leaders regarding the importance of taking ownership for the change initiative that was being articulated by the COO. I found it interesting that the CEO of the company, who was present, never got up to publicly endorse the change effort throughout the retreat nor to take ownership for it. What's more, the CEO never spoke to the COO at any time during the retreat when I was in attendance. Just the optics associated with his lack of engagement might cue some in the audience to potential challenges with moving this change effort forward. Moreover, and equally troubling, during the time I was at the retreat and seated with the COO, only a few of his direct reports stopped by to talk with him. This seemed very strange given this was a campaign for change with lots of questions to be addressed as to why this approach made sense to this audience. Moreover, it was a campaign event, and the CEO was clearly not shaking hands and taking selfies with his legion of leaders. In many organizations, when employees have a unique opportunity to interact with their senior leadership at a retreat, they take advantage of the opportunity to get some face time with key leaders. Not at this retreat.

In the retreat, I used an electronic polling system to have the leaders present at the retreat rate their readiness and support for the change initiative being championed by the COO. As the results of this anonymous polling appeared in graphs on the screen in the large ballroom, it became evident the majority of the people in the room were not prepared to lead this change effort and were not seeing themselves as owners for doing so. These data were clear evidence that the group of leaders, who were supposedly essential stakeholders in the change process, were either ambivalent about the changes being proposed, uninterested, or against the change. A minority of attendees seemed to be able to suspend judgment and give the proposed changes a chance—a small minority.

After spending the remainder of the day trying to address the data that had been generated in the electronic polling, as well as discussing the initiative in small and large group exercises, the COO returned to the podium to close the day's session. He acknowledged there was a lot more to do given the reactions shown in the electronic poll and vowed to spend time considering the next best course of action.

Two years after that event, with the change process stalled, there has been no evident campaign or plan to move this initiative forward in any different manner than what was going on at the time of this retreat. Indeed, the CEO of this health care system has continued to acquire more and more hospitals while the COO has continually failed to find a strategy that would adequately integrate those new hospitals into a seamless operating company. The communications officer kept coming up with new labels to market the initiative—and then decided to retire.

About two years after this retreat was held, I ran a senior leadership development program for top leaders across the same health care system. At this point, there was tremendous uncertainty in the organization. The organization had started a rolling layoff process, creating a great deal of anxiety throughout all of the operating units in terms of who was going to be cut next. For many of these leaders and their followers, it wasn't a question of whether the change would be successful; it was how long they would all be there before they were laid off. Still, it was evident in this workshop that this group of leaders wanted to try to help the COO be successful. They said so repeatedly in open forums and in the presence of the COO and his senior managers during an evening Q&A event hosted by the workshop attendees, who were prepared to share leadership success stories with their senior leadership.

The group of workshop attendees had a lot of legitimate questions about the changes being promoted in their health care organization. For example, they asked why they were being asked to reduce patient numbers in their hospitals by promoting healthy communities while the CEO of this same health care system continued to purchase more hospitals, adding more beds. This made no sense to this group of workshop attendees. Their questions remained unanswered throughout the evening. The COO spoke to the group and asked them to raise questions but then showed very little capacity for listening to their concerns. This whole situation was unfortunate, in that these leaders were some of his best field agents for change and could have been enlisted to take ownership and accountability for the change process, if the COO had simply listened to their concerns. Hallway conversations after the close of the day confirmed this missed opportunity.

Perhaps even more unfortunate is that another senior and highly respected leader addressed this same group on the proposed changes months later and said to many astonished attendees that even the top seven leaders, who directly reported to the COO, could not agree on the change being presented or on how to initiate the change. This sent a resounding message that the group of top leaders had not identified the need for change, nor had they identified the campaign that should be implemented to support and sustain the change initiative. If you can imagine a political campaign, where your campaign surrogates and campaign staff are each articulating a different platform for change (for example, we are raising, no we are lowering, taxes), that's about as close as it gets to representing this health care organization's focus on change.

What might be some clear warning signs that this organization was not ready to initiate the change process, let alone to campaign for it with its leaders?

- The CEO and COO were never on the same page in terms of the proposed change.

- The senior leaders were confused and could not decide what to change nor when.
- Many of the 500 leaders rated that they were not ready for this change and did not fully understand its goals or their roles in the change process.
- The COO admitted he needed to rethink the strategy for change but never did.
- Detractors were able to easily identify conflicting messages that literally sapped all of the positive energy from the change initiative, as well as its credibility with the leaders.
- The organization couldn't downsize quickly enough to keep up with all of the acquisitions, which made no sense to the cadre of leadership across the different operating units.
- The COO got so deep into his commitment to the change that, instead of seeing just about every possible sign that it was failing, he marched ahead, doubling down on resources, rolling layoffs, and eventually one day, far too long into this failed change effort, he was summarily asked to "retire." The change initiative described didn't reverse the fortunes of this health care system; it destroyed them.
- The COO of this organization could have not come up with a more efficient strategy to lose his best people, who were deeply committed to this organization's mission as part of their self-concept and narrative.

AIRLINE TAKEOFF

The Alaska Airlines change initiative we studied is a contrasting case characterizing the Initiating State. This story builds on their Identification State, discussed earlier. Alaska Airlines had two very enviable assets to draw on. First, it had a hometown following in Seattle, with a long list of very loyal customers who spoke about the airline as if it was their own sports team. Second, its senior leadership followed a collaborative model, had a lot of experience working together, and, even though the chairman and CEO had a strong, deliberate leadership style, the top management team largely recognized that the senior leaders had to be on board in the change process to move the organization from being a nice airline to an efficient one, while still retaining its respect for all of its customers.[8]

The senior leadership collected clear and compelling evidence that, if Alaska Airlines did not start to stem the tide of declining revenue and customers choosing to fly with other carriers, in the near future they would be bankrupt. Yet, like most change efforts, even when the data are clear that change is necessary and the organization is teetering at the cliff, it doesn't mean people will change their narrative in alignment with the proposed change initiative.

Bob Kegan, who has written some very good books and articles on individual and organizational change, described why individuals, and indeed organizations, frequently build up immunities that will fight any change effort, as if it is a foreign element entering one's body.[9] In one case, he described a client who was not in the best of health. To sustain his life, he absolutely had to take heart medication. Kegan was interviewing this man, who was in his late fifties, trying to find out why he was not taking his medication.

It is very common that individuals who should take medication to save their lives end up not doing so. Kegan tried to establish that the data presented to this patient were clear and compelling in terms of the risks to his life. His client totally agreed with the data and understood the ramifications of not taking the medication. As Kegan continued trying to understand why this individual refused medication that would save his life, he finally got to a competing commitment his client had against the taking of his heart medication. It was not physically taking the medication that bothered the patient, but rather it was the act of taking medication that made him feel just like he was an "old man." He did not want to be an old man like his father or grandfather—certainly not at his current age. Taking the medication was inconsistent with his self-concept at this point in his life. He did not see himself as an old man who needed medicine to survive. His immunity to the change was centered on the image he had of himself—"I am not an old man, and old men take these types of medications!"

For Alaska Airlines, being nice was at the core of their employees' self-concepts, and being efficient, like taking medication (that is, process improvements), was thought to detract from their identity, self-concept, and narratives about themselves. This meant that part of the campaign launch in the Initiative State had to address this core facet of their self-concept. Perhaps for the client in the preceding paragraph, one might ask, can't you take the medication, which is a compromise, but still see yourself as a relatively young robust man? In the Alaska case, can't employees be nice *and* efficient?

In a small retreat involving the top leadership in Alaska (one of a series that unfolded during the early state of identification), there was a lot of discussion about the problem and what solutions needed to be pursued to sustain this airline's viability while building a new narrative for change. Indeed, after recognizing the strategic challenge already noted, one of the senior leaders was charged to investigate the airline's challenges with a task force supporting him.

He was asked to then come back to the senior leaders to report on what should be done next.

The study was done very well, but, for a variety of reasons, the Initiating State fell short early on because there was insufficient buy-in for the change effort. Some of the leaders would later suggest that the "campaign staff" were not fully ready to be deployed and the focus on the effort was not as strong as it could have been in terms of what the initiative should start focusing on within the organization; it may not have been the right person chosen both to study and then to implement the necessary changes.

How were these problems overcome when the senior leaders stepped back to initiate change process 2.0? There were several key differences that demonstrated how these leaders had to circle back to the Identification State, before redoing the Initiating State. First, a decision was taken to "fix Seattle," which was the hub for this airline. They made an assumption that if this effort was successful, the rest of the organization would follow along with the change process. Interestingly, this didn't mean that the campaign for change waited in other parts of the airlines network. To the contrary, the other geographic locations within Alaska Airlines were kept informed regarding the progress of the changes being made once the change initiative began, with data that depicted a myriad of improvements in their operational process.

The new leader selected to be responsible for the strategic change would say again and again that improvements in the process would produce the results they desired and that they had to create a high-quality repeatable process to produce efficiencies to compete in an increasingly competitive market and then, at the right time, show their progress to others in Alaska Airlines' other locations. There was a continual campaign going on by the senior leaders and their surrogates to explain what they were doing in Seattle to fix the hub.

There were some other changes made early on in the Initiating State that were consequential to the change process moving forward. First, the CEO designated the senior VP of Operations chosen to lead the change to be responsible for the entire change process. That VP would report directly to the CEO and chairman, and everyone else in the organization was required to report directly or indirectly to that VP. Of course, this placed tremendous pressure on one individual to suc-ceed with the change process, as he later recounted. He would say that many of his peers were quite disgruntled for having to report to him, but they did so out of respect for their organization. In their narrative, "my organization" meant sup-porting him because the change was about their airline, even if they disagreed with the new leadership structure.

The CEO and chairman also made his support for this VP of Operations very visible, by being by his side walking throughout the terminal, baggage processing centers, above and below the plane's wings with ground crews, and so forth. As this campaign unfolded, he wanted to make sure the VP was seen as the person in charge to drive change forward in the most visible manner possible to all key stakeholders.

The VP also created a group of senior leaders who met every day to review a long list of measures that tracked every element of the airline's delivery process from booking a passenger to landing that person safely at the gate and helping him or her to disembark into the terminal. I attended one of these morning meetings. The metrics reported in each daily meeting ranged from how many bags were lost per flight, the time it took to return bags to customers, the turnaround times for each plane, to why a plane closed its door late (for example, in one instance a customer had failed to inform the gate agent that he was coming to the gate in a 400-pound electric wheelchair that needed to be put in the hold). Every detail was combed through, discussed, and addressed, including a very minor scratch on the plane's exterior.

In the beginning of this change process, the VP's daily measurement meetings were referred to affectionately as "food fights." Each day they had knock down and drag out blaming sessions. The VP of Operations would continue to say that it is not who did something wrong, it is how the process needed to be changed to yield the desired results: blame the process, not the person. The VP also continued to move the goal posts in terms of each time the group achieved a milestone for performance. After being successful in meeting the targeted goals, he upped their game with a more difficult goal, which caused some consternation but, in the end, built pride in how much they had achieved in terms of early wins.

There are two interesting points about these daily meetings that are worth considering in terms of taking ownership for change in the Initiating State. First, if the leader of a unit could not attend these daily morning meetings, then his or her supervisor was responsible for attending. That one rule led to a very high attendance rate among these senior leaders. Second, well into the next state of Impending Changes, the VP of Operations no longer chaired these meetings but had different leaders in the room rotate responsibility for doing so. Also, when the VP suggested in one meeting that he didn't feel it was necessary to have this meeting every day because he felt that the processes were being routinely repeated, the group turned him down. They said they would own the convening of the meeting going forward on a daily basis.

Of course, there were many elements that went into moving this campaign squarely into the Initiating State. One included working with the ground crew to reengineer how they brought in and released planes from the gate. The VP had them study every move on the ground, including having them paint boxes on the tarmac in which tools should be placed for ease of recovery. When you are down under the plane's wing, there are lots of tools strewn across the tarmac, which, if not put back in the same place, results in lost time in turning a plane around, as well as accidents where workers are tripping over objects that are not properly stored.

Most significantly, the VP ordered that a scoreboard be put on the wall behind the gate that included key metrics on how well the ground crews were performing in turning around each plane (for example, the board included a timer that showed the minutes left before on-time departure). These scoreboards got so popular that the flight attendants asked for ones to be put in the ramp where passengers entered the plane, because they couldn't clearly see them in front of the planes' nose.

On a broader organizational level, the next hub for Alaska Airlines was LAX. As already noted, the employees there were carefully tracking the change initiative in Seattle; as the Seattle campaign unfolded, they moved from being detractors to becoming key stakeholders, if not outright competitors. What was happening during the Initiating State in Seattle was seen as forming into a friendly competition with LAX. The staff there increasingly wanted to know more about what was going on in Seattle and kept asking the VP of Operations if they could start their own similar change initiative. Consequently, even though the VP of Seattle had done relatively little work to initiate changes within LAX, there was some campaign momentum forming down south that would lead to LAX being in the Initiating State before the official launch of the change effort in that location. This might be called a cascading effect of the initial campaign.

Another factor in moving the change initiative past the typical cases levied against change frequently observed in the Initiating State was the launching of an all-employee training program that focused on how the change process would unfold and the implications it would have for how Alaska Airlines performs its services to customers. By "all employees," that meant at the time all 12,000 employees.

Ostensibly, the purpose of these one-day workshops was to teach everyone in the company how to bring a plane in and then send it off onto its destination as quickly and safely as possible. They even used a game simulation, called "Flight Path" in the workshop to teach everyone from accountants to IT personnel how to bring a plane in and out safely. Most important, the instructors in all of these daylong workshops were the very top leaders in Alaska Airlines, who didn't just stop by to meet and greet the group. They taught their employees the change process, answered their questions, and discussed why this change initiative was so important to the future of *their organization*. There were no surrogates used in this campaign stop; this was the candidates at the top themselves, championing the change process.

One very powerful exercise they used to promote being an "accountability" owner for the change initiative was called "One Thin Dime." In this exercise, the leaders demonstrated the importance of a having a repeatable and reliable practice, by showing their margin of profit was one thin dime for every dollar. It was clear that to achieve the one thin dime margin, it would take all hands on deck to make this change process work. It wasn't the pilots, the flight attendants, mechanics, baggage handlers, or back office staff—it had to be everyone in Alaska coming on board for the change to be successful.

To reiterate what has already been said about the importance the top leaders placed in these workshops, the current CEO, who was then the CFO, ran numerous workshops over the life of the training program. We should ask what sort of signal would this send to you about the seriousness of this type of campaign in your organization, if the future CEO was running these workshops with you in attendance. How serious would you take their appeal to coming on board with the change process?

In terms of achieving a repeatable process, the baggage handlers, who were a contracted crew, took over from the original baggage handlers, who were all Alaska employees. This contracted company had to take over literally overnight, when the top management fired every baggage handler after repeated attempts to get them to come on board during the Initiating State. Baggage handling had gotten so poor that there were fists fights among customers at the baggage carousels, resulting in the police having to be called in to break them up. When the decision was finally taken to bring in an outsourced company to take over the baggage handling, what the Alaska leaders discovered was that this contracting company was not ready for prime time, as they had indicated to the leaders. Nevertheless, Alaska's top leaders had to stick with these contractors and continued to place pressure on them to achieve a repeatable and reliable practice.

Over time, the baggage handlers did improve, and they were sporadically hitting their goals, which they wanted to do to receive the bonus rewards promised by the airline. However, the contractor might hit the goals one day, and expect to receive their reward, whereas on the next day they would fall short. During this time, the VP in charge of the change process would fine the contracting company for not meeting goals consistently day in and day out. This led to the senior leaders of the contractor company to file a protest with Alaska Airlines, followed by flying in from Great Britain to get an explanation as to why they were not receiving the rewards on the days their baggage crews were successful.

The contractors met with the VP for Operations and presented their case, regarding their expectations to get their bonus. The VP of Operations listened intently to their concerns and then simply explained that he was clear to all of his contractors that they had to achieve a repeatable and reliable process, and when they did achieve that goal, they would be rewarded. In his mind, you don't reward crews for having some safe flights but not others; to create a reliably safe airline, there was going to be a repeatable process established here as well with the baggage handlers. The meeting adjourned with the senior leaders of the contracting organization agreeing to achieve this goal, which they subsequently did as an organization over and over again, resulting in a new customer offering—getting your bags at the carousel in twenty minutes or less or Alaska Airlines pays you a fee.

In contrasting these two organizations, it is fair to say that we are oversimplifying the Initiating State and could fill this entire book with the details associated with these respective change processes. Also, there were many stumbles along the way for Alaska, and, as the senior leaders repeatedly have said, there were likely other strategies they didn't choose that could have made the process more efficient and effective. However, it was their sense of not having the only strategy for change, and a humble understanding of their mistakes, that was also a significant factor in contributing to their success. The COO of the health care organization was guided in large part by his own hubris and believing he had the *right* strategy that his employees hopefully would be smart enough follow in the future.

We would also like to highlight a term that we have been using throughout this chapter that is pivotal to successful change efforts. The term is *ownership*, not necessarily financial but rather psychological ownership. In the Initiating State, the leadership of an organization responsible for the change has to campaign effectively to engage employees in the change process.[10]

We have also been using the idea of each person's narrative as part of his or her self-concept, making the connection to how the individual describes "my organization." At Alaska Airlines, employees were nice to their customers but not always efficient. When they talked about the airline, they described "my organization" as being nice in taking care of people, as characterized by numerous stories of what they felt was great customer service. One such example involved a young consultant who had flown on Alaska late one evening into a small airport in the Midwest region of the United States. After getting to the hotel, the consultant realized that she had left her laptop on the plane with all of her materials for a very important presentation the next morning starting at 7 am. Without her laptop she was totally unable to give her talk and likely would lose a major contract for her company.

It just so happened that the flight attendant who was on the same flight was in the hotel lobby and noticed the young woman's distress. She approached her to find out what was up and heard how the consultant had left the laptop on the plane. The flight attendant said the airport was now closed, and the plane was locked up, but they could recover the laptop in the morning. Unfortunately by the time they went back to the airport in the morning, the consultant would have missed her window of time to present the proposal to her client. The flight attendant then recalled that she had a friend who was an operational manager at this airport and had his cell phone number. It was now about midnight, but she turned and called his cell, and he answered. He realized the dilemma, lived close to the airport, and said he would go in and retrieve the laptop, and they could then meet him outside the airport—and this all happened.

This was vintage service for Alaska and something they never wanted to lose in terms of the type of ownership the flight attendant took for servicing this young consultant. However, there are times when you have to do the least harm to the most people in a bad situation, such as holding a plane for one person who is late while all the other passengers on the plane miss connections at their next stop. "My organization" for Alaska employees was to hold that plane, because that is what nice people do. And in doing so, among other inefficiencies, they were causing the airline to perform poorly—having no practical, reliable, repeatable process.

In terms of full disclosure, the preceding story is absolutely true. I heard it while waiting for a delayed Alaska Airlines flight at Newark airport in New Jersey. The person telling the story was trying to calm down some irate passengers who could not understand why their damn plane was late and were berating an Alaska Airlines gate agent. Here, in this instance, it was the customer taking ownership to champion this airline. Nice. By the way, that customer was the consultant in the story, now ten years older and still flying Alaska Airlines.

As may seem obvious from our discussion, the Initiating State requires a lot of instrumental and transactional leadership.[11] It requires that employees move from being territorial owners to thinking about accepting new goals, roles, and expectations that will result in a greater level of being accountable for the change being initiated. Complementing this ownership, you can assume that the leadership has been able to envision the future state in which they are attempting to lead employees. Also during the Initiating State, there will be a lot of updates to the change process to adapt to varying contingencies, and the leader will have to promote a high level of agility and adaptability in the workforce. At the same time, people will want to be reminded by the leadership why this change is really necessary.

What can we take away from this Initiating State as we enter into the third and perhaps most challenging state of change, which I have labeled the Impending State?

- One of the critical elements to initiating change is making sure you have a comprehensive campaign strategy for that change process.

- Engaging individuals in the change process is not sufficient to foster change; you have to create a sense of ownership for the change, which ultimately coincides with how the individual perceives "my organization."

- Developing and initiating a repeatable and reliable process for change is essential to sustaining the change process, in that it helps to reinforce the narrative that is being scripted in terms of what the change process means for each employee's self-concept and narrative.

- The two change processes we discussed are not only different, but they also occurred in very different organizations dealing with very different circumstances. Consequently, the changes that you might produce and the methods for doing so could be very different. However, the core principles regarding campaigning, onboarding, building ownership, including key stakeholders, and presenting key arguments supporting the change process all remain the same but are just applied in different ways across different organizations.

In our next chapter we focus on how change emerges when it is impending but not yet institutionalized. By *impending*, we mean it has already started in terms of being the next way of how individuals think about themselves, but it is still impending and not yet firmly wired into the narrative of each employee or into the collective self-narrative. In many ways, this is by far the most challenging state, in that there are some people who have already turned the corner and realized the need for change, while others may still be back in the Identifying State, wondering what all of these initiatives mean to how they view "my organization."

You can almost guarantee that in a large and geographically distributed organization there will be parts of the organization that have already turned the corner with individuals aligned around a new way of thinking and doing while, in other parts, you may find the change is just a theory, nothing really serious, and certainly not something that is going to stick in the minds and hearts of people who work in or with that organization.

Please reflect on the following question before you proceed with the next chapter:

- Do you feel you are ready to move into a state in which there will be more things unfolding and changing in terms of how people view the change effort and what impact it has on their self-concept?

- Do you feel your campaign has reached and influenced enough employees to take accountability for ownership regarding the changes you desire?

- Are you ready to adapt and change, as your employees will look to you for being a role model for the change, as they will in themselves?

- What are you most concerned about in terms of fostering the change process, and how can you mitigate those concerns?

RESEARCH LINK: A DEEPER DIVE

We started out this chapter discussing true field experiments. In one true field experiment that I conducted with the Israeli Defense Force, we compared two weekly training programs focused on transformational leadership development. The unit of analysis for this study was the platoon and its commander. In Israel, the platoon commander takes the unit through basic training. In our true field experiment we randomly assigned platoons to either an eclectic and popular program on training transformational leadership or to a targeted behavioral intervention with a specific focus on how to change leaders to be more transformational. This latter program was more tightly linked to both the foundational model for transformational leadership, as well as to a lot of prior research. To be even more rigorous, we randomly assigned trainers to each condition.

Over the course of basic training, we found that the platoon leaders in the behavioral training program improved more significantly in their soldiers rating them on transformational leadership versus the commanders who were assigned to the more eclectic program. Moreover, those platoons in the targeted behavioral condition were also seen as being more effective by the trainers in basic training.

What this field study showed is that with a very rigorous design and true field experiment, we can clearly demonstrate that complex forms of leadership, like transformational, can be developed. Finally, for the participants' perspectives in the training, they just saw it as training, not some field experiment.

6 THE IMPENDING STATE: BREAKING BETTER

Employees in my unit are always ready to lend a helping hand to others around them.

There was a very popular show that ran for six seasons, from 2008 through 2013, in the United States and globally called *Breaking Bad*. Starring in the lead role in this show was the actor Bryan Cranston, who played Mr. White from Albuquerque, New Mexico. In his recent biography, *A Life in Parts*, Bryan Cranston discusses how his life unfolded and how he ended up in acting. The core organizing idea that Bryan used to structure the narrative in his book was that his life had unfolded in parts, which he described as a series of episodes that formed into the arc of his life story. It reminded me of how I view organizations and how change occurs sometimes in parts, one self-concept at a time.

Cranston's approach to describing his narrative is very similar to how we have described the way organizations change—that is, in a complex sequencing of parts, when they go from a change in an individual's self-concept to the collective self-concept and identity of the organization. As you will see in our following brief overview of the show *Breaking Bad*, there are changes that occurred in this series that were very carefully scripted into the overall show's narrative by its creator Vince Gilligan. The core organizing concept underlying this show depicts a man who goes from being a decent public servant to an outright murderer, albeit ever so gradually and carefully across years in show time.

One of the unique aspects of *Breaking Bad* related to what ethicists call the moral slippery slope. What ethicists mean is a person does not necessarily break bad overnight or even in one specific critical situation. This sort of change occurs in an individual's moral compass as he or she gradually shifts from being able to imagine thinking and behaving in an unethical way to rationalizing why it is necessary and important to do so.[1]

The premise of the show is that a relatively obscure, rather dull high school chemistry teacher finds out he is dying of cancer and goes from being an ethical individual to someone who builds a criminal empire developing and selling the very best crystal meth. This meth has a distinctive, deep blue color and ultimately becomes the top-selling global brand.

In the moment that Walter White found out that he has been diagnosed with an incurable cancer, he was confronted with his mortality. He realized that he had not prepared for this dramatic turn of events either emotionally or financially, and with a new baby coming along and an older child with some physical challenges, he feared that he would leave his family and wife behind without sufficient funds to sustain them—a moral dilemma that resulted in some rather difficult choices for Mr. White in what appeared to him to be his remaining time on Earth.

The writers and actors in this show obsessed over this core organizing principle that underscored every aspect of the arc of this show's story over a six-year run. In his biography, Bryan Cranston discusses how scenes were rewritten to make sure they maintained an authentic arc, one that doesn't move too quickly to the dark side in terms of breaking bad.

Why would this gradual shift be so important to the arc of the story? Consider that it is hard for most viewers to contemplate that a nice high school chemistry teacher, living a normal middle-class life in New Mexico, with seemingly good moral values, will in a relatively short period of time become the largest and most notorious meth dealer in the country, referred to by his nickname Heisenberg. The writers and actors could have taken Mr. White and walked him directly into the dark side, but if they did so too quickly they firmly believed their story would not have been as authentic to the show's viewers. Also, they were worried that a dramatic shift to the dark side could turn the audience against Mr. White too early into the arc of his changing moral values, resulting in the viewers abandoning the show. There were clearly artistic and pragmatic reasons for managing the arc and velocity of change to Mr. White's character.

To make a great long story short, after his diagnosis, Mr. White meets a former high school student of his named Jesse. Jesse knows a lot about the drug trade but not a lot about chemistry. Together they form an unholy alliance to develop a meth business where Jesse first serves as the mentor for Mr. White, his mentee. However, as the arc of the story unfolds, Mr. White becomes more ruthless, unethical, and determined to make a lot of money quickly, even beyond the expectation of his delinquent comrade. At some point in the breaking bad arc of the story, he has acquired much more wealth than his family will ever need, but for Mr. White there is no longer any turning back to his earlier ethical base. He has broken bad too far.

As Bryan Cranston describes in his biography, there is one scene where Jesse is sleeping with his girlfriend, both of whom are heroin addicts. They are both completely passed out on his bed when Mr. White arrives to find out why Jesse did not show up for an important appointment. Mr. White surmises that his girlfriend, whom Jesse actually loves very much, will turn him into a helpless drug addict, making him worthless to Mr. White's business. It's all about business, power, and wealth for Mr. White.

In this pivotal scene, the original script depicts his girlfriend dying through asphyxiation by vomiting in her sleep. In one take, Mr. White is supposed to come into the bedroom and move her onto her back so she will suffocate when vomiting. However, Bryan Cranston feels that if Mr. White does that to her, this pivotal action would be seen by viewers as too ruthless and calculating as a murderer. The concern he had for the arc of this story was that by breaking bad too fast, he would lose that semblance of still being a "good guy" in a bad situation, where he was simply trying to take care of his family, albeit by being a notorious drug dealer. Bryan Cranston gets the director and writers to adjust the scene, so that Jesse's girlfriend is already on her back, and without taking any action he lets her die by failing to act. It was this subtle shift in narrative that years later Vince Gilligan, the show's originator said, that allowed the arc of this story to unfold in a much more authentic way.

I must admit that I have rarely seen such attention to the arc of a story's authenticity regarding organizational change and transformation. I believe that if there were such attention and focus that the campaigns for change in organizations would have a much higher success rate than we have witnessed in the past.

I now move into describing the third state or phase of change with the components of that phase, depicted in Figure 6.1.

BREAKING BETTER

To reiterate, in all of my years working with organizations and people undergoing change and transformation, I have never seen an organization or its leadership handle the arc of change as judiciously as the producer, directors, writers, and actors in *Breaking Bad*, that is, by carefully sticking with the core organizing principle associated with and driving the change process. Of course, some might say, anyone can do this with a TV show because one has a lot more controls including retakes and technical support. Yes, there are many ways to control the scene as presented, but the writers, directors, producers, and actors have very little control over their audience and their receptivity to the arc of the story. Indeed, for the millions of

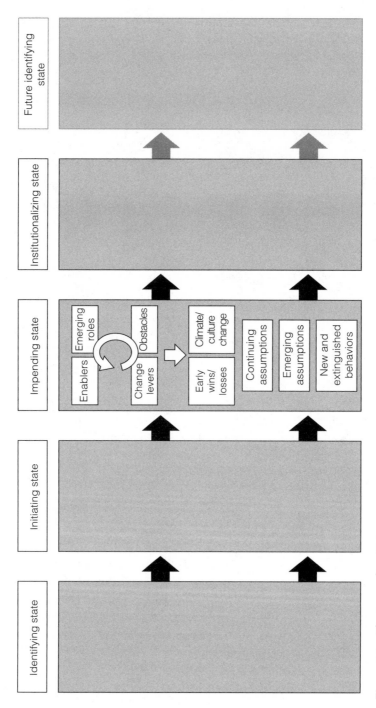

Figure 6.1   The Impending State.

viewers of *Breaking Bad*, I suspect that Bryan Cranston met only a small fraction of them during the show's six-year run.

In the following narrative, I demonstrate that a story line like the one in *Breaking Bad* and the nuance applied to nurturing the arc of that story provide valuable insights into how we can and should view organizational change and transformation stories properly unfolding in the impending state. Let's see how this works.

Like Mr. White, there are typically signals that trigger and/or launch the process of change that results in initiating and impending states of change. So let's return for a moment to the signals of change in our earlier chapter that end up identifying the need for change.

For Alaska Airlines, one of the most significant trigger events was the 9/11 terrorist attacks on the United States, which sent the airline industry into a financial tailspin.[2] For Mr. White, the trigger event for the moral slippery slope was his unexpected cancer diagnosis. Here are some other organizational trigger events not unlike Mr. White's event as a lead in to discussing what constitutes the core elements of the impending state.

Starbucks's revenue and growth began a precipitous decline in 2000 when Howard Shultz left the company after being in the top leadership role for eighteen years to pursue his philanthropic interests. Soon Starbucks had lost its edge—adding new stores worldwide but unable to create a consistently positive customer experience despite premium prices for its coffee. Though revenue was growing due to new store openings, in-store sales were declining.[3] It was clear that Starbucks was nearing an operational performance cliff and revenues would plummet once new store growth ceased. Howard Shultz decided he needed to come back as CEO and chairman to refocus Starbucks on its core values, which included brand integrity and creating a great customer experience every day and in every store. On one pivotal day in 2008, Mr. Schultz mandated that all 7,100 stores in the United States would close at 5:30 pm and all 135,000 employees would go through three hours of training to revisit why the Starbucks experience was paramount to this company's viability.[4] Every store was shut down to reset itself and to learn how to return to its core business principle. This sent a very clear signal to both the workforce and to customers, who showed up to the stores for their lattes and found a sign saying, "Closed for training."

For the U.S. Army, a pivotal trigger was the loss of the Vietnam War and the end of the draft: "The Army that left Vietnam and returned to America and its garrisons in Germany and Korea in the early 1970s was at low ebb of morale, discipline, and military effectiveness."[5] Subsequently, the Army and the Department of Defense would enter into several decades of investing in "breaking better" to establish an effective all-volunteer force: "Except for a short period of time immediately after World War II, the Army had not had a volunteer force since just before the United States entered World War II."[6] What ensued is perhaps one of the greatest organizational turnarounds in military, if not human, history, as the Army transformed itself from a conscripted force to a volunteer force and a highly professional one. The Gates Commission, appointed in 1969 by President Nixon, was charged with developing a comprehensive plan for this transformation. Project Volunteer in Defense of the Nation (PROVIDE), undertaken by the Army, looked at enlistee compensation, staffing (needs, costs, and social impact), comprehensive improvements in military service conditions, and improved recruiting. Ultimately, leadership philosophies and practices that would succeed in an all-volunteer force were also addressed as part of the effort to attract and retain the highest-quality recruits, including expansion of the number of women willing to join the service.

For Japan Airlines (JAL), the trigger that signaled the need for transformation was the deadliest single aircraft accident in history. The crash of Flight 123 in August 1985 killed 505 passengers and fifteen members of the crew. This doomed flight left with a full load of passengers over the Oban holiday break. Early on in the flight, the plane completely lost control of all of its hydraulics and then circled around Japan helplessly for forty-five minutes before crashing into a mountain, killing all but four passengers. This flight became an event that triggered a strategic focus by the leadership of this airline and their employees to become the safest airline to fly. To make sure the accident was not lost to history, JAL built a safety center in 2006 that houses the complete narrative of this doomed flight, along with artifacts such as pieces of the plane, bloodied clothing, watches all stopped at the same time, rings, wallets, and family pictures of passengers. The narrative for this accident continues to evolve in all of the employees' self-concepts, because the leadership of JAL committed to putting every employee through safety training by going through in vivid detail the narrative of this doomed flight. Today, many at JAL would say that the arc of their narrative has been to continually break better in terms of leading the aviation field in its focus on safety in their industry. By the way, after several years of investment in training employees, the leadership decided it was time to have all employees go through updated training again, to reinforce the importance of never forgetting this horrible accident, as well as bringing new employees on board to their core principle regarding safety. I also recently discovered that Boeing was building a similar facility near Seattle, to have its employees go through the same training to understand why their plane had crashed.

For the Wells Fargo company I hope a trigger event (this is still a evolving story, even as of this writing, which is December 7, 2017, with recent evidence uncovered that the bank's employees sold to their customers unneeded insurance) that occurred in 2016, regarding the uncovering of millions of fake, unauthorized bank and credit card accounts opened by employees for their unwitting customers, has changed how this bank now operates. Employees secretly opened these accounts to hit sales targets and earn bonuses. This trigger event may well represent one of the darkest periods in this bank's long arc of its narrative. In 2016, we learned that 5,300 Wells Fargo employees colluded to cheat their customers out of fees and, for many, their good credit rating by falsifying PIN numbers and e-mail addresses. These actions were taken by enrolling those customers in on-line banking services they had neither requested nor authorized. It has been estimated that bank employees opened over 1.5 million unauthorized deposit accounts.[7] This scandalous behavior was linked to the bank's scheme to increase productivity. Today, the new leadership of this iconic bank is trying to build a narrative that is not based on brutal economics, where managers threatened employees each month if they were not meeting unrealistic goals for opening new accounts, to one where customers are respected and treated ethically. The campaign for change has involved full-page ads in the *Wall Street Journal* discussing what this bank is doing to right the wrong that had a negative impact on their customers. What they will need to do is convince their employees and the public of the authenticity of this breaking better narrative before it crushes the bank. The latest news was another major setback and highlights that these unethical acts were fueled by a deeply damaged culture of leadership at all levels, especially including the top.

The narratives of breaking better are not just tied to individuals or organizations. They can also be tied to communities or nations. For example, take a look at the arc of the narrative for a country like South Africa. Their system of apartheid had been breaking bad for 300 years. Then a group of black leaders came along, one better known as Madiba or Nelson Mandela, who wanted to end the apartheid system in which blacks and coloreds were horribly treated and discriminated against. Over time, Mandela's country's story of severe suffering and discrimination started to become known to the outside world. The pressure on South Africa to change was increasing and became more focused when IBM publicly stated in the 1980s that it would no longer do business in South Africa until it abolished the apartheid system. Many other companies followed IBM's lead in terms of not doing business with the apartheid government. This trigger event was a shout heard around the world that eventually led the man who had lived in a cell on Robbins Island for twenty-seven years to become the president of South Africa. The country broke better after he assumed the presidency, based on many transformative events. One of the most pivotal events was when the president arrived at a Rugby championship match, wearing the jersey and number of the captain of South Africa's team. One might ask: why was this act on the part of the president such an important trigger event in terms of breaking better? Rugby in South Africa was synonymous with the white minority or Afrikaners, who had ruled South Africa for centuries. Moreover, unlike soccer, the black man's sport, it was considered the national team. Wearing that jersey signified that this black president was a president for all people whether they were black, white, or colored. Many of his party's leaders were concerned that, by wearing the jersey, Mandela might be breaking better too fast. They may have been right, but it turns out their narrative was wrong, and the arc of change representing his story was correct. Unfortunately, with the current president, Jacob Zuma, we are seeing this country break bad again, with the African National Congress (ANC) displaying many signs of being unethical while padding their own wealth at the expense of their nation's citizens. Sometimes the arc of the story unfortunately becomes a circle.

As you can see, there are many trigger events, some more subtle than others, that become part of the breaking bad to breaking better narrative that we can use to understand how change unfolds, using the terms *impending* or *emerging*.[8] Now let's move into describing our third state of impending change.

ENABLERS AND OBSTACLES TO BREAKING BETTER

In the Impending State, it becomes important to identify the enablers and obstacles to the proposed organizational changes, as well as levers that can be used to nudge the change along the arc of breaking better. I examine how wins and losses factor into the change process, as well as changes that occur in processes, goals, and systems that result in more wins than losses as the change effort unfolds.[9]

During this state of impending change, as noted at the outset of this chapter, some people will be moving into the change process by developing their self-concept in terms of how they change their view of "my organization," as well as what they can achieve next if the changes are successful. With this group of early adapters, there are already changes occurring in their assumptions and how they make meaning of their work, which is not necessarily fully part of their identity, or what I will refer to in the next chapter as being institutionalized. That sort of change breaks more slowly. In this state, for some, new assumptions are emerging regarding how to work better, but for many the old assumptions remain the norm.

This results in competing perspectives and priorities and the development of factions within the organization that can easily delay or derail transformative change in organizations.

Some organizational members still can't see the need for change or even recognize that change is occurring around them within their organization, whereas others are undergoing self-concept and narrative changes, as new behaviors emerge while old assumptions and behaviors that go against the change process are extinguished. So, what makes this change phase so challenging is that old and new behaviors can coexist for a long time before those old behaviors are completely extinguished by all members. Frequently, this transition fails, and old behaviors prevail. It is incumbent on the leaders to manage conflict so that it is adaptive and continues to produce new insights versus being destructive. The leaders also have to be patient because this is the Impending State, and the arc of the change story may not always unfold as cleanly, quickly, and predictably as in earlier or the subsequent states.

In the previous state, we recognized that a lot of things are being initiated, and there is change occurring in terms of accountabilities and transactions among organizational employees. These changes are more tangible than what might unfold in this Impending State. Recall, for Alaska Airlines, the VP for operations was working on getting his direct reports to change from blaming the person to changing the process through which work gets done. The VP argued that if the process could be changed, then Alaska could create a repeatable and reliable practice with higher efficiencies, quality, and performance. As stated earlier, changing that core assumption from people being the problem to processes and anchoring it in the way that employees made sense of challenges and problems is exactly what I mean by an emerging assumption that results in a different way of thinking, behaving, and performing.

In a hospital in the Midwest of the United States, where employees were taking greater ownership for patient care, the change in their core operating assumption could be characterized as going from being a renter of sorts to being an owner, one who was accountable for patient safety. The assumption guiding this change effort was based on owners taking greater responsibility for patient care and safety, in that each individual was pivotal to owning the process, whether that person changed bedsheets or did brain surgery.

Being an owner in this health care system meant crafting one's job to include all those aspects that would contribute to the overall quality of patient care and safety. Indeed, one of the mantras often heard at meetings with "all hands on deck" was to act like an owner, not a renter. Owners take care of their property, whereas renters typically just use it and pay the rent. Many stories were shared about what that meant to their patients' health care so that the narrative continued to break better as new stories were added that reflected the mission to be the very best health care facility for their patients.

On the breaking bad side, a story was shared early on about a patient who had been taken to the emergency room in this Midwest hospital system by his daughter. The patient had been waiting there for hours to receive care, and his condition was deteriorating rapidly. The situation got so bad that his daughter feared for his life, and out of sheer desperation called her uncle. The uncle told his niece to call 911 to get an ambulance to pick up her father. She was stunned by this suggestion; she was already in a hospital emergency room. The uncle was adamant that she had to call 911 to take her father by ambulance to another hospital. She did. Her father survived and fully recovered.

This story was brought up again and again in meetings at the Midwest hospital that failed to provide his care, to make sure it became part of the hospital's narrative that this organization and its employees were determined to leave behind as they changed their system of delivery. On a much smaller scale, this is not so different from our previous JAL example. Indeed, nothing appears to send a stronger signal to health care staff than having an ambulance pull up to their hospital's emergency room and then whisking their patient away to another hospital. This event will certainly do a lot of damage to the collective self-concept of one's staff and, in this instance, was a massive trigger for change.

In another health care organization not yet mentioned in our review of cases, there were two "never events"—errors in medical care that are serious and avoidable, indicating a real problem in safety practices—within a fairly short time frame. In one event, occurring in September 2010, a nurse accidently injected a child with 1.4 grams of calcium chloride rather than 140 milligrams. Though the child, who was already critically ill, did not die immediately due to the overdose, the mistake contributed to this baby's decline and death five days later. The hospital put the nurse on leave, and her employment was terminated within weeks. She was subsequently unable to find other work as a nurse. In April 2011, distraught and depressed, the nurse committed suicide by hanging herself in her home.[10] This became a very prominent trigger event for not only the hospital where these "never events" occurred but for another hospital and its leadership across town. Though no similar events had happened in their health care system, other health care system leaders realized the reliability of their safety practices were also questionable and that it was time to get out ahead of the curve to change them permanently.

The story that we told in the preceding paragraph was the same story the hospital across town used as the basis for launching their patient safety initiative. Seeing what happened in that other hospital system and knowing they were equally at risk if they didn't change the way they viewed their safety practices, one senior vice president, along with other colleagues, began a campaign to get their hospital to recognize the importance of creating a repeatable and safe practice of getting their patients through safely and satisfied with their treatment.

In the Impending State, there are rules, procedures, systems, and people who work in parallel with other people who have changed or are in the process of changing. This is what makes this state so dynamic and tricky, in that you have multiple and competing narratives in play at the same time, sometimes within the same units and teams. However, if you are in the Impending State, you will learn there has already been a lot of attention invested in the need for change, along with considerable resources that have gone into the campaign. It is very likely that numerous and perhaps well-crafted messages about the narrative have gone out to the larger organization. Of course, there are already numerous initiatives typically underway if you are in this state, such as "fix Seattle" in the Alaska case. And, if you are lucky, there are entities like LAX that also have caught the narrative for change and are already working ahead of your plan to both initiate change and to embed that change in the Impending State.

If you feel that you have now moved into this Impending State with regards to your own organization, then it is important for you to think about what the levers are that you can use to enable and foster the change process. Ask yourself repeatedly, how will the set of roles I have within my job portfolio, as well as in my view of "my organization," change as the arc of the change narrative evolves over time? What are the obstacles that I can anticipate and address as we shape the narrative to accommodate the new directions that have been set by me, and "my organization"?

REFLECTION AS A LEVER FOR OVERCOMING OBSTACLES

Going back to the U.S. Army after the Vietnam War, there was one huge assumption out there that had to be considered, challenged, and changed. Some soldiers believed the war could have been won if President Johnson had just avoided micromanaging the combat engagements. Others believed the war could have been won if only we had better comrades to work with in the South Vietnamese government, in which corruption was rampant. Still others felt the rules of war had restricted the U.S. Army to such an extent that their hands were tied, and in retrospect there was no way the United States could have won the war under those conditions.

Indeed, many soldiers would remark that we won every battle, so how could we have lost the war?

We are in no way making light of this tragic point in arc of the history of the United States. Moreover, those who served in the war and those who died should be respected and honored for their service to their country. But the war was not won, and one could argue perhaps it should never have been fought, but in the end recognizing that it was lost helped to fuel a dramatic transformation of the U.S. Army from one that was somewhat broken to the most formidable military force in human history.

The core assumption that had to be challenged and changed was that many thought the United States could have won the war, which was irrelevant to the impending change state. Soldiers had to realize that, to move to a professional and all-volunteer army, they would have to learn and understand why they didn't win the war and how they had to be part of rebuilding the U.S. Army one assumption, practice, self-concept, and narrative at a time. If the mission of your Army is to win all of your nation's wars, and you don't, that can have a very debilitating effect on your soldiers in terms of them bouncing back and changing. Winning all of the nation's wars is the core mission of the U.S. Army.

There were certainly many other obstacles in the way of changing the U.S. Army, such as the soldiers' unwillingness to challenge their officers if they saw something done wrong. In fact, during the Vietnam War, soldiers would sometimes get so frustrated with their leaders that, seeing no other recourse, they would resort to "fragging" their leaders, which meant killing them—a rather brutal form of performance feedback.

Of course, when dealing with a nation's army, the complexities of change require us to consider an enormous number of complex processes. Yet, at the very core of what constituted the change process that unfolded was that the most significant change had to occur in the self-concept of each soldier, and by soldier we mean from Private Snuffy to General Big Britches. Each soldier had to think about what it meant to be a professional in the new and emerging U.S. Army, first going back to the founding of this country and its values and then reconsidering what it meant to be a professional, like doctors and engineers.

One of the key obstacles to overcome was building a reliable practice for feedback on up through the entire system. Over time, there were many mechanisms that emerged during the Impending State, including the creation of the Center for Army Lessons Learned, through to what became the foundation for feedback called the After Action Review or AAR. The AAR was created as a lever for allowing individual soldiers to address superiors by providing valuable feedback to improve their processes and performance. The process involved first identifying what the intent was of an order, what happened, how it happened, and what could be done differently and then deciding what was next. The AAR could be used at any level for any situation, and the process was the same in terms of motivating a healthy exchange and debrief.

The AAR symbolized changes in assumptions that were emerging regarding that every individual solider mattered in terms of operational success, as well as to function at the highest level of ethics and integrity. Soldiers at every level were trained to facilitate an AAR, and this debriefing process was embedded in all of the schoolhouses around the military from the U.S. Military Academy through to the ROTC and what were called the Joint Readiness Training Centers (JRTCs). In fact, it is not uncommon to find the AAR process included in many organizational learning and development processes today, in the same way that the soldiers were trained within the military. This includes companies like General Electric, who embraced the debriefing process to such extent that its leaders thought they had invented it.

What became ubiquitous about the AAR process is that it could be used to improve the number of successes individuals and units experienced while reducing and addressing mistakes and failures in a way that was generative rather than punitive. The emerging assumptions concerning this developmental process were that learning and feedback were important to how people behaved in the Army and that, if you were a good commander, you gave orders, you expected a lot from your soldiers, but you were also expected to listen to them in debriefs and be an owner, as well as a motivator of change and transformation.

I was asked to attend a Joint Readiness Training Center in Fort Polk, Louisiana, as part of a project I was doing for the U.S. Army. The Army allowed me to embed with a platoon for several days as it worked through eleven missions over a two-week period, including combat, peacekeeping, peacemaking, rebuilding, and the like.

During one day at JRTC, an observer controller named Mike, who had been accompanying me in the Humvee, asked if I wanted to attend the AARs being done that day for a squad, platoon, and companies on up to the battalion level, which comprised the leaders of 5,000 soldiers. What was amazing about my experience was that the same AAR process was cascaded up the organization, or battalion in this case, so that one could see the mechanisms that worked and didn't work throughout the entire battalion. I was able to observe a sample of the entire leadership development system, at every level of the battalion, for the missions under review. With Mike's help, I was also able to see the holes in that system, the breakdowns, the lack of alignment around the narrative and mission, the misinterpretations and consequences on that battalion failing in mission after mission. It turns out, that this battalion was one of the worst to come through JRTC training, according to Mike, and it became evident as the day wore on that the leadership at the top was clearly in over their heads in terms of running this battalion and not listening to their soldiers' feedback. The soldiers affectionately called their leaders "cement heads."

What is amazing about the JRTC experience is that when you are embedded with a platoon, you are in terrain that feels like a real battle context, in which there are bombs going off, flames coming out of rifles fired, people falling off trucks breaking their leg, the opposition forces overrunning your defenses, and people really, really stressed, sleep deprived, cold, as well as being a bit angry with their leaders and situation. In fact, one soldier told me several years later, that absent the real bullets that fly by your head in combat, JRTC was much more difficult in terms of the logistics of fighting, as compared to what this soldier had experienced in the first Iraq War in the early 1990s, when the United States invaded Iraq after it had invaded Kuwait.

COMMANDER'S INTENT AS A LEVER
FOR OVERCOMING OBSTACLES

Another mechanism the U.S. Army has used to change their narrative is something called commander's intent. With commanders' intent, there was a subtle shift emerging toward breaking better, which allowed commanders to say what they intended to happen to their soldiers, and what they desired, while also leaving some of the execution details of their mission to the expertise and discretion of their soldiers. This shift in going from orders to commander's intent allowed soldiers to discuss what their commanders really wanted and the degrees of freedom they had to achieve their mission.

They also added to this mechanism something they called an informational versus a decision brief. With informational briefings, soldiers were encouraged to be more casual with their superiors, so that they could offer a broader range of views, along with conflicting opinions to intellectually stimulate the thinking process. Then, when it came time for a decision brief, the mood changed toward a more disciplined selection among several proposed options. These briefs were done at different points in time, so as not to confuse the messages that were shared.

Consider that if one is going to build a more adaptable and agile force, it is critical that the soldiers own and understand the commander's intent. By the way, commander's intent works well with any organization even if not comprised of soldiers. Discussing your leader's intent in terms of some directive allows their followers to more fully understand their role and to take ownership for their own actions. The mechanism of commander's intent showed that the leaders were exhibiting more respect for input from their soldiers, while at the same time allowing for feedback and to be challenged by them.

Of course some soldiers then and now would say that there are still many commanders whose intent is simple: do what I have told you to do. However, we know that the type of commander who behaves in that way is typically one who does not do such a great job in developing the next generation of leaders or professionals to be agile and adaptive.

LEADERSHIP AS A LEVER FOR OVERCOMING OBSTACLES

In terms of the type of leadership we all see in this Impending State, there is still a lot of instrumental or transactional leadership, as employees within the organization move to change how it does its work. This requires that expectations are made as clear as possible, that the process is built for work that employees can understand, embrace, and replicate reliably. Also, what employees are accountable for and how they are evaluated will likely change, as will the rewards for doing so. With these types of changes in play, it is crucial that the leadership is clear with their intent and that they create an environment where people feel safe to provide feedback, where employees are given the time to practice doing things differently—sometimes failing, learning, reiterating, and then succeeding.

I typically find that organizational leaders are impatient with the pace of change, and they may have every right to be so because these organizational changes typically are behind schedule in part because they were not properly implemented in the earlier phases. Yet, it is imperative the leaders stay the course and allow employees to practice and fail in that, to learn a new way of doing work, employees must explore new ways of behaving and interacting with each other and their customers, suppliers, and other stakeholders. This requires that leaders plan to spend time in investing in developing and supporting their followers. Anticipate that you will have to invest more time in development in this phase than in previous phases to sustain the changes and to achieve a new and higher standard of performance. People don't just extinguish one way of thinking and behaving and move to another; it is an unfolding process, similar to how employees turn over.[11]

The type of leadership described here must have started in the Initiating State; otherwise, by the time the organization has entered this emerging state there are a lot more things in motion, more confusion, and of course missteps. In addition to a heavy focus on transactional and instrumental leadership, the leaders must also add both authentic and transformational leadership. In the following discussion, I describe some specific ways this leadership is manifested prior to and into this phase.

Authentic leadership contains four components: being self-aware, transparent, fair or balanced, and ethical. As an organization enters into this dynamic state of change where new processes are being tested and implemented, it is paramount that the leadership team build a sufficient level of goodwill to get employees to listen to why the change is important, including articulating their intent. Leaders need to be sufficiently self-aware to understand when they are not connecting with followers. They also need to be aware of their followers' signals in terms of their feedback regarding what their leaders need to do to move the change process forward. Analogous to the notion of agile programming, you need to keep iterating till you have mastered what you have chosen to do differently with respect to how you want people in your organization to change.[12]

Leaders also need to be as transparent as possible because, as change unfolds in this state, things tend to get a bit cloudy and uncertain for many people, especially those who are more risk averse. Expect there to be some cynicism from employees because everyone will not be equally ready for the changes proposed, nor will they understand the rationale for the change process/outcomes even if it has been told to them several times. In fact, some may start making up stories and narratives that are not real but perhaps support their concerns or fears regarding the direction of the change process. This reaction occurs in part because many of us have gone through changes in our respective organizations where there is very little transparency, and we wonder, is this going to be another one of those so-called "change efforts" to go nowhere except toward the next state of confusion or conflict?

Leaders need to be very fair and balanced in how they judge their employees because in a new and emerging state where many things are impending, employees will make mistakes and leaders have to be judicious in terms of how they treat their employees to keep them motivated to support and sustain the change process.

Try to consider, when making your judgments about followers' performance, that there are recoverable and unrecoverable mistakes. And there are many more recoverable mistakes that can be corrected to foster improvement.

You can be transactional in pointing out how mistakes are addressed, which helps your followers understand your redlines not to be crossed. Paraphrasing Phil Knight, the founder of Nike, you can make mistakes at Nike, but don't make the same mistake twice—that was his redline. We suggest that this may be a tough bar to get over in terms of doing something new and complex right the first, second, or even third time, but at least Phil Knight made the standards clear to his employees. Importantly, if employees feel and believe you are fair, they will be more likely to tolerate the stress that goes along with change, as well as being tolerant of your mistakes, and you will no doubt commit some throughout all four states. Just keep in mind that you don't want to add any additional unnecessary stress, and yet too frequently I have seen situations in most organizational change processes where leaders invest way too much time waiting to catch an employee doing something wrong, which could, in many cases, be seen as practice, not ambivalence or being against the change effort.

Having an ethical and moral leader allows employees to suspend judgment about the change process in that such leaders are genuinely trying to do something that benefits everyone and not just themselves. However, we also witness leaders doing the opposite of what they are asking their employees to do, during complex change processes. For example, they will state how important it is to cut costs and watch margins while they themselves are staying at expensive hotels and flying first class on business trips. Rest assured that your employees always find out and know this is occurring; more important, they will determine their leaders are not worth following through this difficult transformation given their bias toward self-interest. This might suggest the need for leaders to think about what it means to be a servant leader, as was described by Greenleaf back in 1970, in service of their followers.[13]

Building on a base of authentic leadership, it is also important for leaders to be transformational. These leaders recognize that individuals will have different acceptance levels and capacity for tolerating change, and they will work to find ways to help employees achieve their optimal development and performance. Such leaders will challenge the way things get done and will encourage their followers to do the same to change the way they perform and transform their organization. Ultimately, if the leaders can be inspiring role models for change, the change will be more likely to stick.

OWNERSHIP AS A LEVER FOR OVERCOMING OBSTACLES

With lululemon, Christine Day challenged the assumption that employees couldn't own their respective stores by putting them in the position of being decision makers about how the stores were designed and managed. The manufacturing CEO whose company built chrome pipes for Harley-Davidson challenged the assumption that employees, often with very low educational levels, couldn't be owners who were enabled to make critical and costly decisions. In one case, the CEO demonstrated his own willingness to challenge assumptions with his senior staff, when there was a payroll snafu that led to a large number of employees who were either significantly under- or overpaid. His staff suggested they deal with this snafu quietly and work through getting the payroll adjusted, so as not to upset the so-called apple cart. He challenged that assumption and said, "If we cannot be open with our employees and transparent on this issue, then how could we possibly expect them to be owners of any complex and even more expensive change process?" Based on his viewpoint and values, the company disclosed the mistakes transparently and over a relatively short period of time corrected the mistakes in the distribution of their payroll—without any complaints from 1,500 employees—actually, there was one because they miscalculated the change in an employee's pay, which was quickly corrected.

PSYCHOLOGICAL CAPITAL AS A LEVER
FOR OVERCOMING OBSTACLES

During this state of change, it is also important to maintain the level of positivity of one's workforce to stay with the change initiative. It is going to be hard to do this if it is a very significant change, certainly requiring that the employees know why the change is important and be inspired to stay the course and to remain hopeful and optimistic that the change will be for the betterment of the organization and its employees. Of course, given the focus we mentioned on letting employees fail and then recover, the leadership has to build some hope, optimism, and resiliency to achieve sustainable success with the overall change process.

The capital referred to earlier has been called psychological capital or resources, and it is critical to sustaining change efforts. Psychological capital can be remembered by the acronym HERO: hope, efficacy or confidence, resiliency and the ability to bounce back, and, finally, optimism. In combination, these resources can be as valuable as every other form of capital being invested in the change process, including financial, social, and intellectual.[14]

What I have described and will go into more detail about in the last chapter, where we provide a more specific "exercise plan" or "diet" for experimental change, are a number of leadership styles and ways of thinking that have to be balanced for change to be successful. You will have to balance being very transactional in setting goals, being authentic in terms of being self-aware, and being transformational in terms of understanding that not all employees will understand and come on board with the change process as it initially unfolds, or even partway into the change process, to keep breaking better.

CULTURE AS A LEVER FOR OVERCOMING OBSTACLES

As part of the change process, there must be a sufficient level of psychological safety in your organizational climate and culture to have employees provide critical feedback on how the change process is unfolding. By psychologically safe, we mean the ability to offer your opinion, even when that opinion contradicts your leaders' points of view. To be successful, the leader cannot build this type of safe climate in the third state; he or she must start this earlier to leverage it when the changes are most difficult. It doesn't mean that everyone will feel psychologically safe going into or throughout the change process; it just means that you have to have a sufficient number of stakeholders who do to provide you with ground truth and reliable feedback.[15]

In terms of the organization's culture, this requires that we tinker with deeper mechanisms associated with the change process to go from breaking bad to breaking better. In the Midwest hospital that nearly closed due to its lousy performance standards, there was a need to move from having employees being renters with little concern for the hospital or patients to people who were owners of the complete cycle for health care delivery to each and every patient. Before the change unfolded, if you asked employees whether they would recommend this hospital for their own family, the response you would receive is, absolutely not. No one was willing to risk the care in this facility for loved ones.

As the change process unfolded and broke better over a three-year period, the ownership value became a deep taproot and a core value that employees began to understand and embrace in terms of their self-concepts, narrative, and behavior. In the beginning of the change process, they saw ownership as being something more akin to territorial ownership—it's not my job, you do it. Patients could languish in the system for days or months because no one took ownership for their service—that was someone else's job. As the culture began to shift to a more inclusive ownership base, there was more of a focus on being accountable to taking care of the full spectrum of patient care. This accountability started to become a badge of honor that individuals sought out and felt a great deal of pride in when receiving it. Employees were recognized for meeting their targets and milestones and then teaching others how to do the same in terms of building and then sustaining a repeatable, reliable process.

From this point on, the culture shifted from being accountable and complying to being committed, whereby employees and their culture began to change into being identified with quality care for all patients. As they became more committed, the employee's self-concepts were changing such that they were coming to identify with a new set of professional norms in terms of the way they delivered patient care each and every day. In many instances, we heard employees in conversations talk about the care *I* give, which is the only care *I* consider acceptable for our patients. And, if they saw care being given below their new standards, they would address it at its source, now even challenging their leaders and the occasional surgeon holding a sharp instrument.

As the culture of ownership evolved, employees were collectively seeing themselves as being able to provide the very best care in the overall health care system to which they belonged. It wasn't just *I* care about *my* patient, it was shifting to *we* care about *our* patients. This shift in perspective or self-concepts was also being reinforced in terms of important outcome metrics. For example, prior to the changes, their organization was ranked 130 out of 132 health care organizations on most of the critical patient outcome measures. Over a three-year period, they had moved from being the lowest ranked to one or two in almost every category of health care performance. Overall, the employee workforce narrative was shifting to a point where they could not think of themselves as providing anything but top health care treatments for their patients.

At Alaska Airlines, senior managers well into their change process in Seattle and beyond that hub location found that when they told their employees that, in the current year, they might not be #1 in their industry, many employees' reactions were—no way! In their minds, self-concepts, and narrative, they had become a number one airline. Also, they truly believed they had the human, operational, social, psychological, and financial capital to win every year, not one or two or seven. One manager said that when he first arrived at Alaska, he would often hear from employees that Alaska was a good middle-range airline, but certainly not major league. Now it was clear to him that when new employees came to Alaska Airlines, they no longer saw themselves as minor league players; they came to Alaska to work with the best airline and would not easily accept being in second place.

REVIEW OF THE IMPENDING STATE

In this chapter, I have covered a lot of territory in that one panel in our change model and also in the last section, where we started to look back at what had to accumulate in the first two change states for the change to go from an individual self-concept change to a collective self-concept that changed or broke better over time. By way of summarizing, here are some important things to consider:

- You have to lay the foundation for the type of change you will observe in the Impending State from the very outset of the change process; otherwise, by the time you get to this point, you will likely end up derailing the change process. Building a requisite amount of goodwill to suspend judgment on the merits of the change as it is emerging is also critical to the ultimate success of your changes.

- In my research, the Impending Change state is usually where most organizations get stuck and fail to achieve the last state of collective identification associated with their change process. We find this can happen if there are too many people who have self-concepts that have not changed sufficiently enough and who still challenge those who are trying to promote and sustain the change process. With these competing forces in play, the change may simply languish at equilibrium or, worse, spiral into chaos, with the forces for and against ending up in a stalemate.

- The discipline required of leaders at all levels is even greater in this complex state of change than in the previous ones. Why? Leaders have to use a variety of leadership orientations and styles that help to promote higher levels of individual and collective ownership. For leaders who are accustomed to one size fits all, the change effort is likely doomed.

- Consider that it's not just an individual's direct leader who matters but rather the indirect leadership experienced during the change that will have a huge impact on the change process and its sustainability. What I mean here is that the CEO who is promoting the change must get surrogates/direct reports to carry that change through the organization at all levels in a repeatable and reliable way. First, these surrogates must know why the change is important in terms of the leader's intent, and they must also know how it is going to unfold. Equally important, the surrogates have to oftentimes provide brutal and direct feedback upward in the organizational hierarchy when the change is slightly or largely going off the rails. The cascading of leadership is like falling dominoes, except that it can and should go both ways, making it even more difficult to continue with and sustain the change process.

- Related to my previous point, I believe if the organizational leaders want to make sure all of its leaders are working in concert, then it is likely they will have to invest in developmental interventions that resource the leader to be better able to lead using a variety of orientations. A big mistake that organizational leaders make when going through any transformative change is that their leaders will learn how to make this work on the job as it is unfolding. Of course, they will to some extent. However, it is important to give them support, education, coaching, resources, and an opportunity to share stories with each other, in terms of how the change is or is not working. This is where you can take leadership development and make it a critical process that leaders work through as part of the strategic change process. In fact, instead of doing role-plays and using cases of other organizations for leadership development, the leaders should use their own organization as the case attempting to do real change, not reading about someone else in an organization they do not fully understand or identify with. This is the process we use in the Center that I direct at the University of Washington called the Center for Leadership and Strategic Thinking.

In our next chapter, I move into rarified space, where a very small percentage of organizations have entered, representing organizational change that has completely altered the individual and collective self-concepts of its workforce. I am confident that we can all dramatically increase the success rates of organizational change if organizational leaders consider that transformative change does come about, one self-concept and narrative at a time. I repeat this for emphasis.

Some points to reflect on as you move forward:

- Have you developed the leadership styles you will need to move you through the Impending State? Of course, you will have some time to practice, but if you have not started developing the styles associated with this state, your chance of success diminishes greatly.

- Have you built up a sufficient level of goodwill to get you through the parts of this state where individuals will challenge the very basic logic for the change process and direction?

- Are the people who work with you willing to challenge your ideas? Do they feel psychologically safe to do so with all leaders?

- How developmentally ready are your employees to learn new ways of thinking and behaving? Are they so risk averse that it will be difficult to encourage them to experiment?

- Have you identified key milestones that will mark your arc of change as points where you can celebrate success?

- How will you evaluate the changes you intend to institutionalize in the next state, while you are still moving toward those changes in the Impending State?

- Is the change you are proposing worth the effort, or should you perhaps think about other changes, as this is the state where most organizational changes derail? We are just testing your resolve here.

It is now time to really break better.

RESEARCH LINK: A DEEPER DIVE

There is a broad and deep literature on organizational change and transformation. In this literature the unit of analysis is typically the organization, and that is where authors tend to focus their attention in terms of describing what triggers, promotes, or deters organizational change. At the same time, there is also a literature on leadership development that focuses on how events and experiences shape the development of leaders across the life span. In both literatures, there are different types of positive and negative events that can trigger change. For example, for organizations, these events can be associated with the markets in which organizations operate, as well as events based on what one's competitors are doing. For leadership development, events can be difficult experiences a person goes through in life that build a greater sense of self and resilience. On the positive side, there are respected leaders who come along who can trigger a completely different way of thinking about how to influence those being led.[16]

It suffices to say that we must understand how different categories of events shape the way individuals and organizations grow and change. In both instances, neither leaders nor organizations are born to lead or to be successful.

7 THE INSTITUTIONALIZING STATE: DEFINING "MY ORGANIZATION"

The successes of my organizational system are my successes.

At the risk of losing total credibility with you, I want to resist saying that this is probably the most difficult state for organizational change and transformation. Perhaps I can just say that sustaining the institutionalization of change is really the ultimate challenge, with institutionalization being the end goal for completing a transformation. What I mean here is that change can be more tactical and not necessarily transformative, and I associate the latter with institutionalization, along with the highest levels of ownership.[1] Certainly, organizational leaders can change some processes and methods for doing business without fundamentally changing the organization or its business model. However, in institutional change, how one's employees view "my organization" will, as a consequence of the change process, fundamentally change the way they make meaning out of explaining what they do and why they do it. That's a big difference we need to keep in mind as we move into describing this fourth state. See Figure 7.1.

In the Institutionalizing State, we witness the formation of fundamentally new beliefs, roles, expectations, goals, and performance metrics. These all represent some of the most obvious aspects of the changes that have occurred and become institutionalized in the organization's identity.[2] For example, one of the most successful change efforts in the long history of organizations has been associated with just one of two words, that is, *agile* or *lean*.[3] In fact, one CEO recently said to me that if we were going to be successful with an organizational change, then we would have to come up with one word that totally represented the change we were working toward . . . as the word *agile* did for software programming/project management or *lean* did for quality and efficiency. He said, "That is all you will need to say; just one word, and then your people just get what you are trying to change and then

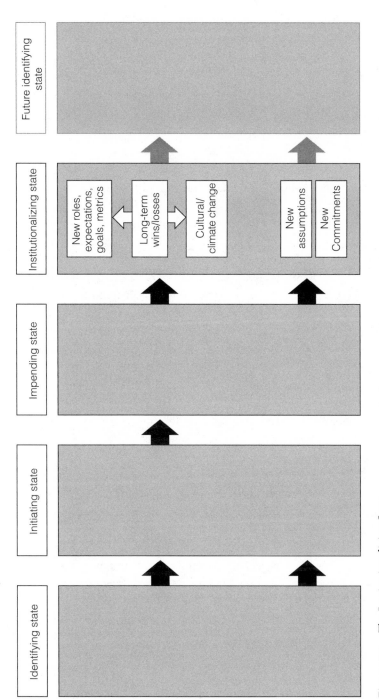

Figure 7.1 The Institutionalizing State.

Identifying state

Initiating state

Impending state

Institutionalizing state

New roles, expectations, goals, metrics

Long-term wins/losses

Cultural/climate change

New assumptions

New Commitments

Future identifying state

work to implement it." I thought perhaps he was on to something here. However, there also needs to be a lot of work that goes into making sure the one word means the same thing to all individuals for them to be aligned around the change effort. The one word also has to have a lot behind it, such as with *lean*, when we add to that word *processes*. Someone who has gone thru lean process training will understand what those words mean and can likely discuss in detail how those processes have changed his or her beliefs about how work is best done in terms of roles, expectations, goals, and performance metrics.

This is odd because, a year earlier, I had heard essentially the same thing from a senior programmer who was describing how he had been trained in agile programming and how all of his programmers are now "doing agile" or, more appropriately, are agile programmers, shifting from doing some task to agile being part of their identity as programmers. With that one word, people get exactly what is meant. To be agile means being nimble, quick, turning things around rapidly, and so on.

Also, in his description of agile programming, it was obvious that you don't have to get so caught up in whatever program version you are working on but rather you can focus on iterating quickly, doing what we have referred to in the initiating state as tryouts and moving on, fixing, updating, and then iterating again. It is clearly a fail forward process that an individual expects to fail, iterate, fail, iterate, fail, and succeed, as with experimentation and tryouts.

One might say the same thing if we hyphenated *design-thinking*[4] and made it one word. When using design-thinking, you are weaving into the fabric or architecture of your work design principles regarding how you create something from a hybrid MBA program that meets both virtually and face-to-face, through to building a new office complex, park, or restaurant. The design principles are drivers and guides for the intervention and what you are trying to manipulate in terms of different ways of configuring the program or physical space. This thinking is at the core of what you are trying to alter, and it is threaded throughout what you are attempting to build and execute.

I visited Umea, Sweden, about an hour's flight north of Stockholm. I was there for a TEDx conference where I presented, in eighteen minutes, "Showing up for Leadership."[5] Umea is a unique small town that attracts a lot of design-thinkers to its university, along with being the so-called capital of the European Union's cultural center. At the university in Umea, there were a number of rooms designed to promote different ways of design-thinking. One room had multiple levels built into it, similar to ledges on the side of a mountain. Sitting in different parts of the room, you would have different vantage points and views of whatever you wanted to create in that workspace. At the bottom of the room, instead of a typical floor they had what appeared to be a tablet that could bring in any context into the room, for example, lake, field, river, lava flow, or whatever. The room was designed to let you imagine things.

You may not have heard of Umea or its university, but likely at some point you have seen a Volvo drive by on the road, or you have been to IKEA to look at some furniture. If you have observed either of them, then you will have seen some of the products and their design features that came from Umea. A great deal of the Swedish design movement can be sourced to this little town in the northern part of Sweden.

Here is another thing that happened in Umea. After the TEDx conference, there was a dinner held in what looked like an old armory, a place where Swedish military officers met. There were about 100 people invited to this dinner, all were sitting at long tables. The unique thing about the dinner was that there were two presenters throughout the meal. One presenter paired beer with your food and the other wine. These two national experts in their respective fields worked throughout Europe together, competing head to head for the audience's ratings. For most people, the idea of pairing is generally associated with good wine and food. This is a brand that is very strong in the self-concepts of people around the globe. These two individuals were challenging our self-concepts to show that both beer and wine could be equally paired with specific foods. What occurred at the outset of the dinner that was interesting to me was one of the first statements made by the brewmaster. He simply said, "Every time we do this together, I never lose. Well, maybe just a few times," but he said that we looked like a bright audience who would no doubt vote in his favor.

I could see that the wine "experts" around me were at the very least quite skeptical. The brewmaster's first challenge to our way of thinking was when he said that there are far more types of hops and grains in the world that make up beer than varieties of grapes that make up wine—by a long shot. He provided data to challenge what for most of us was an assumption based on how we have been trained by our restaurants, friends, and family. Unless you are in a brewpub, how often is the beer list longer than the wine book? Rarely! So, out of the gate in our sort of Identifying State, we got a signal from him that maybe our assumptions about beer were incorrect.

Second, as we entered into their competition, which we can call the Initiating State, aligning with our states framework, we were given an explanation of the wine and beer pairings for each part of the meal, and the rationale for that pairing from a gastrointestinal perspective. We had a very explicit rating system we had to use to make our judgments: a new initiative for all of us. As we all worked through the meal, I could sense the people around me were shifting their views. In fact, some were turning to their tablemates saying, "That appetizer did taste better with this beer versus that wine." As we progressed through the meal, the wine expert was racking up some wins, but it was clear by the time the dessert came that the beer expert was closing in on a huge victory.

In terms of my reaction, being amenable to drinking both beer and wine with my meal, I felt and still do each time the server provides the wine list, with a few beers on the other side of the page, that the Umea dinner event triggered a fundamental change in my thinking based on what I learned that evening. Beer can be paired with food and wine also—why not? By way of example, it appears that a transformation had occurred in my thinking and in the thinking of my host, who said the very same thing happened to him when he first met this duo in competition. Also, please keep in mind that my colleague was a big beer drinker—literally. He said that, for him, drinking beer had always been associated with pub food, not fine food, and this event had also changed his way of thinking about pairing of beer versus wine. At the very least, beer could be number one in pairings and so could wine, perhaps leading to a change in narrative. I digress, but for a good cause.

In our work on organizational change, I have struggled to find one word that represents the type of change we are referring to in this book. For now, we can certainly call it *transformation*, as in the title of this book, in that if we change an individual's self-concept and narrative to something that is completely different in terms of a different state, that's what constitutes a transformation. Going back to our discussion of roles, self-concepts, and identities at the outset of this book, in the current state of change, we witnessed a change in employees' identities, as noted earlier with Alaska Airlines' focus on being a major league player in their industry, while not thinking of themselves as ever being number two, to perhaps being like beer pairings with food.

I see the same sort of transformation having occurred in the Midwest hospital example that went from being asked to close by the local newspaper editor, to being a top health care system within several short years. I therefore feel comfortable suggesting that the change in the identification state is so fundamental as to be a *transformation*. As you and your organization enter this state, neither of you are the same as you were in your past state in terms of how you consider what constitutes "my" or "the organization."[6]

One way that I have personally recognized that this type of transformative change had occurred at Alaska Airlines came from a conversation I had with a new pilot trainee. Meeting me at a social event, he described Alaska and its new narrative as an airline organization that was past the change processes that I discussed earlier and certainly not prechange. What I mean here is that he only described an airline that was in his self-concept the best in its class. Indeed, when we talked about the history of the airline and how it had gone through this change process, he was actually quite amazed that I was talking about the same airline. In retrospect, I realized we weren't talking about the "same" airline.

As depicted in the panel in Figure 7.1, if change is successful and it's the right change for the organization, then we start to see longer-term wins and lesser losses. For example, with lululemon, when Christine Day was brought in by Chip Wilson, the company's founder, the organization had leveled off in terms of its growth and was not performing well. Within a couple of years of implementing her change processes toward an ownership culture, lululemon had become one of the hottest brands and was considered one of the fastest growing retail chains in history.

If Satya Nadella and his leadership at Microsoft are successful in institutionalizing change at the individual and collective self-concept level, then what we would expect to observe in terms of the identities of Microsoft's employees and its leaders in the future is a perspective shift that good ideas come from every source, and "not invented here" is as good as "invented here" in terms of what is recognized as being innovative and useful within Microsoft. We would then also see a climate in Microsoft more characterized by a learning orientation and a desire to experiment and try out different ways of working and performing. People who are newcomers to Microsoft would be expected to be more comfortable offering their ideas and challenges even though they have limited tenure with the organization. That is to say, these people would assume their ideas would be valued based on their own merit, not based on the source of the idea, which has been a very strong assumption guiding Microsoft's founders and comprising their culture. For example, the leaders throughout Microsoft's organization would be expected to bring into the company a more diverse range of ideas from different industries and acquisitions. As a consequence, employees would feel a deeper sense of commitment to speaking up and having voice, particularly when it comes to promoting innovation. By having voice, we mean that any employee could offer an idea or perspective that might change the way Microsoft functions and the options it considers for future growth.[7]

When people feel their voice matters, they are more likely to stand up and offer their perspectives, which is something that Christine Day certainly advocated in her organization. If people feel they will be ignored, or worse yet targeted, then the likelihood of their ideas being put forth is significantly diminished.

There is evidence that directly contradicts what I said earlier, in terms of most companies not creating the conditions or climate that would foster open and transparent exchanges of ideas. For example, over three-quarters of the entrepreneurs who have had successful startups created their original ideas for their new company's mission or products when working for their previous company.[8] Time and time again, these individuals had to leave their prior organization to be able to initiate their new ideas and businesses. This might explain why the former editor of the *Harvard Business Review* once said in his final editorial for the journal that the way innovation happens in most organizations is through subterfuge and cunning. It may also be why a lot of students leave college early to start up their firms because they may not feel their academic institutions and instructors listen to their ideas.

We might conclude from these comments that to change one's identity, the individual needs to leave his or her organization. Yet, in many cases, and for many individuals, that is simply not a choice that is available to them, so they have to remove themselves mentally by leaving their brains home when they come to work, until they decide to actually leave their job. In fact, that is exactly how one worker described his experience at a Bausch and Lomb sunglasses plant in upstate New York.

In this manufacturing plant, the workforce of 600 employees had worked under a series of plant managers who treated them as equipment more than as human resources. Their opinions were neither solicited nor valued. The climate and culture for offering new ideas was not safe by any means. Into this well-established narrative came Peter, a new plant manager. Peter was keenly interested in improving this manufacturing plant, in that it was the lowest-performing unit in the overall organization. He made it clear to his employees from the start that he was committed to building a culture where people felt respected and engaged with their ideas.

After spending six months identifying the manufacturing facilities challenges, Peter initiated a campaign that was squarely focused on respect, and he became chief campaigner for this cause day in and day out. Rarely did a day go by that Peter was not in the plant on all three shifts, trying to understand what his employees needed from him and their organization to be more effective. Working with his supervisors and their surrogates he provided a consistent message: we will respect you and expect the same in return. Respect became his campaign initiative.

About two years into the process of change, Peter was convening an entire shift for an awards ceremony in the middle of the sunglasses plant. He had started these awards to recognize good ideas and changes promoted by employees, often recommended for these awards by their peers. In this instance, 150 people were standing around on the manufacturing floor, with Peter and two employees next to him. One employee, a young Korean chemist, was dressed in a lab coat. The other was a very muscular blue-collar worker, who worked machines that lifted heavy racks of sunglasses that were then dipped and plated in vats of gold.

After Peter finished his recognition presentation, he asked the blue-collar employee when he had first noticed a problem with the gold-plating process. He said the problem was identified when they measured the gold-plating process, which involves bonding a thin layer of gold to the sunglasses frame. Based on their measurements, they concluded that on average they were losing several hundred thousand dollars of gold down the drain each quarter using the old process. The worker said he had noticed several problems with the process about three years earlier but had not said anything to his manager or to the chemist who had designed the process.

Peter then asked why it had taken so long to change the process to achieve these savings in gold for the company. The manufacturing employee indicated that before Peter came along, no one cared about what he thought, and each day he said, "I would come to work, put my brain on a hook outside, go in and do my job, and then at the end of the day, pick up my brain on my way home." Peter said he had been there in the plant now almost two years and had worked very hard on convincing every employee that they all were respected by him and his leaders. The employee and chemist next to him nodded, and said, "Peter, you do respect us, and I waited till six months ago to speak up because I wanted to make sure you were serious about that . . . we have had so many plant managers over the years tell us one thing and then do something else, so I can now say, you have passed the test!" After Peter had passed the test in his mind, the manufacturing employee, who had never taken a chemistry course, began meeting with the Korean chemist to brainstorm some changes in the plating process.

Just to add one more note to this story, Peter had been suffering from cancer over the previous year, and not only did people come to respect him, they completely identified with his work ethic and concern for others. Peter had made a huge impact on these employees, in that he was authentic and committed to making this plant the best it could be, and by the time I left his work with this organization, he had turned the plant into one of the top facilities in this global organization. It is also important to add to this narrative that he accomplished this transformation without changing the actual facility or the machinery; rather, the most institutionalized changes in this plant were in the culture and climate of the organization and the respect employees now had for one another.

I often tell groups the story about Peter, and it sounds a bit like a fairy tale even to me. Yet, there is never anyone we have talked to who can't identify a Peter in their life, who had a similar impact on them, and that leader usually represents their idealized leadership.[9] That might lead you to ask: do we just need more Peters? Well, that would be nice, but what we really need is all leaders thinking about their self-concepts and narratives and how they impact the way people come to work for them—either leaving their brains at the door or bringing them into work. A simple question you might ponder concerns what your preference is. Do you want to work with renters or owners? Do you want employees to leave their brains at the door, because it is easier for you to give them directives and to be done with them? These are choices you and your organizations make, and I just want you to be completely self-aware regarding the type of narrative these choices create for your organization and for you. In Peter's case, there was clearly a stigma associated not only with leaders early on his leadership but also with the organization itself being seen as a bottom feeder in terms of performance.[10]

Here are several stories about institutionalization in rapid fire.

At Alaska Airlines, the leadership was able to institutionalize a culture that was efficient, lean, focused, and still quite "nice." In terms of institutionalization, employees collectively identified with the airline, following the establishment of this state, as now being a major player in the airline industry. It is interesting to note that a few years ago, Delta Airlines wanted to shift its long-term and collaborative relationship with Alaska to becoming an exclusive partner. These two airlines had one of the most positive and collaborative relationships in this highly competitive industry, but that changed in 2016. In an article written by Ben Mutzabaugh,[11] he described how the two airlines, as of April 30, would eliminate their partnership. Alaska traditionally had many partnerships with other airlines and felt an exclusive partnership didn't make sense in terms of their business model; it also was not part of their culture to have exclusive partnerships. The leadership at Delta was not happy with the decision, which led them to competing head to head with Alaska Airlines in its main hub in Seattle. Now everything Alaska has done to promote its business, Delta, which is a much larger airline, was trying to match or beat on price, service, brand, available routes, frequent flier bonuses, and the like. The competition has ranged from Delta buying the rights to be the Seattle Seahawks football team official carrier to attempting to buy the naming rights to the sports facility at the University of Washington campus, changing it from Alaska Airlines to Delta Airlines. As of today, Alaska is not only beating Delta in head-to-head competition, but they have recently closed a deal to acquire Virgin America, which will make Alaska the fifth largest airline in the United States. Alaska has institutionalized its thinking that it is a major player in the airline industry—not a second place finisher.

None of the hospitals that we have mentioned earlier, except the one in the Midwest, has moved into the Institutionalizing State. All of them were languishing in the Impending State, with some hovering around a neutral point and others sliding backward with more initiatives piling up that were not successful and increasingly rushed and ill-conceived.

The COO of the one hospital who did just about everything wrong in terms of a formula for changing an organization has now been replaced, and the layoffs continue in terms of its current status that is still unfolding or, more appropriately stated, declining.

The U.S. military has institutionalized changes in terms of becoming a professional army to such an extent that its retired officers are now highly sought after, not only by the public and private sectors, but also by colleges and universities who feel they have a different way of thinking about leadership and organizations. We can see the AAR process and commander's intent are part of the very fabric of this organization's culture and how it operates day in and day out. As we watch veterans get on planes in the United States first, those of us who have lived through the Vietnam War have to think how profoundly different the brand of military service members are today versus forty years ago when they were met with utter disdain when disembarking from their flights.

Another example, referred to early on in this book, is the Cleveland Clinic. This health care facility has gone from having an abysmal record of care to being considered one of the top global brands in the world today, particularly around cardiac care.

SUCCESSFUL INSTITUTIONALIZED CHANGE—
AND THE ORGANIZATION STILL FAILED

I want to make sure we are painting a balanced picture in terms of actually being successful at institutionalizing change, given how many change efforts summarily fail. I have seen a number of organizations get way downstream on the change process and show strong signs of institutionalized change before failing, or right before the old or new leadership decides to move in a new direction before change is firmly embedded in the collective self-concepts of employees.

For example, there was a General Electric plant in upstate New York that was designed to be a completely team-based organization. The plant was built to develop high-end computer circuit boards with a total workforce of about 300 employees. GE invested a considerable amount of money and time into building a world-class state-of-the-art plant. GE also invested a lot of money into selecting a workforce that would understand how to work in a team-based

culture and environment—literally millions of dollars were invested in the selection process.

In this same region, there was another older GE plant that was not designed
based on a team culture platform. This plant had 1,500 employees, and the GE
leadership felt they could easily recruit most of the 300 people who were required
for the new plant from this established workforce. However, they found that very
few of the GE employees could make the switch from a hierarchical organization
self-concept and identity to one where there were three plant managers in charge
with equal authority as part of their collective identity of leadership. The employees simply had a hard time wrapping their heads and self-concepts around this
type of design thinking. Consequently, even though the new plant was in a more
desirable location and the starting pay was actually higher, GE could select only a
handful of employees from the older plant who seemed to fit the new team organizational design and emerging culture. And, even among this subgroup, there were
some who ended up asking to go back to their old jobs after only several months
in the new plant. Eventually, by doing a national search, GE was able to find its
requisite number of employees.

What was extremely interesting about the hiring challenge faced by GE was that
the employees from the old plant did not have a team mind-set as part of their self-
concept and narrative. It's not that people didn't cooperate with each other in the
old plant. They did cooperate, and they were highly skilled. However, they didn't
think of work as a team sport but rather as individual contributors in subordinate
roles to their leaders.

The team-based plant and its leadership thought about all aspects of their
work using a team perspective, ranging from taking time off to how work was
accomplished throughout the day. In this new plant, employees were able to determine their vacation schedules, as well as when to take time off work. If they
violated agreed-on policies, they quickly realized that their actions had an impact
on their team, rather than having a more nebulous concept of their organization.
For example, in the early days, some employees would use their sick days as vacation days. However, by using sick days as additional discretionary or vacation
days, these employees discovered that they were affecting their team's ability to
get work done, in that their work process was totally based on members being
there to support each member of their team, which means taking full ownership
for their work. In this environment, team members were encouraged by their
plant managers to provide those team members using their sick days as discretionary days with feedback about the impact their actions were having on the

team. This was not considered a management problem; it was considered a team problem to be solved.

Unlike many other organizations, the three plant managers, who equally ran this facility, delegated the problem to the teams to resolve, which they did in rather short order with different approaches based on the capabilities and needs of their respective teams. This was actually becoming a very common practice within this organization, where teams could make the final decision on many aspects of work that typically had been in the domain of their managers, including whom they hired, rewarded, and fired.

What happened next provided one of the clearest examples of the institutionalization of a self and collective concept in terms of the GE facility working with a team mind-set.[12] After investing considerable resources in building out this plant and its workforce over a two-year period, the leadership of GE decided it didn't want to remain in this business. Even though this plant was operating at the top of its industry standards in a period of less than two years from start-up, GE's leadership made the decision to close the plant.

To say the workforce was devastated with this decision would be a huge understatement. For many of the employees, this plant had become a sanctuary organization where people could really work in teams, not just call groups a team, as many had experienced in other facilities and jobs. The three plant managers tried to convince GE to keep the operation open, but the decision was final. The next step was to bring in monitors to audit the closing of the plant over the next twelve months, without loss due to theft or damage.

The three plant managers contacted GE headquarters and asked that they allow the plant to monitor itself and not bring in external auditors. They indicated that their employees would never steal anything from their organization because, in their mind, they were the organization. They agreed to cover any cost of thefts if there were any losses. GE leaders agreed to let them monitor and audit themselves, as long as they were able to close the three lines of operation down in the next twelve months with as little disruption as possible and without any damage or theft to equipment or products.

What happened next was the systematic closing of this team-based organization line by line. Each month, there would be a few more pictures from the gallery of employees removed from the front lobby, of people who had been laid off. You could see there were pictures on the wall there before by the shadow in the paint where it had faded. One employee described the process as going to a funeral each month, month after month after month.

In a number of interviews that I did with employees, we found that some employees were having a very difficult time getting a new job. When I asked one employee why this was so, he said that people keep asking him what he did at this plant, and he said that he never did anything alone. He then handed his resumé to me, and in every part of it, he had used the word and/or statement *we did this* or *we did that in our work.*

People outside this plant of highly skilled workers simply did not have the same self-concept and narrative that represented the fundamental team mind-set that had been developed among these GE employees. Many of the employees were very fearful of having to go back to that "other world of work" that was so focused on individual contributors. These employees had learned that just about everything you do at work relies on someone else, and they did not want to go backward.

At one meeting I attended several months into our project, which was initially focused on reviewing this facility's team model, I watched as some employees chose to be laid off sooner, not because they had a job, but because they had fewer expenses than someone else working in their job role who may have also had children, college loans, dependent parents, and/or an overdue mortgage. Repeatedly, I saw employees sacrificing their own self-interest for the good of their fellow teammates.

What happened next was even more remarkable. A group of employees got together and decided that before they closed this place, they were going to get a commercial realtor to develop a plan with them to market the facility to other organizations. They in effect would start a campaign to sell both the building *and* its amazing workforce to the highest bidder. From GE's perspective, they were fine with the plan as long as production continued until the last line was closed.

The employees found an experienced realtor to represent them, whom I then interviewed. At first, he thought the idea was not worth pursuing and that the employees would have to come to the realization that the plant would close. However, after spending time with these employees, the realtor realized that it was not just the physical plant that was special; it was also the workforce that was really special and clearly ready to take on a new team challenge with a new owner. He started to market this idea around the country focusing in on a *team-ready* plant.

Although this is not quite a fairy tale ending, before the plant was fully closed, an aerospace company came along and bought it and offered to hire many of the employees who had worked there previously. Before I left this project, the new company had hired back 150 of the original employees, after which they grew the workforce back to the original 300 plus.

What was amazing about this story was the dramatic shift that one could see in the self-concepts of employees to one that represented a team mind-set. We interviewed over forty employees during the time the plant was closing, and every one of them thought about how they worked in terms of a team guided by a collective mind-set. In fact, these employees were more articulate about things like team mental models and collective identity than any other workforce I had ever engaged with except for the one described in the next section.[13]

I want to be clear that having this team mind-set did not mean they were not operating as unique and very talented individuals. What they were doing was thinking in terms of their teams and, more important, as a fully integrated team system with a lot of dependencies that helped them to work more collaboratively and efficiently, including how to best leverage each individual's talents and experience. It was a very pure example of viewing the world through the lens of unity via diversity.[14]

THE HERD ON WALL STREET THAT RAN TO TAMPA

Back in the 1990s and prior, one of the preeminent Wall Street firms was named Solomon Brothers. This brokerage firm was known for hiring some of the best and brightest people in the world, and they were never ashamed to tell you so again and again. A typical story one heard on arrival at the firm was that *this firm* hires really smart people, and it is their responsibility to find out what they're supposed to do at work. If you were smart, the expectation was that you would figure it out. There were other stories about people who had started in the mailroom and then ended up being highly successful traders and millionaires, which was also part of this company's history and folklore.

During this period of time, what was considered a "financial or trading desk" represented a very sophisticated technology platform for trading stocks. The desks employed the financial types, but supporting each desk were the BTO (or Business Technology Organization) employees, run by a guy named Peter. The BTO probably had 1,800 employees or more working for it, and it was at that time the largest on Wall Street.

Peter was a remarkable leader, who was charismatic, inspiring, intellectually challenging, and individually considerate with employees, which according to the leadership literature would qualify him to be called transformational.[15] You also knew when Peter had visited a site by just looking up at the ceiling. Peter was an expert magician and somehow he could stick a playing card on any ceiling, sort of a calling card that Peter had been in the house.

Marc was a senior partner in Solomon Brothers, and he worked on a lot of innovative projects over his career. Most people estimated his IQ to be somewhere north of 200. Mike was his OD consultant, who was engaged to help interpret what Marc had just said and to make the changes he proposed work. Mike fully understood the four states of transformation in this book.

Marc proposed to Peter that the cost of running technical support for the various financial desks could be substantially reduced if they were to build a more team-based environment to support these complex technology systems. Peter was very much in favor of developing a team orientation, as represented in the way he treated his own workforce, as well as his stakeholders. For example, in one year Peter decided to give bonuses to employees who were not part of BTO but had been recommended by his employees as great collaborators. Although Peter funded this initiative entirely from his own budget, the other executives whose employees were getting bonuses from Peter were extremely upset with him. Why? In their view, he had crossed a silo line that he didn't own. He was asked to stop providing these tokens of his workforce's appreciation, and Peter reluctantly agreed to do so.

Marc designed a plan to move about 600 employees, who supported technology, to Tampa, Florida. His vision was to set up a completely team-based environment in Tampa. The heads of Solomon Brothers were skeptical that hundreds of Wall Street employees from New York City would move to Tampa, Florida, and then be able to support their trading desks from a distance. The numbers that Marc presented in terms of cost savings were impressive and enough to win the argument to move the back office operations south—at least as a tryout.

The agreement to go to Tampa was made because it was in the same U. S. time zone but far enough away to keep the executives in New York from interfering with the team experiment. The distance would allow some autonomy, and it aligned with what Saturn had done to get away from the General Motors executives in Detroit, who also did not think with a team mind-set. Saturn went to Memphis, Tennessee, in part because it was far enough away from the epicenter in Detroit to create some freedom to experiment. The Saturn managers knew that the GM top executive team, who had an exclusive elevator for their executives in the GM tower in Detroit that did not stop at any floors until it was safely at the top, would very likely not move toward supporting a team mind-set. The same logic applied to Tampa.

The plans were put in place to move a significant number of key employees to Tampa, and then afterwards they would hire the rest of the required staff at substantially lower salaries, given the cost of living and labor in Tampa, Florida, versus New York City. This was an audacious move in that they would have to literally turn off the lights in New York City on Friday at the close of trading and turn them back on in Tampa on Monday morning at the opening bell of the stock exchange. This was the type of audacious goal that characterized Solomon Brothers, and many of the New York employees were betting thousands of dollars it could not be done—yes, betting in effect against their own fantasy team.

Looking back in time, on February 26, 1993, there was a bomb detonated in the World Trade Center across from 7 World Trade, which housed Solomon Brothers before the 9/11 terrorist attacks took their building down. The bomb had taken out a rival's trading floor. Perhaps unknown to those outside of Wall Street, when something happens like this, New Yorkers jump in and help to fix things, even for their competitors. The BTO team in one weekend set up a complex trading floor in their own facility, so that by Monday morning their competitor was up and running.

The team of Solomon Brothers employees who knew how to run this technology was on the ground for months building their team model and mind-sets in Tampa. They were hiring people, just as GE did in building their teams, now at Solomon Brothers under the supervision of Mike and Marc, who each fully understood what it meant to first think "team." Mike did a lot of innovative training, not unlike that done at GE and also Saturn at the time. Mike also tried to come up with appropriate titles that would reflect a team-based organization. For his title, rather than VP of Organizational Development, he was a Master Team Builder. He told us that he would submit the title to the printing shop in the New York office, and each time he did, his business cards came back "VP of Organizational Development." What the New York employees thought about Tampa was that it was some type of socialist or communist plot, and they would have nothing to do with it, including changing titles on business cards.

Initially, those who bet against Tampa lost. Over one weekend, they went from lights out to lights on and were up and operational. With a relatively new workforce, and a cadre of experienced New Yorkers, they had done what many thought was impossible. Realize that this success was based on a lot of hard work on the part of Marc, Mike, and their team, to inculcate in the self and collective mind-sets into their Tampa team, an authentic team mental model. Like the GE employees, every employee we met and interviewed was incredibly articulate about what it meant to operate in such a team-minded context, and like those employees they feared going backward from this sanctuary organization

There were many stories during the initiating and impending states that indicated that those outside of Tampa were very suspicious of this experiment and were confident that it would eventually fail, which it did. For example, top financial traders would call Tampa and ask who is in charge, so they had a name to scream at over the phone about some problem they were experiencing with technology in New York City. The voice in Tampa would talk team and would indicate the team would resolve the problem, and it did. However, this was very unsatisfying to those in New York, who were more oriented toward finding who screwed up versus what went wrong. Marc was able to provide a lot of cover during the first two years of operation, as he was highly respected among the top leaders and his Tampa facility was performing great.

For two years, the Tampa facility was meeting and indeed exceeding all of Marc's projected savings. However, the whole effort was taking a toll on Marc and his family, and after two years, due to health reasons, Marc had to take a leave of absence. Without Marc there, who in the eyes of New York was "the guy in charge," the experiment was attacked at every turn, until finally the leadership of Solomon Brothers decided the facility had to close.

Here again was an experiment where the employees who had moved from New York had actually become identified with the power of team design and thinking and were in the Institutionalizing State, but the others who were not in the experiment found ways to continuously undermine what was actually a successful change project—because they were not in this state of mind nor, as an organization overall, in the institutionalized state of team mindedness. It is actually quite interesting to see how much subterfuge and cunning went into sustaining Tampa, as well as killing it. Realize that, at the end of the day, whether you were in Tampa or New York City, you all were supposedly playing for the same team, but in reality it became as Saturn was to GM, a war of the parts against the whole. What it represents is something that Bob Kegan, whom we referred to earlier, called an immunity to change. If it is a foreign element in the body, then one's immune system is supposed to attack and eradicate it as quickly as possible. At Solomon Brothers, that is exactly what happened.

PULLING TOGETHER ALL OF THE PIECES IN EACH STATE PLUS LEADERHIP AND OWNERSHIP

I have now fully covered all of the elements in the four-state model. In Figure 7.2, I have added to the bottom of the figure and model the types of leadership and ownership that I have been referring to throughout the last four chapters associated with each state. At the bottom of this figure are the psychological ownership states, going from territorial to accountable to a sense of belonging to finally identification. At the highest level, we see that individuals have a collective sense of ownership that comes to define who they are to themselves and others.

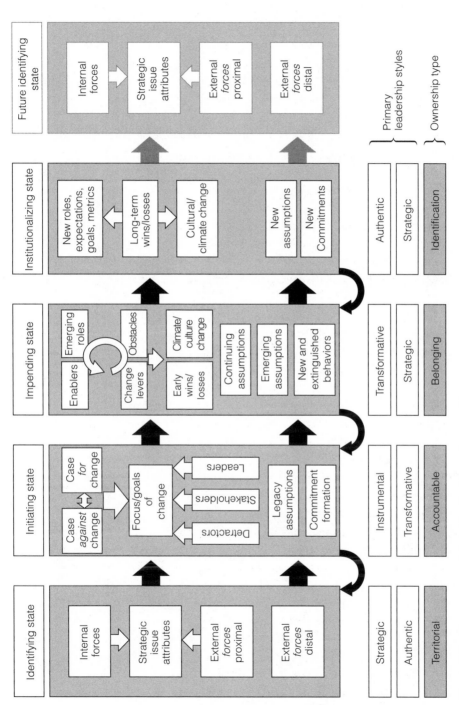

Figure 7.2 Four-state model plus leadership and ownership.

In terms of leadership, we begin in the Identification State with creating an authentic leadership base, along with strategy to capture the signals that are out there, and move through the Initiating State by initiating actions, transformative as those actions build out fundamental change, into an Impending State with fully transformative changes, followed by solidifying the strategic focus on into the fourth Institutionalizing State, where authenticity is now firmly rooted and leadership is looking forward again to new signals and directions.

I now would like to highlight and summarize some of the key points made in this chapter, as we prepare for our next chapter, which will go through two examples to demonstrate the complete process associated with the states of change.

The Institutionalizing State represents a transformative shift in thinking and doing. For those who did not grow up in the old system, if there has been institutional change, they do not know that other previous organization. For them, how they make meaning is based on what they think and do in their current organization.

In this state, the culture and climate, which are each mind-sets that people use to make meaning of how they are supposed to work together, have fundamentally changed. This means that assumptions about work and about interactions, roles, expectations, evaluations, and rewards have also changed in alignment with the way the individual makes meaning in this new state of operating.

Of course, if the culture and climate changes, so do the assumptions the individual is guided by in terms of beliefs, thinking, and action. For example, with agile programming, one of the assumptions is that you iterate and fail and then continue to iterate. So, failure is not seen as so consequential but rather as a stepping-stone to something a bit better—like breaking better. People in this state also form new commitments as to how they go about following this cycle of development, with a different commitment in terms of the thresholds for accepting failure.

In the fully Institutionalizing State, we expect there will be a high degree of authenticity on the part of the leadership and followership. Leaders and followers will be more self-aware of their new beliefs and commitments, transparent in how they interact with each other as a consequence of these new commitments, and balanced and just when addressing deviations from the new state; they will display a high level of collective interest for others in terms of ethical standards.[16]

This state also tends to coincide with strategic leadership in that there will be new signs and signals on the horizon that will appear as you move into a new state of operating that will require yet further considerations of what the individual might change or not change as you enter into the next cycle. In fact, the way of thinking that has been developed will provide you with a keener sense of the glide path for change and transformation that needs to be followed. This leads to a clearer understanding of what you can expect in the Initiating State.

You will have noticed before, and now in Figure 7.2, there is now a fifth state, which represents going through the Identifying State. I want you to recognize that the model is perhaps like agile programming in that it is iterative and continues to cycle through states of development. There is no end state per se, in that organizations, like individuals, continue to evolve over time and make adjustments to the changing needs and demands in their markets. This is true for governments, for-profit, not-for-profit, and volunteer organizations. All of these have to change to address the needs of their clients, customers, and stakeholders. This is why it is so fundamentally important to recognize that at the very center of the change process is the individual's self-concept, which must evolve over time to come up with and then address these changes. It is not so different, then, if I focused this entire book on individual development, which I address in more detail in Chapter 10. Consider how you viewed the world prior to being a teenager, being a teenager, in early adulthood, and now if you are further along in your life stream. At each point along the way, I know that people's self-concepts change, and that continues throughout the entire lifespan for some, but not necessarily for all, individuals. You have to have discipline to work at that sort of change, just as you have to have discipline to work at organizational change.

Now let's set up the example for our next chapter. I want you to be comfortable with using the framework that I have provided in the previous chapters and to be able to apply that framework to your own organization. To do so, I will create some prototypical generic change efforts that will be used to exemplify the process that unfolds with change across the four states. These cases are based on real organizations that I have fictionalized in that I am using examples from multiple organizations to create my narrative to review the four-state framework covered throughout this book. Please think about the dynamics of your own organization and how they apply to my examples to bring it more to life for yourself.

I ask you to reflect on the following questions, as you move into the next chapter:

- Think about a transformative change that has altered your thinking and self-concept with respect to work, and how that change unfolded from identification to institutionalization. What were your first thoughts about the change? Were you against it? Did you not understand it? How did you know it was institutionalized?

- What were some of the most successful aspects of the campaign process that stand out in your mind? What discipline or focus seemed to have the biggest impact on sustaining the change?

- What were some of the strategies used by folks to derail the change? Could those individuals have been changed before they went against what was being changed?

- What did your leader do to support or inhibit the change? How about other leaders? Why?

- Do you feel that there were too many initiatives to sustain the change effort?

- Has the change been sustained over time? If so, what do you believe were the most consequential elements of the change process?

RESEARCH LINK: A DEEPER DIVE

A case study was done to examine how the New York Port Authority transformed itself to address a massive homeless problem affecting their facilities. Back in the 1980s, the police who worked for the port were continuously being notified of homeless people sleeping around their facilities, including train and bus terminals. They thought this was not "their" problem, in that they were not social workers. Yet, the social work community was not able to take this problem on and solve it for a variety of good reasons, including shortage of resources. Because identity is the lens we use to make sense of our world, their world of policing and identity did not include homeless people; this just was not part of their self-narratives or concepts.[17,18] Yet, over time, the leadership of the port and its workforce realized that the challenges they faced with the homeless were their challenges to own and something that they would have to address as part of their roles and their identity. This step was taken, and processes were put in place that became institutionalized over time, changing what the port and its officers did as part of their work.

8 A TALE OF TWO TRANSFORMATIONS

We all have a clear understanding of our organization's vision and strategy.

In this chapter, my focus is on helping you walk through the process of transformative change in an organization, based on all four states that we have discussed in our previous chapters. Because readers of this book will come from many different types of organizations and cultures, I wanted to compare two generic organizations in this chapter, which in some capacity and form exist in every society, culture, and country. The first organization, Foodie Inc., comes from the food industry. The second example comes from a more recent addition in terms of industry and organization and represents a computer software company. I will present each organization, in pieces so to speak, taking you through their respective arc of change. For each one, let me start with a brief history of their founding.

FOODIE INC.

Foodie Inc. is a company comprised of 417 employees. The organization is responsible for working with organizations who process and package seafood for distribution throughout your country—any country you may want to add in here for a local reference. The company is celebrating its thirtieth anniversary this year and has grown into being a major player in the seafood industry. Foodie Inc. got its start in a little shack shop on the waterfront where its founder Max worked with other fishermen to buy and process their catch for the day.

Max built a reputation for being a tough and fair negotiator. Everyone who worked with Max knew that he was very particular about the fish he bought, so that his customers could be confident that he never would sacrifice quality in what he bought, sold, and delivered. Throughout the early years for Max's business, there were many stories about him not being able to provide enough fish to all of his customers, which happened when the quality of the daily catch was not up to his standards.

Over the years, Max's business grew larger, to the point where he had to move from the waterfront to a larger facility. Max was very particular about whom he hired for Foodie Inc., as he wanted to make sure they fit the culture and values of the company, which he repeatedly would say was always working toward one common goal—providing its customers with the very best product, at the lowest price, in the most efficient manner. It was not uncommon for recruits to go through numerous rounds of interviews addressing structured challenges related to the work in the company before they were finally hired. Even after the rigorous hiring process was completed, all employees remained on probation for six months, which Max liked to refer to as the Foodie boot camp. Being an employee for Foodie Inc. was considered a badge of honor that was associated with being a very high-quality individual. It was not uncommon for someone to say after hearing where a Foodie employee worked, "You work in one of the best companies, bar none!"

The mind-set Max wanted to develop in all of his employees was what he referred to as "a calling for taking the gifts we receive from the sea and then providing them through the best selection and care to Foodie's customers." For Max, fish were not a commodity; they were something very special and essential to our existence on this planet. This may seem silly to an outsider, but to Max, this was a calling, and he wanted people who worked with him to feel their jobs were special, they were special, and they were providing together a very, very special service to humanity.

Many of the people who came to work at Foodie stayed there for a very long period of time. The early hires were held in very high regard by all employees and were expected to model the organization's core values for others. Many employees remarked that if you were talking to any one of them, you were talking to Max. Max had given them very special status and called them his "Knights of the Cutting Table."

NEAR SOFT

Near Soft's two founders started their company in the Northwest town of Pullman, Washington, after they had both graduated from college. Jim and Jean had developed software that allowed any two devices to communicate with each other, and their patented source code had quickly become a universal standard in the industry. The timing of their firm's launch was perfectly aligned with a growing need corresponding to the rise of the Internet of things, where everything will have Radio Frequency Identification (RFID) chips embedded in them for easy tracking. This meant that devices from refrigerators to your car could also speak to each other using their standard operating code.

Two years after their launch, Jim and Jean decided it was time to move their company to a larger city and chose Tacoma, Washington. Tacoma had gone through a downturn in the late 1990s and still had a depressed real estate market, providing Jean and Jim the opportunity to get a lot of space for future growth at a very low cost. There were also a lot of software engineers in the region due to high-tech industries in nearby Seattle.

Near Soft grew very rapidly during its first eight years, and by its eighth year it had a workforce totaling 3,015 in Washington alone, along with employees in small offices around the United States, as well as in Brussels, London, Dubai, Tokyo, Tel Aviv, Jakarta, Singapore, Bogota, Sydney, and Christchurch.

EMERGING SIGNALS AT FOODIE INC.

Foodie Inc. had very little absenteeism, turnover, or theft, and year after year they were at the top of the industry in safety, efficiency, productivity, and quality. Foodie managers oftentimes had to encourage employees to stay home when they were sick, because they were so committed to the business. Max placed a great deal of importance on investing in education that was focused on being lean and agile. Max's contention was that if you had a best friend at work, he or she would certainly never let you get hurt by letting you be careless and inattentive to what you were doing. Also, Foodie employees knew their customers and the histories of their grocery stores and/or restaurants. Max always said, "You ought to get to know the person who is eating at your table," and the customers were the ones who were coming for dinner. Employees felt stimulated by the challenges they faced, even though a lot of their work was tiring and repetitive. This was a work environment where you could expect the employees would be cynical, overworked, and not very engaged, but this would be exactly the opposite of what one observed at Foodie.

As times changed in the industry, consumers became more educated about where the fish came from and how they were processed. If it was not "free range" versus "farmed" fish, then Foodie's customers were not buying it. The pressure to qualify suppliers for sourcing their fish became increasingly more challenging, as did the regulations one had to follow in this industry. These changes plus the higher-maintenance customers were taking more and more of Max's time. Max had certainly groomed people who worked with him to do what he did when he was gone, but the employees really liked to have him in the plant, in that he was the deep taproot for their core values.

Max would rarely fire someone, but if he did, it was because they compromised on a core value or treated an employee or customer with disrespect in ways that were unacceptable at Foodie Inc. Everyone knew Max's redlines for bad conduct, and if you were inexperienced and made a mistake, you were typically given another chance or two, but not much more.

CHALLENGES ON THE HORIZON FOR FOODIE INC.

As in most industries, the fishing industry was going through consolidation ranging from the catching of fish through to their processing and delivery to customers. Small, high-quality companies like Foodie Inc. eventually had to decide whether they would organically grow to compete or be acquired. Of course, there were rumors that some large companies had approached Foodie Inc. with acquisition offers. Max's style was to discuss such events, when something serious was happening, but in this case, the employees had not heard anything directly from Max. He was also aware of the rumors because people were very transparent in Foodie Inc., sharing their opinions with each other and him.

Max typically studied challenges for a long time. However, once he knew what was required and had gotten input from many people, he was very quick to act, and bring people on board with what needed to be done. The go/no go decision was something he would hold close to the vest for a long period of time before announcing.

Increasingly, the costs of doing business were mounting, whereby Max's company was being squeezed by its large competitors on the pricing of its products in their market. Several of Max's very loyal customers were contacting him to see what he was thinking, as they too were witnessing the changes happening in their industry. They all wanted to stay with Foodie Inc., but they were coming to a point where the costs would outweigh their loyalty to Max and his workforce.

CHALLENGES FACING NEAR SOFT

Jean and Jim realized a year back that they needed to bring in a more professional management team to run their business. Jean was still hesitant to move forward with the hiring because she felt that bringing in new senior managers from different technology companies might have a negative impact on the culture of Near Soft. Jim felt that was a risk they had to take with Near Soft.

After months of discussions, they both agreed to move forward with the hiring of a new team of leaders and brought in a new CEO, CFO, COO, and CTO to run their business. Each of them had come from a different company, so at the start of their employment, initial concerns about what would be the culture of New Soft under this new management team began to emerge.

For some time, the new management team blended well with Jim and Jean, who each took on new roles within their company that were more aligned with their expertise and passion. Jim became the VP of Innovation, and Jean was VP for Customer Services and Development. They were both okay not running the company and felt the new management team had their collective interests at heart. Jean and Jim could also see that, with the pace of growth Near Soft was experiencing, the workforce was not as cohesive or aligned as it had been in the past. This was partially a function of too rapid growth, as well as new employees coming from a much broader range of organizations, cultures, and backgrounds. What they saw emerging at Near Soft was a company that had different territories and boundaries in terms of their divisions, products, services, and cultures.

The differences that were emerging in their company were also coming at a time when its flagship products and services were under increasing competition. This was putting pressure on other divisions to innovate, whereas the main product division with the largest workforce was feeling pressured to keep increasing their sales targets. Several senior leaders in those divisions had already left Near Soft, as they felt they were not trusted by the new team members. This was causing rifts among the top management team and with Jean and Jim. The arguments were coming to a head, leading the board members of Near Soft to decide to change the leadership at the top, before moving forward with an IPO. The individual they chose was one of Jean and Jim's longtime employees—a very highly respected engineer in their company. Sam seemed like a great choice because many employees felt she was someone who respected the old culture of Near Soft.

INITIATING CHANGES AT FOODIE INC.

One golden autumn day, Max came into the plant and asked for an all-hands-on-deck meeting the next afternoon. Max was a person of few words, so the employees knew that he would be brief, to the point, and would answer any questions posed, and then they would be back to work. He started by indicating how proud he was of what this company had become over the last thirty years. Max then went on to talk about the purpose of meeting, which was a decision he had to make on going ahead alone with the goal of growing bigger organically or being acquired. He said that he and his leadership team had been tracking the trends in their industry for some time now and also had been talking to lots of experts. He said what was now clear to him was that over the next five years the industry would undergo some dramatic changes in terms of using technology, along with the scope and size of companies that would survive, while also reducing the cost structure required to continue to do business.

Max then said that he came to the conclusion that Foodie Inc. would have to go through some significant changes. This would involve being acquired by a larger organization, several of whom he had been talking to over the last year. He then said, "I know from rumors that some of you have already heard about those conversations, so let me tell you today: they are real."

Max then said that it had always been the case that their workforce had moved forward together in terms of taking on whatever challenges were necessary. This would also be the case in this instance. Max committed to making sure that everyone understood exactly what was going on during the change process, which had not actually started, except in terms of identifying the critical signals that would affect their business and how they operate. Max wanted them to consider that today is day zero on the new trajectory of Foodie Inc.

Most of the forces that were causing this shift in thinking within the industry were distal in the sense of their overall industry around the globe. As the supply of quality fish became more limited, companies like Foodie Inc. would have to adapt and change. Of course, there were also signals from their own local industry, customers, and government that things were going to change in their industry, so there were also proximal forces at work. By delaying action, Foodie Inc. would be putting the whole company at risk.

Next, he said that the solution for Foodie Inc. was to join forces with a larger entity that could provide the company with the resources it needed to compete in new emerging markets. Max also said he wanted a company that would acquire them to be like them, in terms of their core values and respect for both their employees and customers. Clearly, Max had built up a tremendous amount of goodwill in his workforce that afforded him the opportunity for his employees to suspend judgment, place their trust in him and their leaders, and then allow the process to unfold under their guidance. Max promised that he would tell them everything he knew, when he knew it, with the exception of any legal obligations he and the company might have going through an acquisition process. Max then indicated that he had one more bit of information to share with all of them. Max needed the entire 417 of them to own this change, and he realized that was asking a lot. Max said, "I am asking you to make a psychological contract with me, to figure how we can make this transition work, and come through the other side, perhaps with a different definition of what my organization means, when we say Foodie Inc. However, at its core it will still be the organization we have all known over these last thirty years."

With that, one of the doors opened, and waiters came walking in with large silver trays with white envelopes neatly stacked on top. They walked through the plant and asked each employee to take one envelope. Once the last envelope was delivered, Max said, "Let's open this chapter together," and each employee held his or her envelope up and ripped it open. Inside was a ticket with the number of common shares each employee had received based on years of experience with Foodie Inc.

FOODIE INC. ACQUIRED

Foodie Inc. was in deep negotiations with a large global food company called Fishbone LTD. Fishbone was well known for being a top-quality company that was growing rapidly. During the past five years, Fishbone had acquired four other companies, and from what Max could find out through his due diligence process, all of the acquisitions were thriving. Fishbone was also a very lean corporation with only fifty employees in its Netherlands headquarters. Their model was to operate as a holding company and to find synergies across their operating companies that could be leveraged. They also preferred to keep the top management teams in place and to give them a great deal of autonomy to run their businesses. The CEO and founder of Fishbone LTD, Stefan Sauder, over his career and now in his late seventies, had a great reputation as both an industrialist and a philanthropist.

CHANGES BEGIN AT NEAR SOFT WITH THE CAMPAIGN

Sam came on board and over the next few months built her management team, keeping Jim and Jean in their current positions. Sam was largely promoted from within and grew up in the Near Soft culture, but she did bring in a new COO, who had a lot of experience with lean manufacturing and also worked for a company very similar in values to Near Soft. Every two weeks, Sam would hold an all-hands-on-deck meeting to give her employees updates on their business while also covering trends and challenges emerging in their industry. Sam was clear that she was meeting with folks outside Near Soft to get their ideas about the future directions within their industry while trying to map out the next phase of development.

About six months into her tenure, Sam signaled to the employees that she would present their new manifesto for future growth and development on the heels of their announcement to go public with an IPO. Sam and her team appeared to be very aligned around this new manifesto and presented it in a very compelling way in terms of the future directions the company would take over the next ten years. There were some significant changes that would take place in the near future that would shape Near Soft for years to come. One of those changes entailed investing in three new lines of businesses by acquisition. The other big shift was away from their core legacy business, which had been the cash cow for Near Soft since it was founded. This came as a big shock for people in that division, while for others this move seemed long overdue. Sam and her team specified very compelling reasons for their decision, supported by data as to why that business was becoming a commodity, and the shift in focus was to new growth areas. Going forward the strategic positioning of Near Soft would be to provide the most advanced software solutions for any technology device, and although building software that connected everything was still at the core of their business model, they were now concentrating more on customized software development services, including emerging areas such as augmented or mixed reality.

At the end of the session, there was a brief period of questioning that followed. The employees didn't necessarily argue with the projections provided. They also felt that Sam was a leader of high integrity and had the company's interests in mind; nonetheless, they still felt betrayed, and over the next year many ended up leaving Near Soft.

Over the next several months, there was a noticeable increase in territorial behavior. As promised a few months back, the distribution of money in Near Soft was changing, where the core division's budgets were declining while more resources were being allocated to new and emerging businesses. It felt as if the leadership had created the haves and the have-nots, and there was a great deal of tension associated with the overall change process.

FOODIE INC. MOVING INTO THE INITIATING STATE

As part of Max's change campaign, he periodically sent voice messages out to all of his employees that were brief, to the point, and focused on where Foodie Inc.

was in the acquisition process. Max began his campaign for their transition into Fishbone LTD. He gathered his Knights and talked to them about the phases that would unfold and described that they were now entering into the initiating state of this change process. He gave each of his Knights the following talking points that they had collectively crafted:

- There are pros and cons to the change process, and in the end the list of pros is longer than the list of cons, but both should be presented to all employees and discussed in what Max called dialogue circles. For example, one pro was the opportunity to bulk purchase new equipment with the other organizations in Fishbone, and to then negotiate a better price for new technology. One con was that they would likely have to compromise sometimes on which particular brand they bought, as Fishbone wanted the decisions across their organizations to be consensus based.

- Max had 4 explicit goals for moving into this change process including:
  - To take advantage of being the very best partner with the other Fishbone companies.
  - To be transparent with any challenges they faced and to address those challenges together.
  - To go through this process with people saying they felt as respected as they did when it started.
  - To change how future Foodie employees would describe "my organization" to their friends and family; it would be an organization with a global and a local culture.

- There needed to be clear communications with all stakeholders, and that included employees, clients, customers, and their suppliers and distributors. There also needed to be one point of contact for communications, and each communication would build on the next, helping to create a very clear narrative for the change process.

- Foodie Inc. also had some legacy assumptions. Max discussed with his Knights what they felt were some of the most important to retain and dismiss. For example, the diversity of companies in Fishbone required Foodie Inc. to think like a global company and to understand cultural differences. Many of Foodie's leaders would be interacting with a diverse array of cultures. They would have to learn the cultural ways of these other companies and to keep them in mind in terms of how they did business.

- Max asked his Knights to think carefully about the commitments they were all making and to keep the list lean, as they moved through this initiating state.

- In the midst of massive change, employees needed to have a very clear line of sight as to what they had to do going forward. Max also said they should all remember each day that they were not only dealing with employees now, they were also addressing owners, so they needed to show them the individualized consideration and respect Foodie had always been known for . . . plus a little more.

- Max also wanted his Knights to know that they all have to be inspired to pursue this change, to see it as worthwhile and meaningful; at the same time, all of them needed to "fish or cut bait" and be accountable.

BEGINNINGS OF THE INITIATION STATE FOR NEAR SOFT

The new businesses were given leaders who had the title of president of their divisions, which signaled they would have a lot more decision authority over strategic planning, operations, and their budgets. Each business was required to put forth its own strategic plan, while figuring out how they would align with the new business model that Sam's team had put together. They were also encouraged to be agile and to iterate their plans each quarter, making the necessary adjustments required to grow and succeed, even if that led to some failed or false starts.

Employees throughout Near Soft were offering very different narratives about the strategic change process. Many were dead set against the new directions and felt as if the presidents who were chosen did not deserve those positions, given their tenure and experience. These employee groups tended to block initiatives or slow them down as much as possible. This led to some very uncomfortable circumstances, where Sam had to step in and fire some of the executives who were being distractors or, worse yet, undermining exactly what had to be done. This all came to a head when Sam fired someone who was very close to Jim and Jean, who Sam felt was the ring leader in blocking the new organization. Both Jim and Jean were upset over the firing and were informed after the firing happened, at the same time that everyone else in Near Soft heard about the dismissal. On hearing the news, Jean decided to go on an extended sabbatical leave. Jim stayed on, but he became more remote and rarely was seen around the office.

Sam and her close set of leaders began to push really hard on growth goals of 10 percent per year in the new business divisions. These goals were placing a lot of pressure on the workforce, resulting in higher turnover rates. Near Soft had had a very stable workforce for years, but now they were going to their competitors. Also, with the increased pressure by Sam and her team, managers at all levels were being asked to be more accountable to the growth goals and to support one another. This recommendation went out to the leaders as a mandate rather than a request, leading some employees to not get on board with the change process. Others felt that they should give the change process a chance, even though it was not uncommon to hear about a growing level of confusion across the company in terms of where they were in this strategic change process.

As the initiating state unfolded, there was increasingly a lot of conflict around what were the new assumptions guiding the business and those legacy assumptions of how Near Soft had always operated. In terms of legacy assumptions, Near Soft had emphasized writing code that fit with the universal standards that Near Soft had become famous for in the industry. Now it appeared that there were many different standards being used across products, which frustrated some of the old-time employees, who felt the code wasn't as good or up to their standards.

Sam and her team's consistent focus, and their ability to adapt, kept the changes moving forward, with the new divisions starting to get traction in their markets. This forward movement coincided with a very successful IPO that hit the market at $31 per share but soon rose to $53 given the confidence in their top management team and plan. These events helped fuel a stronger commitment to the changes that Sam and her team had been pushing within their organization.

Sam was noticing increasing accountability in the organization as managers continued to push their goals and milestones within their divisions. Sam also encouraged her leaders not to forget how much of a change they were going through and that being patient and supportive was what they needed to keep in mind when they met resistance.

THE ARRIVAL OF FOODIE INC. IN THE IMPENDING STATE

The financial acquisition now done, it seemed that the workforce was moving along relatively smoothly with the transition. However, for the first time in thirty years, Max was not the guy who had the last word, and in some ways he was not their leader, as he had been in the past. He was no longer fully in charge and could be asked to leave if the leadership of Fishbone changed.

Given the age of the Fishbone LTD founder, Foodie employees were understandably worried about what might happen in the transition given that he was nearing eighty years of age. They even started to worry about the possibility of what might happen if Fishbone were acquired. The more the conversations unfolded, the more concerned a lot of the employees became, with some opting to leave Foodie to either go on their own, retire, or find another more secure job.

Max realized these concerns were bubbling up in his workforce. He started monthly all-hands–on-deck meetings to ramp up the campaign to stay the course in terms of change. He would also invite others to speak on the transition underway, enabling them to have an audience with the plant's workforce. He brought Fishbone leaders in to talk directly to the plant's employees, and he would always spend time with them the day before, so he could get to know those leaders, asking them lots of questions about the future direction of the company.

Max also created what was called the Green Go Team, or GGT. This team met every morning to touch base on any new news that needed to be communicated throughout the day to the workforce. The GGT was responsible for getting that information embedded in all aspects of the plant's workforce.

Although Fishbone had great intentions, there were times when they were communicating corporate-wide messages that seemed to go against or at least were not fully aligned with Foodie's messaging. This was bound to happen in that Fishbone operated in a much larger global pond, and their leaders needed to address issues that were not always equally beneficial to every organization in their corporation. They too were doing their best, but there were nonetheless some hiccups along the way that created a bit of confusion and angst.

There were also cultural issues to be addressed because Fishbone LTD was a Netherlands-based company. The Foodie Inc. employees found that the corporate leadership in the Netherlands tended to operate based on a social democratic model of decision making, which they were trying to understand in terms of their own leadership and decision making. Hierarchy clearly took on a different meaning at Fishbone LTD.

Max was adamant throughout this state on creating and executing a performance dashboard so that Foodie employees would see every day any incremental declines or improvements in their performance. The dashboard was supposed to represent the progress being made during this transition state in terms of having greater economies of scale while also underscoring the importance of transparency. For the most part, there were a lot of small wins, but there were losses as well. For example, with the fluctuations in different currencies across global markets, sometimes the "taxes" being placed on Foodie Inc. by their holding company seemed larger than what they should have paid.

Some employees were also posting on the blog that the culture and climate was changing in Foodie Inc. as it became part of a larger enterprise. For example, the speed at which decisions were made that had an impact on other member companies was slower than in their own past. On the positive side, the culture was evolving to be a more global one that was changing the way Foodie Inc. employees thought about people from different cultures and themselves. A change to having more of a more global mind-set was something that was being promoted.[1] Working with a company that did cross-cultural training, periodically all employees would receive some short podcasts on interesting facts regarding how to engage in very different national cultures. For many in Foodie's workforce, who neither had a passport nor had traveled outside the United States, these were huge changes in the way they thought and behaved at work.

In the past, it was not uncommon to hear some off-color jokes about other cultures, what they ate, how they dressed, and how they treated their partners, spouses, and so forth. It appeared to Max and his Knights that their employee workforce was becoming much more open to cultural differences and also were displaying a growing level of inquisitiveness to discover more about these different cultures. There were even very serious discussions about expanding their lines of food into areas that were very nontraditional cuisines, at least in terms of America and Foodie Inc.

Max encouraged his Knights to keep focusing on being positive and inspiring about the change but also not to shy away from challenging assumptions they disagreed with or had a different opinion on. He would also bring in problems that he was confronting during the transition into this state and would ask employees if they could reframe the problem to think in different ways about a broader range of solutions.

Sometimes these discussions also became more strategic, and Max could see his leaders were leveraging a broader range of ideas and data than in the past, as well as navigating through them in terms of coming up with different perspectives and actions. Max continued to motivate his Knights to cascade their messages about change across all levels of the organization and with all of their stakeholders outside, including Fishbone employees.

Max was starting to see a sense of belongingness and ownership growing toward being part of the Fishbone family of companies, even though at the grocery story every employee probably still said when asked where they worked, "My organization is Foodie Inc., but we are a bit bigger now." Max saw them struggle with this distinction, and that was okay, because it had taken thirty years to get to where they had been before the acquisition.

NEAR SOFT'S MISALIGNMENT IN THE IMPENDING STATE

Near Soft's foundational division started to gain traction in its markets again, and sales were growing by 4.5 percent year over year. This was partly due to the many legacy systems that were upgrading software without having to completely change their source code. The upbeat and unexpected projections were viewed very favorably in the markets, but internally it was emboldening leaders to push their old agenda again. Leaders were building coalitions with their counterparts in other divisions, who felt that Sam and her team were pushing too hard on numbers and not hard enough on the quality of services. There were more backstories passed around that did not always reflect how things were unfolding at Near Soft or with their competitors.

Sam and her team were aware the change process was at a precarious point in time and were trying to come up with strategies to rebuild their campaign to support the initiative. At the beginning of the year, a new campaign was launched entitled "Turning the Corner." Sam and her direct reports created a set of talking points and went out throughout the company to hold small meetings comprised of fifteen to twenty employees to address the change process and the progress being made and then to sit and listen to the questions, concerns, issues, and in many cases rants. At each meeting, the managers committed to gathering up all of the issues raised and then getting back to employees with their responses. Some managers were very diligent in responding in a timely manner to employee suggestions and complaints, although others were not. Over the next six months, the sessions were making headway in getting a more coherent message out into Near Soft, but there was still a lot of confusion and resentment.

Sam asked some of the champions around the organization to attend the employee listening sessions in their divisions, so that it was not just her senior managers carrying the load, as well as to boost their credibility in the eyes of her employees. Also, the top management team had come up with a new performance dashboard that everyone in Near Soft could download as an app to track on a daily basis how the company was performing. The app also allowed for anonymous input from any employee on the change process and was set up along the lines of Glassdoor.com, where employees could rate any leader. Although for many leaders it felt very uncomfortable to receive such feedback, over time they got accustomed to what one manager called his "Yell" rating, playing off the popular Yelp site. In the beginning, ratings and comments were not so positive, but over time the tide was turning and the ratings were beginning to show an upward trajectory.

One of the biggest obstacles to the change in this state was the fact that the message was often being diluted by those who wanted to distract attention from the changes underway. Although progress was being made on performance goals, there were setbacks from time to time, leading some of the employees to comment that they perhaps should have stayed with their original business model and focus, although a growing number of employees realized that you either change or fade into the history of countless fallen organizations.

The increasing levels of tension were causing some competing priorities in Near Soft. Many employees were beginning to see a new Near Soft emerge that was growing in terms of brand equity in the new and exciting markets of mixed and augmented reality. In the newer divisions, the culture was shifting to one that was more edgy and collaborative. Teams were becoming the norm for units of work, and many employees were requesting to work in open-space environments, even if their job allowed them to have their own office. What it felt like was that there were two or three Near Softs operating at the same time, with some transforming before the leadership's eyes and the others seemingly stuck in a time that no longer existed.

At least in terms of the markets and the new divisions, the strategy that had been launched several years back was being positively received, and there was a greater sense of ownership in the future direction than in the past. In fact, there were many employees in Near Soft who had a much greater sense of ownership to the new divisions, and there was some talk that the company might even spin these organizational divisions off into separate privately held companies. This would be a bold strategic move for Near Soft, but one that might actually make sense.

FOODIE ENTERS THE INSTITUTIONALIZING STATE

Max would regularly attend new employee orientations, finding that the workforce was increasingly becoming more diverse in terms of cultural background and identity. Many of the new employees seemed to convey a sense of being part of something bigger, that although Foodie was the proximal identity, the overarching identity they felt was more aligned with Fishbone. For them, Fishbone was a brand that was quickly becoming a global brand, and they liked to describe how that defined who they were and what they did at work.

Max and his Knights were now pretty comfortable with how they needed to make decisions in terms of being part of a larger entity. Their process for making decisions was lengthened as they realized they had to go through more steps than in the past, so they wanted to be sure to account for more decision-making time.

They also appreciated how important it was to have a dialogue with their partners in other companies and that, even though consensus took longer to achieve, it usually provided a clearer understanding of everyone's position.

Over this time span, Fishbone had also acquired four other new companies, so there was a growing internal market for ideas and collaborations and economies of scale with purchasing resources. Fishbone leaders were putting out quarterly briefings on the status of all companies to create some friendly competition. Also, given its scope and size, there were new company-wide goals coming out in terms of proposals to increase market share and to move into different countries. In addition, Fishbone had brought a few of the Knights into the corporate headquarters, thus providing them with greater opportunities for career growth. The assumption that you could go as far as Max's office in terms of growth no longer applied, and Max was in some instances reporting to his former Knights.

Max also saw that commitments among his leaders did not include only the specific goals of Foodie but also those for Fishbone. For some individuals, he felt that answering the "my organization" question might now start with the vision and mission of Fishbone. This seemed like a good transition, as long as the core values and beliefs of Foodie Inc. were never lost, or at least that's that what he hoped for in the future.

The founder of Fishbone was still in charge, and many of the Foodie employees were comfortable enough with the transition that, even if he did step down, they felt that life would go on and that Foodie would adapt and grow. In fact, the workforce was just north of 625 employees. What they appreciated about Fishbone was that the leaders were aware of their concerns, transparent with their intentions and expectations, and very fair when hard decisions had to be made. They were an ethical group of leaders who had some sense of vision and mission that worked really well with Foodie and with the company in the arc of its life cycle.

THE DISTANT HORIZON FOR THE INSTITUTIONALIZING STATE IN NEAR SOFT

There were some parts of Near Soft that had turned the corner on change, and if you asked new employees in their division to describe "my organization" it was not the old Near Soft but rather the new organization that had emerged in terms of their individual and collective self-concepts, identity, and narrative. These employees were now thinking about the revolution that was facing them in terms of augmented, virtual, and mixed reality. There were lots of competitions emerging among employees to think about the most far-out applications in these new market spaces, and then they were asked to answer the following question: Would VR or AR or MR change the _____ (fill in the blank for industry such as education, health care, military, manufacturing, safety, house construction, dance, art, music, and space exploration, and in what specific ways?) Often, people would say the two industries most interested in MR, VR, and AR were the military, and, of course, they would then say pornography.

As time unfolded, Near Soft began to build out its R&D capabilities in this new space and was racking up discoveries and patents. Over the next five years, with the current pace of development in Near Soft, it was expected the company would emerge as one of the top three players in this industry. What this meant was that Near Soft had to build out an employee workforce that could work within and across any industry. A critical aspect of their growth was not only building the new software for this emerging industry but also learning about the different industries and how one could adapt what was developed in one industry to another. This was based on the assumption that VR or AR or MR could be used to advance any industry. This led some of the old-timers in the original division to feel that they may be heading back into a more universal code as a basis for the work being done.

At the present time, Near Soft is still growing into its new businesses, and even though they are five years into the change process, there remain some segments of the workforce who still believe the new strategic direction will not sustain. If you went out with this group for dinner, you might still find a very strong desire to go back to the good old days, when Near Soft dominated the industry with its universal code.

Sam and her team remain committed to the change and each other, which has gone a very long way toward transforming Near Soft into the organization it has been becoming over time. They are clearly aligned with each other and a cohesive unit that has open and transparent interactions.

In this chapter, I have attempted to show a more or less smooth transition through these four states of change. For Near Soft to get through all of the states, the storyline and narrative had to be positive enough so that there remained sufficient momentum to get through to the Institutionalizing State. What you should have noticed, however, was that there remains within Near Soft significant pockets of employees who have never changed the way they would have responded to "my organization is." For those employees, the changes that Sam and her team have promoted came from some foreign entity not within their own organization. It seems fair to say that they will be stuck in a territorial ownership focus for some time to come, if not indefinitely. This is often the more common reality of complex change processes occurring in organizational systems and why they take so long to complete before the next change unfolds.

What we also wanted to accomplish was to present a more positive transformation in the case of Foodie Inc. and its acquisition. With Foodie Inc., one could see the new narrative becoming more of the norm than the exception. Also, I tried to portray how the leadership had to keep adapting and iterating to model the changes for all other employees.

I know that I could have provided a lot more detail to explain the unfolding of the change process. However, at some point, the narrative would have become more fictional and remote to your own work situation. So I elected to provide enough detail to explain the potential states and then allow you to fill in some of the details that are associated with your own situation. By doing so, I felt that you would get a much deeper appreciation for how change actually unfolds in your own organization.

In sum, I have tried to convey all of the facets that are part of Figure 3.1, the four states of change, with two organizations that I felt could be scalable in terms of the narrative provided to bring these different states to life. There are several things I would like you to think about now going forward.

Although I tried to provide you with rich detail about the transitions, there is certainly information that was not provided. Try to consider the narrative I provided and think about how it applies to your current organization and where it is with respect to any change process underway and fill in the details.

Think about how your leadership would have responded to each of the states in either Near Soft or Foodie Inc. What might they have done better or worse?

I presented a rather positive change process and believe it may be a bit fairy tale–like; however, the model I actually used to describe Fishbone was Berkshire Hathaway, run by Warren Buffett. Much of what I described here parallels his work and successes in bringing in companies into the Berkshire family of corporations, whereby he does tend to keep the top management teams intact to continue to run their own organizations. Similarly, many are worried about what will happen when Warren Buffett is gone. Near Soft represented a collection of companies I have worked with from medical devices to large IT and manufacturing companies.

In the end, ask yourself: what would you have liked your role to be in the process? What would you have struggled with, and what might have come easy for you in going through one transition to another?

SOME LESSONS HOPEFULLY LEARNED

There are a few basic lessons I hope you've picked up from this discussion.

Change is dynamic, sloppy, personal, and often still successful.

You have to provide people with a reason to be the agents of change, and part of that reason is linked to the individual's self-concept and part is to the rewards if change is successful.

There will always be a lot of tension associated with any successful and, for that matter, unsuccessful change process. Often, in the early states, you have to count on failures piling up and that performance will improve only slowly, while people are learning how to do things differently. Many people may also not like what you are doing, nor like you.

It takes a very strong emphasis on campaigning to overcome those groups who become obstacles to change and also processes and procedures.

One of the advantages in these organizational narratives was a strong and coherent top management team that seemed to learn from its mistakes and who also were willing to change course if things were not moving forward.

Organizational change is a lot like gaming in that you have to have some rules that need to be followed, some rules that you can break, rewards for achievements, and punishments for failure. Every organizational change will accumulate wins and losses, and having a .500 record is likely naïve thinking, but one doesn't have to assume that the record will be awful either when you are batting .100. To continue with the baseball analogy, you will, as a leadership team, certainly have some slumps; you will lose some tight games; you will have things happen that seem like random events going against what you are trying to do; and you will hopefully learn from mistakes and win enough games to successfully change and transform.

I want to emphasize, which is also depicted at the bottom of the four-state model, that the nature of leadership will encompass a broad range of positive styles from instrumental to strategic and transformational. These styles can emerge in any one of the states, so don't feel you have to rigidly follow the model presented in Figure 3.1. The placement of leadership styles corresponds logically to the state, but someone can be transformational, instrumental, authentic, and strategic, all within the identifying state. My goal here was to help you understand the states and what the leadership looked like within a state. We suspect with that understanding you can easily apply what you have learned across different states of change, which we recognize is an assumption that needs to be tested by you.

The best form of reflection is to think strategically about the arc and flow of the states we have gone through and think about a series of thought experiments in terms of how you could systematically walk through each state. Now, give that a try and see what unfolds.

9 BECOMING THE CHANGE AND SUSTAINING IT

My job roles and responsibilities have changed.

The world is definitely round when it comes to organizational change and transformation. What I mean by this statement is that once you get to an end point in the final state, you are typically seeing signs of a new state of change emerging. Also, these states will overlap with each other and are not as clean in reality as they are in the text included in these chapters. Hopefully, you may be seeing these signs even earlier, so our depiction again is perhaps what might be seen as normative or average patterns of change and transformation. Ultimately, I want this way of thinking to become part of the way you always think, so that it eventually would not be as mechanical or formulaic.

Also, please keep in mind that within the different states there can be a lot of circular movement where forward progress is more iterative and does not always seem evident or actually to represent moving forward. This often occurs with change efforts, and too often the leadership wants to change the campaign message as they get concerned that the change process has stalled. This may be the case, or it may be that people are still trying to figure out and make sense of how the change is altering their roles, goals, and expectations and what that means for the changes to their self-concept and identity formation.

Staying the course with one's campaign and making appropriate adjustments by using levers of change that have not been tried is fine, but changing the core message for the campaign only serves to signal employees that the leadership may have bet on the wrong new direction. So be cautious as to whether you really need to change your campaign message or focus.

CHANGE HAPPENS EVEN WHEN YOU THINK
YOU HAVE STOPPED

If you think about the changes that occur to your body over time as you age, there are some clear analogies we can draw to changes in organizations. For example, there are some of our friends who say, "At my age, I just don't feel exercise is going to do much for me." Sometimes these are the same people who were athletes in high school but forgot to keep in mind that life is a long-distance run, and sometimes, if you are just keeping up, you are actually changing, whereas when you claim defeat, it is likely you will be growing in directions you would prefer not to be growing, such as around your waist or chin.

If you have the discipline to stay in shape, eat right, and exercise, then you can maintain a lot of the muscle mass and form you have had throughout your life. So it takes a constant campaign to stick with a strong focus on your health and well-being. Of course, things can happen to derail this plan, including health issues that are more genetically based and accidents. Yet, we also know that if you choose not to exercise, things change by your omission. In our general life trajectories, like those in organizations, one might argue that there is really no state of equilibrium. There may appear to be within these states, but as I already noted, inside the states there can be a lot of disequilibrium unfolding even when the change processes are reasonably successful.

Extending our model to your own leadership changes and development, perhaps we can more firmly establish the language that can be applied to your own organizational change and transformation. Let's give this a try.

You can see the job you have been doing at work is increasingly being taken over by automation. These signs are becoming very clear to you because in other countries where advanced technology has moved along more rapidly you are seeing jobs like yours being eliminated. As you read books about the future states emerging, you can see that your type of job is not one of the ones that seem to survive change.

The signals you are picking up that are on the distant horizon are also occurring in your organization if you look to how some of the new emerging divisions operate.

What you need to be doing now is seeing who you are and what you must become to sustain and survive. I realize that for many people their identity is inextricably linked to their jobs, but times change, and you have to realize that, by holding on to the old job, you may in effect be sinking or at least diminishing your future opportunities.

Realizing that change is happening in your industry or chosen career, you start to read more about new opportunities in your industry as well as other industries. You have started to attend meet-ups around your community, some of which are exploring new industries emerging on the horizon. You can see that there is a lot of excitement within these new growth industries, and you want to learn more about them, so you start to sign up for some on-line classes that take you to a future state in fields of interest.

You also start to realize that you have actually become a legacy system, and, like the work you currently do, you may need to lead yourself to a new version if not a whole new product line. Some of your colleagues think you are worrying about nothing and that it might be years or decades before things change, and you will be long gone into retirement.

You are holding yourself accountable to your new learning and career goals, and you are finding that you have been inspiring some of your peers to do the same things you are doing. In fact, you realize at one point that you could create your own peer learning group to continue to focus on new avenues for change.

Now the changes that seemed not too far back as theoretical are actually unfolding in front of you, and you are feeling positive about the goals you have set and achieved to change. You also are finding that the peer group that you created has become an incredibly important sounding board to future directions you are currently pursuing. You can see that, as you go further into your own development, there seem to be more opportunities for advancement and movement into other organizations. People you work with who spoke against the changes you had seen on the horizon are now becoming champions for change themselves. You feel validated in the direction you have pursued.

One of your core values was to be the "stable one" among your peers, but now you feel that a new value has emerged, to "seek differences," which forces you to question your assumptions and the way ahead.

You were recently at a meet-up outside your region, and when you were asked to introduce yourself, it appeared to you that the person doing the talking was not the person you used to know, but the person you were becoming. You felt more comfortable with that new version of yourself than the old version, and others around you who hadn't known you did not seem to detect the difference.

You have come to the realization that the new self is really the possible one you had envisioned just a couple of years back, and now that new self is the one who holds the narrative that represents how your self-concept is being defined.[1] The descriptions and the narratives also don't seem strange or threatening, but rather they seem comfortable to you.

Can you think of a time in your life where that sort of change happened? For me, one key pivotal state was going off to college and realizing the people you grew up with were not the entire world, and they would become over time a small part of your worldview and value system. Like most changes that transform our worldviews, changes in one's identity and self-concept will not occur from one moment to the next but will unfold for different people across different trajectories of development and time.[2]

I have been able to apply the overall change model first in its entirety, then broken down by the different states, followed by two examples of very different representative companies that underwent significant change and transformation. Now, let's take a look at the model in Figure 9.1 and how it applies to your own development as an individual and leader. Of course, as is true of this entire book, the narrative we described in these last several chapters is my narrative, and I know for change to work it has to become your narrative. The only way that will happen is when you go through your own change process, knowing the states and how they unfold, but inserting into the description of those states your own narrative and ultimately how you operationalize your self-concept and identity.

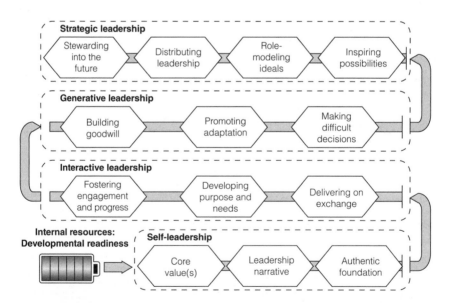

Figure 9.1   Blueprint for sustainable leadership development.

Source: © 2014 UW Center for Leadership and Strategic Thinking.

I want to help you with that process of change in you, so what I will do now is bring in what I call our "Blueprint for Sustainable Leadership Development," shown in Figure 9.1.[3] We introduce this second framework because we want to make the change process personal for you. We will then follow the description of the blueprint with a diet for changing your organization. By diet, we mean a change in what you do to change the way your organization consumes, feels, operates, and produces. So we will use the analogy of a diet as a way of saying: change requires that you stick to a new regimen of eating, and of course some exercise to support that diet.

In Figure 9.1, there are four phases of development you move through going from self-awareness to instrumental change to generative change on up to strategic change and transformation. This process model is meant to guide you from self-leadership to strategic thinking leadership and stewardship. The model is not a hierarchy per se but rather states of leadership that you can work through over time based on the last fifty years of research and practice on leadership.[4]

You will notice on the bottom left of the figure that, like organizations, individuals also have varying levels of readiness to develop and change—the energy battery. I view readiness as being both an ability to change in terms of the model you have for how you work and also your motivation for change, such as your orientation toward learning and experimenting with new ways of behaving and performing. Readiness includes how you view your "leader" self-concept and how wired it is into everything you do at work. Motivation includes the probability you have in your head that your attempt at change will be successful.

The first panel, labeled "self-leadership," represents the base on which you build what comes next. This base, like an organization, has values that are very important to you that I have previously referred to as your core value. Recall how difficult it was to change the value set of an organization from one state of change to ultimately the Institutionalizing State. The same is true here with your own core value(s), and in fact the changes that organizations go through will likely affect those values if the changes are transformative. For example, you might have grown up in a work environment where you valued the individual contributor model— something that was fundamentally tied to your self-concept, narrative, and identity. Then you and your organization started to realize that you needed to change to a more team-centered and collaborative environment, which was a huge shift in the way you described yourself to others.

Perhaps you can now see why I started this book focusing on the idea that to change an organization you have to change each employee one self-concept at a time, and now that one person is you, the leader. As the leader, your self-concept is intertwined with the organization's collective self-concept if you have worked there awhile, and to change the organization you have to change the individual, and the blueprint is a useful guide to consider in terms of interpreting how change unfolds.

A leader who once gets to a different view of his or her core values starts to realize that the narrative associated with his or her leader self-concept needs to change to come in line with the new or emerging values. This is no different than what I described with respect to the organization as unit of analysis, except that the change here is primarily about you, not the organization per se. For example, if you feel that being more respectful and positive of others is an important core value, as the leader who was the CEO at the cable plant I described earlier came to realize, then that change in value would change the way you perceive the importance of being kind and respectful in your daily interactions with others as leader.

As the changes filter into your narrative, we also start to see a shift in the way you perceive how you influence others, which affects the third box in the model, labeled "Authentic foundation." This foundation is the one you are building on, and it will now include an emphasis on the new value you have been thinking about and practicing with others. As you shape this foundation, you then become more self-aware of how you treat others, and as a long as you are keeping that value of respect and kindness in mind, we would expect to see a change in how you view what is your actual leader self-concept as it emerges and you make sense of it over time.

What is motivational here is that these are changes in yourself that you can purposively pursue, either self-initiated because of some need you perceive on the horizon or caused perhaps by changes in your organization as depicted in previous chapters. What might be helpful is viewing this self-leadership phase as largely being associated with the Identifying State we described as part of the overall change model in Figure 3.1.

In the next panel up in the blueprint, I use the term *interactive leadership*. Here I can say it is reasonable to assume that the changes are not unlike what happens in the Initiating State. Specifically, you are choosing to create a repeatable and reliable practice of interactions that is different with the people you work with in your organization. To the extent that you are more self-aware of what you are trying to change, you are more likely to show up acting differently— in the case depicted earlier, with greater kindness and respect. To the degree this is changing the way others interact with you, it is then possible to refine the purpose of why you are behaving in this way and engaging others in that conversation. For example, you may believe the best way to achieve exemplary customer relationships is to act in this way, so you consistently model this sort of behavior with others, who may begin to model it themselves to the extent they buy into the new way of interacting.

Much of this phase of initiating new behaviors and getting rid of old ones is very similar to the type of actions that one would see in the transformative organizational change process. It is in this phase of development that we can see and interpret the changes. Perhaps as with organizational campaigning, you must become the candidate for change and you must convince others, through a reliable and repeatable process, that you are serious about the changes being made—they are, in other words, authentic.

The third phase is labeled "Generative leadership" in that at this point in the developmental process things can be in flux and transition, not unlike in the Impending State. By using the word *generative*, I am declaring the change process is transformative and that going from one state to another will require a lot of energy and focus to successfully complete. This will require as noted in that third panel to the right that you as an individual will need to make some difficult choices. For example, there will be times where you are frustrated and tired, and your respect for others and kindness will be tested. It is in these times, when emotions run high and your self-control is perhaps low, that you will need to stay the course.

You may have to, as shown in the next box in the blueprint, consider ways to adapt to the tension in this generative phase of development. For example, you may need to create mechanisms to help you step back from these emotional interactions to get a clearer perspective on what you need to think about and then do. Some might use mindfulness training to help, and some might have triggers they use that can get them to reframe a challenge, whereas others may simply practice suspending judgment.

What you will also need to learn in this state is that you have to build up sufficient goodwill in yourself and others to make some mistakes, to get some passes, and then to continue on with the work you are doing to change yourself and perhaps others. By goodwill, I mean that you will be ready to give yourself a pass if you are not kind or respectful, but at the same time you realize that you were not, and you correct it the next time around. The same will be true for others whom you interact with, as they have to be willing to suspend judgment and to say, "You didn't live up to the value you are working on, but you knew you didn't, and you will fix it next time." Change in us or in organizations or, more important, both doesn't happen alone; there is always some individual or individuals who play a role in our change processes.

Now moving up to our next panel, we can see there is strategic leadership development taking place as one moves beyond the transformations that have been successfully achieved to a new way of thinking, operating, and behaving. At this level of development, the change in you has been out there; if properly practiced and seen as worthwhile, your change will start to inspire changes in others. To that extent, you may become a role model for them to aspire to in their own development as individuals and leaders. You can see perhaps the connection here to organizational champions of change, who come to realize the change is necessary, who reliably move in the direction of change, who get others to adopt those ways of thinking and behaving, and then institutionalize a new way of looking at and behaving in the organization. Indeed, to the extent this does not happen in organizational or individual change, it is very likely that the change will not become institutionalized.

You may also note in that fourth panel that as you become a role model of the change in yourself, and you then inspire others, then what we would expect from you is that the changes that occur in your narrative are also starting to be reflected in the narratives and behaviors of others in your organization. Again, the change process being successful depends on this distribution or cascading process, in that we have said earlier, that the surrogates of the leader, their surrogates and so forth throughout the organization, must carry the new narrative forward in their own self-concepts and narratives as well as reinforce those changes in others who have influence within the organization. This is a process that builds an adaptive organization over time, one that can go through the process of knowing that it needs to change, initiating changes, and pursuing these changes through the state where new and old ways of thinking and behaving coexist until they become so engrained that they are institutionalized.

Ending up in the final box of our blueprint, we see the people who started this change in their values, narrative, and authentic foundation have now become those who have helped to steward the change not only in themselves, but others, so that we have now connected the transformation in the individual's development to the transformation of members of the organization. Hopefully what we have also done is to show how pivotal it is to have as your unit of analysis the individual's self-concept and narrative because, without that focus, there is simply no way you can change an organization. Why? An organization is a collection of individuals who each have a self-concept and narrative that ultimately must be organized to create what constitutes the organization along the arc of its transformation and development—which places us back at the very beginning of this narrative.

And now we have one last step to take, and that is to get your diet set and exercise launched. I will follow the same organizational change model where I will emphasize the kind of diet that is necessary and the discipline to achieve the institutionalization of change. I will use days to represent periods of time that unfold in terms of the change process, but a day could be a month in real time.

Day Zero

- There are signals that you have been thinking about that suggest there is something on the horizon that requires more of your time and attention. You are clearly aware of the need to focus on these signals, but you are not yet sure they really mean anything for you or your organization, although they are interesting to reflect on.

- You try to get more information about the signals by talking to people you respect and who are aware of changes in your industry. You seek out readings and opinions on the changes you see and test them against the current state to see whether they should or should not be pursued.

- You have been trying to consider different hypotheses associated with change, and you have been going through what are called "thought experiments," where you try to consider the state of your organization if nothing were to change over the next several years versus specific changes that you are testing.

Day 1

- You have become convinced that the stronger signals that you have been tracking are significant, and you need to consider actions to take to initiate change, something perhaps specific that really gets to the core of what you believe will have an impact on your business.

- You start to formulate a campaign that is focused on the change you have envisioned. You are building support for that change and spreading the message and talking points with your future champions for change. Recall how important it is for people to know why the change is being implemented, when it actually started, what the core messages are, that they have time to dialogue and ask questions, and that they can be able to communicate the messages to others in a repeatable and reliable manner. To change other's narratives will require a lot of discipline and focus. However, if you have picked up the right signals, the effort will be well worth it.

Day 2

- Initiating what the new "my organization" looks like will follow the changes you have chosen to make in terms of your roles, goals, and expectations. Keep in mind that the expression "less is more" applies very well to initiating these changes. As with any change, I often see people try to change too many things at once, and the propensity to do that is highly characteristic of organizational change efforts. What you need to do is choose your very top priorities for starting change and stay focused on them. In terms of your diet plan, don't try to lose your organizational weight too quickly!

- You need to realize there will be people who are more territorial in their narrative, and they will see what you are initiating as being threatening to them and what they own. Try to understand their perspective, why they feel threatened, and how you might reduce their uncertainties with the change to come on board.

- Be willing to make some compromises in terms of the timing of change and the resources required to so. Also, consider that some individuals or units may not be developmentally ready to change, so you have to figure out what is the problem—is it motivational and/or is it a lack of capability? For each of these two sources, there are different strategies that you can pursue to enact change. For example, if motivational, find out what would reward a change in the way they think and behave. If ability, find out what they feel they can't do, and try to break down the steps required to enact changes, while doing some tryouts or practices.

- It is important that you stick to some of these changes such that they are the new normal way of operating. Realize that it will take a number of iterations to accomplish that state, as well as a tolerance for failure and mistakes. Each and every time that we learn something new, it is going to take time to get to a level of proficiency that is acceptable. Realize as well that people will have different trajectories of learning and development, so you will have to adapt somewhat to working with those different trajectories and adjusting to them.

Day 3

- The state I have seen most organizations stall within is the Impending State. It is not that things just go wrong in this state; it's that the appropriate foundation has not been built in the prior states, and when organizations enter the Impending State, things are really in flux, in which, as I said previously, some new and old ways are operating side-by-side. This is a state

that will require a lot of reflection and debriefing to make sure you are
making the appropriate adjustments along the way to refine your repeatable practice of changing your behavior.

- You probably need to anticipate that, whatever impending changes you are
  working on, you might want to add in some buffer time to achieve a more
  solid change in your narrative and behavior. I would say that, given my
  experience in a very diverse range of organizations, it will likely take three
  or four times the amount of time and effort you thought it would take for
  things to change in a transformative way. If you allocate more time for the
  change rather than less, and you beat your time estimates, the savings will
  be something you can reap and use to build on. However, if you short-
  change the amount of time that is necessary to change, it will be harder to
  recover what you need to continue on with the change process. Moreover,
  those who are not in favor of the change will have a lot more ammunition
  to try to subvert the change if you miss your timeline and goals.

Day 4

- If you have reached this point in the change model, you are in the minority.
  There are lots of estimates that people have made up that say that organizational changes mostly fail, fail at a 70 percent rate, or whatever. I would
  feel more comfortable saying that change efforts more often than not fail or
  fail somewhat, and by more often it could perhaps be 51 percent. What that
  means, however, is ambiguous. Did the change fail in the Initiating State?
  The Impending State? The Institutionalizing State? Usually authors are not
  clear about when the change failed, nor how, and that is also true of the
  organizational leaders.

- Assuming you have gotten this far, you have to try to go back and reflect
  on how much has specifically changed and in what ways. One thing that
  would help is some form of documentation of the changes before, during,
  and after they have unfolded. Having this sort of look back is invaluable to
  your own self-reflections on the change process and, more important, on
  the next case for change and process you enter into within your organization. You may even want to write a good field researcher who does qualita-
  tive research to keep track of your emerging narrative, as it could become
  the case that future leaders in your organization then study before they
  make a transformative change.

- What I might suggest you consider is that, if you think of your organization
  as a business case, most business cases have problems you have to address

that are obvious and some that are not so obvious. Like the business case, there is a narrative that you are guided through by the author, except in the case for organizational change, you and the leaders are the authors making it a bit more complicated. Nevertheless, if you consider the narrative of your own business case, you have its history and with some good thought and reflection on how that has changed your current narrative. You also have in front of you various scenarios and narratives that you could pursue and others that you will leave alone for now. This doesn't mean that you won't try a different pathway for change, just that you can handle only so many experiments at one point in time, so less is again more in terms of changes.

- I actually envision that in fact you are writing your own organizational case and you have to learn your own narrative to envision the changes you want to pursue as well as the narrative of other members of your organization. Like most cases, you can always update them, but you can't change the history that led you to the point where you are in the case. (Please see more details on this case recommendation in our next chapter).

Day 5
- Start over; recall what I said, that the world of change is round, so you are going back to the Identifying State to see what's out there of interest to you and your organization, perhaps with a more global mind-set.

CONCLUSIONS BEFORE LAUNCHING THE NARRATIVE FOR YOUR ORGANIZATIONAL CASE

I set out in writing this book not to oversimplify organizational change, and I hope that now you would judge my approach to not be simple but also not so complex that you couldn't repeat the change process yourself, while understanding the states you traveled through to do so. As you will gather through sheer repetition and examples, I have been focused on starting with the unit of analysis that makes change either happen or not. In no uncertain terms, it's you, or me, and eventually us. The self-concept is our story, and it provides us with the script we follow until we decide to author another chapter to change its direction or meaning.

We can see from earlier chapters that the type of changes that occur to one's self-concept and narrative can be influenced significantly by outsider factors, such as crises, challenges, and opportunities that arise. At the same time, change can start with your own self-reflections, more so from the inside out than from the outside in. And we also know that, in most cases, it is a combination of both forces.

I also have learned along the way that organizations, like people, will change whether we do anything or not. Conditions inside the organization as well as outside can have an impact on a change in organizations, and it may be something that was planned or something that is pure serendipity. Realize that, in any organizational change, at some point you need to be more purposive in terms of the choices you make; otherwise you are at the mercy of events, which we all are from time to time, but you can also take some control to move in the direction that makes most sense for your organization.

In terms of what I have covered in this book, I am confident that the states that are outlined in the previous chapters include what happens when organizations change and transform. Why? I have the data to show that these are the ways change unfolds and that the elements within each state do appear as depicted. Again, it is not always as clean as I have presented in Figure 9.1; in fact, it rarely is, but in the end the figure captures how change happens or not. I have also shown this pattern in the research notes at the end of each chapter depicting the model, and sometimes embedded in the text in the words of those going through these change states.

Well, thanks for coming on this change journey, and good luck with growing and developing your self-concept and narrative. It is worth the effort for sure, in that it is the unit of analysis for life.

In the final chapter, I want to pick up on the idea of your building your own organizational case, and we will do so in several ways:

- First, I will examine what you might measure in terms of readying your organization for change. I am also going to make an assumption: that you have already picked up on the signals for change, so you are into the Identifying State.

- In terms of readiness, I will describe and examine two types of readiness: the individual unit of analysis and the organizational, which can be a department, a division, or the entire organization.

- I will then examine the leadership necessary to move through the states of change building on what I said throughout this book, where I have mainly focused on how the styles and orientations fit into the different states.

- I will then discuss the levels of ownership required to move through each state to end up in terms of collective institutionalization.

This last chapter will also provide some links to some potential survey and other tools that might be useful to how you think through the change process in terms of readiness, leadership, ownership, culture, and climate. Please keep in mind that there are many tools available to you and of course consultants who will want to jump in and help guide you through the change process. One of my ultimate goals was to make you a wiser consumer if you choose to use their services.

In the last chapter, I will also introduce you to a resource center that we call LD Navigator. My hopes and aspirations for this site, which I use in my own work with organizations, is to provide a place where you can design and build your individual and organizational plans for change. I also want you to have a place where you can share your plans and ideas within affinity groups that are comprised of individuals going through similar change processes. In fact, there is an app you can use to help connect you to these affinity groups who have similar opportunities and challenges and are in industries like yours, from whom you can get some peer-to-peer coaching as you move through the change process.

10 DEVELOPING AS A TRANSFORMATIVE LEADER

As a leader I can motivate myself to perform at levels that inspire excellence in others.

Now that you have completed the first nine chapters in this book, you may be ready to engage in some practice regarding your leadership development. The purpose of this chapter is to provide you with some key resources that have been developed for those purposes. Accessing these web-based resources can be done at the links provided in the following pages.

We begin our focus on your leadership development by reviewing resources that focus on the individual unit of analysis and then move to discuss ways to assess developmental readiness. I follow this discussion on your readiness to change leadership and develop by examining a pivotal construct depicted throughout the four-state change model, which is referred to as psychological ownership, and describe the five different types of ownership that are associated with each state of change.

I next elevate our unit of analysis to discuss ways to measure your organization's readiness to change, which could be your team or unit as well as your entire organization. With this web-based survey, you can assess a number of leadership, culture, climate, and attitudinal scales related to levels of readiness to change within the organization.

Following the review of these surveys, I then discuss a resource portal that was developed to support your leadership development, the LD Navigator. This portal contains a number of on-line resources that can further support your leadership development, including a template for leadership development planning, articles, games, and other developmental planning tips.

DEVELOPMENTAL READINESS

In my work with individual leaders, one of the first areas I focus on examining is the readiness level of each individual leader to change and develop. I know that going through the four states of change will require a lot of discipline to change yourself and others, and that is why I begin by first focusing on your own leader developmental readiness (DR).[1]

The Center for Leadership and Strategic Thinking (CLST) has generated evidence to support the idea that leaders are not simply "born" to lead but are "made" into effective leaders through development that occurs over time, experience, and challenges. In fact, prior research consistently shows that 70 percent of what constitutes leader development is "made" through the experiences of leaders, and what they learn from those experiences, whereas only 30 percent of what makes an individual leader effective comes from heritable traits.[2]

Similar to our focus on states of organizational change, I also focus on individual states of development that can be changed. Most people assume that traits are much harder to change, but they are more elastic than we have thought. Also, based on prior research, such individual traits account for only a small, but meaningful percentage of what makes up effective leadership. What I have learned in our research and practice is that there are many, many traits associated with effective leadership, so there are many "types" of individuals who can be developed to be more effective leaders.

In terms of DR, I focus only on examining states, in that these states can change and be developed, as I have argued throughout this book at the organizational unit of analysis. For example, one of the states I examine is your motivation to learn. I know there is quite a bit of variation associated with different individuals' motivation to learn, and this can have an impact on how they respond both to change in themselves as well as to changes in their team or organization. Research has also shown that motivation to learn can be enhanced and therefore is seen as an important input into DR, as well as your leadership development.

Also measured in the DR survey is your level of self-concept clarity. Consider that, throughout the previous chapters in this book, I have discussed the pivotal role that each individual's self-concept plays in changing an organization. So it should not be too surprising that I would also focus on how your self-concept and narrative around leadership contributes to your development as a leader, and that's exactly where I am starting in terms of your readiness.

Leader Developmental Readiness (DR) Defined

This includes your *ability* and *motivation* to focus on, make meaning of, and develop new and more complex ways of thinking that position you to more effectively assume and carry out leadership roles, particularly those roles that involve fostering change. I assume at the outset of your leadership development, as discussed throughout this book, that each leader will follow a unique trajectory of development and change. My goal is to meet you at the starting point of your trajectory of change readiness and to help develop an action plan on how to best foster your development. This is a good rule of thumb to use when working with others, as some will be very ready for the changes being discussed in your organization, although others will need to take time to develop and embrace the rate and direction of change.

Developmental Readiness Survey and Results

The DR survey contains fourteen scales that tap into ability and motivational factors that are foundational to understanding and enacting to accelerate your leadership development.[3] In the report that is provided after you have completed this survey, there are many references to research that supports the validity of each of these fourteen scales. By knowing where you are in terms of your motivation and ability, you will be more capable of launching into your own leadership development journey.

The fourteen scales are listed in Figure 10.1, which includes sample data. The scale anchors vary in terms of ranges, as my colleagues and I have always used the original scales that were validated, and some used five, seven, or ten-point ranges. Also, in Figure 10.1 the vertical line represents the range of scores given for that scale for this particular sample group. Each of the scales in this figure is briefly defined in the following paragraphs.

The main purpose of the DR survey is to identify areas where you can focus on in terms of your developmental readiness as a leader. In what I referred to as the LD Navigator or portal, there are a number of helpful hints and some sample leadership development plans that you can use to start launching your developmental process.

Motivation to Develop as a Leader

There are four subfactors in the motivation to develop as a leader;

1. Learning goal orientation
2. Leadership self-confidence

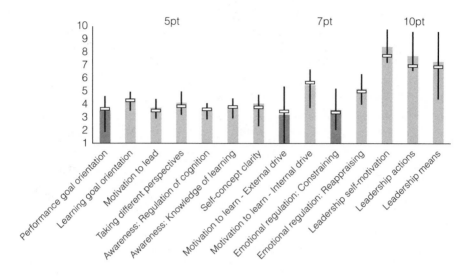

Figure 10.1   Sample feedback profile for developmental readiness scales.

3. Internal motivation to learn

4. Motivation to lead

Learning Goal Orientation

Some individuals take on leadership challenges with the primary goal of simply being successful in terms of achieving a high level of performance. Others take on challenges with the primary goal of leveraging the opportunity to learn something that can facilitate their development and capacity for taking on increasingly demanding challenges. Learning goal orientation has two subscales:

1. *Performance Goal Orientation (PGO).* This scale refers to the extent to which you place a high priority on successful performance and on being viewed as competent. People with a high PGO tend to emphasize the successful accomplishment of results and to avoid taking developmentally important risks.

2. *Learning Goal Orientation (LGO).* This scale is also called "mastery goal orientation" and refers to the extent to which you desire to learn from challenges and are concerned with developing your competence, sometimes even at the expense of performing suboptimally in the short term. A high

LGO score usually indicates that an individual seeks out challenging tasks and continues to strive under difficult conditions.

Leader Self-Confidence/Agency

Leadership self-confidence or agency refers to your belief that you have the knowledge, skills, and abilities that are required to lead others and to mobilize groups toward collective performance goals and change. This level of individual awareness means that you can be the "author" of your own narrative and journey, rather than being at the mercy of the situation, which is represented in your level of agency or confidence. As such, individuals with high levels of personal agency are aware they can plan, execute, and control their own actions to successfully and positively influence others and the context in which they interact.[4] The three scales include:

1. *Leader self-thought.* You believe you can get others to buy into your ideas and to change their ways of thinking about their ideas and perspectives, how they work together, and that what they are focusing on in terms of performance can change.

2. *Leader self-action.* You believe you have the capacity to take the necessary actions to influence others in terms of the direction that you want them to pursue. This capacity can relate to being inspiring, developing others, setting goals, and also in taking a stand on difficult and/or ethical issues.

3. *Leader efficacy.* You believe you have the resources necessary to accomplish the goals and objectives that are in front of you. These resources can be tools, people, financial, or other resources that you feel you need to acquire to be successful.

Motivation to Learn

Your motivation to learn refers to how driven you are to acquire new and more advanced leadership styles during challenges and when dealing with change. Motivation to learn is comprised of two subfactors, which include both external (environmental) and internal (personal) elements that reflect different underlying attitudes and goals driving your quest for leadership development. For instance, a leader can be highly motivated to learn new or advanced leadership behaviors and concepts out of curiosity and interest when experiencing success in more challenging leadership situations. Alternatively, a leader can do so out of a desire to receive a tangible reward and the status increase that comes with a higher-level leadership role and not necessarily because of what is learned.

Motivation to Lead

The strength of your motivation to lead will influence your propensity to engage in leadership development activities both in and outside of work. The survey questions in this scale assess your identification with leadership and your key beliefs about leadership. People with a high motivation to lead may want to lead because they desire to make changes, to inspire and influence others to achieve goals, to achieve power or success, or some combination of these goals.

Ability to Develop as a Leader

Your ability to develop as a leader is comprised of four scales:

1. *Emotional regulation.* Individuals can exert considerable control over their emotions. They also differ in the use of two strategies available to understand and manage emotions, constraining and reappraising. Leaders who can regulate the strength and timing of their emotions, using both strategies as appropriate will remain calm during difficult situations and inspire confidence in others through the example they set.

2. *Taking different perspectives.* Leaders often have to represent and balance the interests of a diverse range of individuals when going through any significant change processes. These different groups of individuals frequently have diverse views from each other and from the leader on the very same issues. Taking different perspectives focuses on your ability to examine the perspectives of other people and see things from their point of view. Taking different perspectives is the cognitive capacity to consider the world from another individual's viewpoint.

3. *Awareness of the way I think and learn (metacognitive awareness).* Your leadership development is accelerated when you can quickly and effectively make sense out of any developmental experience. This scale, Awareness of the Way I Think and Learn, is comprised of two subscales that represent regulation of your thinking and knowing how you learn. This awareness is also known as metacognition, which refers to your ability to reflect on, understand, and control your own learning. Cognition is the mental faculty or process of acquiring knowledge by the use of reasoning, intuition, or perception.

4. *Self-concept clarity.* This scale reflects the extent to which your beliefs about yourself are clearly and confidently defined and are internally consistent and stable. Having a strong sense of identity and knowledge about areas where you excel and areas where you need further development optimizes your leadership development and shows others you understand both who you are and who you can become.

LEADERSHIP DEVELOPMENT PLANNING

In addition to the DR suggestions for development, suggestions are also provided in the LD Navigator portal for building a more effective leadership development plan. You can use this plan in terms of focusing on your own development, as well as linking the plan to whatever state of change you are entering into within your organization. For example, you might set a goal to be more self-aware of your followers' or peers' reservations about the change that is being initiated. As part of your plan, you might then check in with your colleagues to see what reservations they have regarding the change process and future outcomes. Setting a goal to be mindful of their reservations could motivate you to focus on how you engage others who might not yet buy into the changes being proposed or, perhaps worse, are against the changes.

As already noted, one of the scales in the chart and discussed earlier refers to how well you take into consideration different people's perspectives during the change process. By examining your readiness to understand other points of view, this feedback could help facilitate your understanding of why people either don't understand the merits of the proposed change or are against it. It may be that they simply don't know what the change means for them, or they are feeling territorial, both of which are worthy of your understanding.

Similarly, you could work on enhancing your learning orientation goal as you seek out other views during the change process. How? Being open to others' ideas and perspectives is a great way of motivating your own learning about different ways of approaching new challenges and opportunities during the organizational change process.

Another important facet of your readiness is to develop a sufficient level of emotional regulation to deal with the anticipated stresses associated with change. We know that emotions often run high during change, especially where some individuals feel they are winning and others losing. It is incumbent on the leader to develop a sufficient level of emotional regulation to avoid derailing the change process and also not to turn off or alienate followers who need to be coached to get on board with the change for the process to be successful.

In sum, there are many connections that can be made among your own developmental readiness, the goals that you set for your leadership development, and the goals and focus for the change initiative. What I hoped to convey here in this brief overview is that your developmental readiness to change is pivotal to the ownership people will take for change and their readiness to continue with the change process. Again, as I stated from the outset, our unit of analysis at the beginning was the individual level, and that is also true here as we focus on your development as a leader.

PSYCHOLOGICAL OWNERSHIP

Another pivotal aspect of supporting and promoting change at any level of analysis is the level of ownership each individual in your organization takes for engaging in and sustaining the change process. As part of your development, you can use the Psychological Ownership Survey in the LD Navigator portal to assess the level of ownership that your employees have in your unit toward change, as well as your own.

This survey assesses five distinct levels of psychological ownership, including territorial, accountable, confident, sense of belonging, and identification.[5]

Territorial Ownership

This scale assesses how different parties see the change as being divisive, with some winners and some losers. Within this state of ownership, there will be those in favor of and those against the change process and goals, and their positions will be based on knowing that if they don't take a stand, they are likely to lose something valuable to them.

Accountable Ownership

Unlike territorial ownership, being an accountable owner is a more positive form of ownership, and it relates to taking on what you are asked to do and completing the goals and objectives set out for your work. Here the goals and expectations are set for moving in the direction of some new initiatives, and employees feel an obligation to comply with the goals and directives; thus it represents more of a compliance ownership focus.

Confident Ownership

Confident owners have internalized their goals and objectives; rather than seeing them as being just compliant with those goals and objectives, they are now becoming more committed to the change process, in the sense of feeling a greater level of personal agency for being successful. A confident owner will also go above and beyond what is expected to complete the tasks, as he or she has the confidence to search out solutions that perhaps were not initially anticipated but are necessarily required to be successful.

Sense of Belonging

Here we see a shift in the unit of analysis from focusing just on what I own to what we own. There is a greater sense on the individual's part of what that person can do that promotes more of a collective agency and ownership of the change process that is indeed pivotal to successful initiatives, as well as when working through the *impending* into the *institutionalized* state of organizational change.

Individual and Collective Identification

In this higher state of psychological ownership, the goals and objectives have become completely internalized both in the individual and in the groups in which individuals work within the organization. People who are at this level of ownership will take independent action beyond what they have been instructed to do, as it is "my job" or "our job" to get this change done successfully. At this level of psychological ownership, people are completely committed to the change process as they see it as something they fully own.

As you can see going through these states of ownership, just as individuals change the way they operationalize "my organization" from the start of change to its institutionalizing, we see the same sort of change in state as they go from a job they have to do to a job that is "my job" to be successful.

ORGANIZATIONAL CULTURE READINESS ASSESSMENT (OCRA)

This change readiness survey includes a number of scales that tap into the readiness of your organization's employees to adapt and change. The scales included in the survey focus on the type of leadership, climate, attitudes toward change, and culture of your organization. For example, one scale measures the level of psychological safety employees feel in challenging leaders. Another scale taps into the ethical climate of the organization and the extent to which employees and leaders display highly ethical conduct. A third scale measures what employees feel is the motivation for change, as I typically find there are a lot of opinions on why the change is being implemented and who will benefit from the change, particularly where there are low levels of trust in the organization and territorial ownership.

I also measure in the OCRA the extent to which individuals are committed to the changes that are being proposed. Without such commitments, it would be difficult or impossible to develop a sense of ownership beyond the levels of simply being accountable and compliant.

The OCRA also includes scales that tap into the perceived impact the change will have on employees' jobs and careers, as well as the level of turbulence the change will create within the organization. In addition, it assesses the extent to which employees feel they are participating in the direction setting that will promote the change process, as well as having a voice that can affect how the change process unfolds. Both of these scales measure employee perceptions that are pivotal to committing to the change process, as well as how their input will be perceived by their leaders. The OCRA also taps into employee perceptions of whether they actually believe the organization has the capacity to change and sustain the change process, as well as the level of cooperation and support they will have going through the change process within their own units, as well as across units.

In the following lists, I provide a brief definition of the scales and then a sample chart displaying results that show the relationships among various leadership styles and some of the key scales included in the OCRA. I recommend that you use this survey to assess the readiness of the unit in which you work to take on the proposed changes, or you could have the survey completed by multiple units or the entire organization. Generally, I like to measure the readiness of the organization to change prior to introducing any interventions, experiments, and tryouts and then again after a period of time as the change process is unfolding. This allows me to gauge the extent to which the leadership in the organization has been able to move the readiness meter up to facilitate the change processes success.

OCRA Survey Leadership Scales

- *Authentic leadership* fosters greater self-awareness, an internalized moral perspective, balanced processing of information, and relational transparency.

- *Authoritarian leadership* demonstrates a pattern of behavior that asserts absolute authority and control over followers and demands unquestionable obedience.
- *Transactional leadership* clarifies goals and standards that followers are expected to achieve and then to be rewarded for their efforts and performance.
- *Transformational leadership* includes four components: individualized consideration, intellectual stimulation, inspiration, and idealized influence.
- *Ethical leadership* demonstrates appropriate conduct through personal actions and interpersonal relationships and promoting such conduct with followers.
- *Change leadership* acclimates followers to the change and supports them in a way that fosters their understanding of, commitment to, and engagement with, change.

OCRA Survey Change Scales

- Through *emotional commitment to change*, participants feel the desire to provide support for the change based on a belief in its inherent benefits.
- *Organizational capacity for change* is the ability of the organization to establish norms of innovation and encourage innovative activity fostering change.
- *Consequences of the change* are that participants believe the change is more helpful than problematic for the success of their unit.
- Through *participation in the change*, participants believe that they have requisite input needed to support a specific organizational change.
- In *change turbulence*, participants feel that the organization lacks the capacity to undertake the change based on other distractions and changes occurring during the same time.

OCRA Climate and Culture Scales

- *Psychological safety.* Unit members believe they will not be rejected for revealing errors or providing new information.
- *Work group cooperation.* Unit members communicate and cooperate with other groups and members of other groups.
- *Organizational citizenship behaviors.* Unit members exhibit behaviors of altruism or cooperation and directly assist co-workers to support change.

- *Organizational identification.* Participants show a specific form of social identification where they define themselves in terms of their organizational membership.

In Figure 10.2, I present a sample output profile produced by the OCRA that shows the relationship between four different styles of leadership and five outcomes. The *y*-axis represents a correlation, and in this case we use the range from 0, meaning no correlation, to 1, being a perfect 1 to 1 correlation. What you can see is that the positive leadership style relates to and promotes positive outcomes in terms of organizational readiness to change.

The leadership development portal was originally designed to support coaching practices whereby an individual coach could work on-line with a number of clients to facilitate their development. As I continue to build out this portal with my colleagues at the Center for Leadership and Strategic Thinking (CLST) in the Foster School at the University of Washington, we intend to make it widely available to

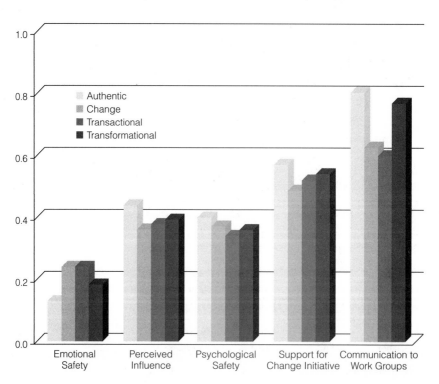

Figure 10.2 Sample feedback profile for organization readiness scales.

users who may not be in coaching relationships but nevertheless are focused on their leadership development.

The LD Navigator can be accessed at by going to https://foster.uw.edu/centers /leadership/ldnavigator/. The resources available to users who access the portal include:

- A leadership developmental planning template along with several benchmark plans that our professional staff have judged to be excellent examples of planning documents.

- A sample of DR and OCRA scales/items you can complete on the web, which can be used to familiarize yourself with these dimensions/scales and items. These are not the full scales or items but are offered to provide you with a better idea of what comprises these measures.

- A select number of articles that are focused on your development as a leader.

- Several documents include tips for your leadership development ranging from improving your readiness to lead to your leadership style.

- Discussion boards that you can use to share ideas with others who have come to develop their leadership to lead change in their respective organizations.

Over time, I will continue to work with my colleagues to build out this portal so that it becomes a more robust source of information to support your leadership development, as well as a community of peers working on organizational change and transformation. Next, I discuss some applications I have worked on to help facilitate your development using gaming technology.

Games

A significant part of the work we do in CLST is to examine how gaming can be used to foster your leadership development. Included in the portal is a set of games that we use to form affinity groups that can work together to anonymously support each other's development. Also, I have included a set of six games that focus on enhancing your self-awareness as a leader. You also have access to some other games we have created focusing on leadership and organizational transformation by going to www.recurrenceinc.com. There you will find what we call gamulations, which combine the best aspects of gaming and simulations into one development process. The gamulations provide you with the opportunity to embed in game play by assuming various avatar roles in different types of organizations, for example, an airline. Each gamulation is built based on the research we have done with real organizations to examine how they have navigated through the states of change and transformation.

I have found in my work on leadership development that one of the most powerful agents for fostering your development as a leader is your colleagues or peers, whether they are in your organization or outside. In fact, in every face-to-face program, I always include a peer learning component in workshops, in between workshops and sometimes following the close of workshops to continue support for leadership development. The peer groups are taught some basic lessons focusing on coaching one another and then how to interact to facilitate each member's learning to lead through change processes.

With our gaming technology, I can put people into affinity groups based on different profiles that individuals produce based on the surveys described earlier. For example, after completing the short DR survey, I could place individuals into affinity groups based on similar levels of developmental readiness. Alternatively, I could also place individuals into more diverse readiness groups to take advantage of the fact that some members are further downstream in terms of their readiness to develop their leadership.

The gaming technology provides not only a platform for organizing these peer learning groups but also a mechanism to continue interacting in a fun way to enhance each other's development. Over time, I will continue to build out the sets of games available in the LD Navigator to support individual leadership development.

I want to emphasize that the LD Navigator portal is a place that we are continually building to support your development as you proceed through organizational change and transformation. The more individuals who opt into this peer learning community, the smarter the exchange of ideas will become, as we continue to seek ways to enhance the tools available to promote accelerating your leadership development.

In closing, the challenge of taking on change in your own leadership or with your team and organization is not a simple one, but hopefully the guidance provided in the previous chapters will make this a less formidable and, more important, a more understandable task. With the task before you, I will leave you with one of my favorite quotes to reflect on as you begin to write the new narrative for your journey, hoping that you reach the simplicity you seek on the other side of your development, as well as the development of your team and organization.

"I would not give a fig for the simplicity this side of complexity," said Oliver Wendell Holmes, "but I would give my life for the simplicity on the other side of complexity."

NOTES

PREAMBLE

1. Y. N. Harari. 2015. *Sapiens: A brief history of humankind.* New York: Harper Collins.

2. K. E. Weick and R. E. Quinn 1999. "Organizational change and development." *Annual Review of Psychology* 50: 361–386.

3. R. C. Wylie, P. J. Miller, S. S. Cowles, and A. W. Wilson. 1979. *The self-concept* (revised edition). Lincoln, NE: University of Nebraska Press.

4. R. G. Lord and K. J. Maher. 1994. *Leadership and Information Processing: Linking Perceptions and Organizational Performance.* New edition. New York: Routledge, Chapman Hall.

5. B. E. Ashforth and F. A. Mael. 1996. "Organizational identity and strategy as a context for the individual." *Advances in Strategic Management* 13: 19–64.

6. G. E. Kriener, E. Hollensbe, M. L. Sheep, B. R. Smith, and N. Kataria. 2015. "Elasticity and the dialectic tensions of organizational identity: How can we hold together while we are pulling apart." *Academy of Management Journal* 56: 981–1011; and D. A. Snow and L. Anderson. 1987. "Identity work among the homeless: The verbal construction and avowal of personal identities." *American Journal of Sociology,* 92: 1336–1371, page 1348.

7. M. B. Brewer and W. Gardner. 1996. "Who is this 'We'? Levels of collective identity and self representations." *Journal of Personality and Social Psychology* 71: 83.

CHAPTER 1

1. McKinsey Global Survey Results: Creating Organizational Transformations. 2008. Available at http://gsme.sharif.edu/~change/McKinsey%20Global%20Survey%20Results .pdf.

2. R. J. Thomas. 2008. "Crucibles of leadership development." *Sloan Management Review* 49 (Spring): 14–18.

3. "*Breaking Bad* is an American crime drama television series . . . [that] tells the story of Walter White (Bryan Cranston), a struggling high school chemistry teacher diagnosed

with inoperable lung cancer. Together with his former student Jesse Pinkman (Aaron Paul), White turns to a life of crime, producing and selling crystallized methamphetamine to secure his family's financial future before he dies, while navigating the dangers of the criminal world." Available at https://en.wikipedia.org/wiki/Breaking_Bad; Poniewozik, James. 2010. "Breaking Bad: TV's Best Thriller." *Time*. June 21; Bill Nevins. 2013. "Contemporary Western: An Interview with Vince Gilligan." *Local IQ*. March 27; and "'Breaking Bad' Finale: Lost Interviews with Bryan Cranston and Vince Gilligan." *The Daily Beast*. September 29, 2013.

4. The title for the TV show *Breaking Bad* comes from a southwest slang for raising hell, defying authority, and skirting the edges of the law. In the show, the hero uses his talents as a scientist to make money illegally. Our use of the reverse idea, breaking good, is meant to suggest that talents can be used to break with convention in a positive way. Posted by Jake Jawesome on September 27, 2011, at www.urbandictionary.com/define.php?term=Break%20Bad.

5. M. B. Brewer and W. Gardner. 1996. "Who is this 'We'? Levels of collective identity and self-representations." *Journal of Personality and Social Psychology* 71: 83–93.

6. J. E. Dutton and J. M. Dukerich. 1991. "Keeping an eye on the mirror: Image and identity in organizational adaptation." *Academy of Management Journal* 34: 517–554.

7. M. G. Pratt. 1998. "To be or not to be? Central questions in organizational identification." In D. A. Whetten and P. C. Godfrey (eds.), *Identity in organizations: Building theory through conversations*, 171–207. Thousand Oaks, CA: Sage.

8. S. B. Frampton, S. Guastellow, M. Naylor, S. Sheridan, and M. Johnston-Fleece. 2017. "Harnessing evidence and experience to change culture: A guiding framework for patient and family engaged care." *National Academy of Medicine Perspectives*: 1–38.

9. D. Ravasi and M. Schultz. 2006. "Responding to organizational identity threats: Exploring the role of organizational culture." *Academy of Management Journal* 49: 433–458.

10. M. Rosoff. June 25, 2015. "The buzzy new term at Microsoft is 'growth mindset'—Here's what it means." *Business Insider*. Available at www.businessinsider.com/satya-nadella-instilling-growth-mindset-at-microsoft-2015-6.

11. Ibid.

12. B. J. Avolio, C. Patterson, and B. Baker, 2015. *Alaska Airlines: Navigating change*. Ontario, CA: Ivey Publishing.

13. A. H. Van de Ven and M. S. Poole. 1995. "Explaining development and change in organizations." *Academy of Management Review* 20: 510–540; and H. Tsoukas and R. Chia. 2002. "On organizational becoming: Rethinking organizational change." *Organization Science*, 13: 567–582.

14. M. Tushman and E. Romanelli. 1985. "Organizational evolutions: A metamorphosis model of convergence and reorientation." In L. L. Cummings and B. M. Staw (eds.), *Research in Organizational Behavior*, 171–222. Greenwich, CT: JAI Press; E. Romanelli and M. L. Tushman. 1994. "Organizational transformation as punctuated equilibrium: An empirical test." *Academy of Management Journal* 37: 1141–1166; T. Peters and R. Waterman. 1982. *In Search of Excellence: Lessons from America's Best-Run Companies*. New York: Harper and Row; and J. Kotter. 1996. *Leading change*. Boston, MA: Harvard Business Press.

15. M. G. Pratt and P. O. Foreman. 2006. "Classifying managerial responsibilities to multiple organizational identities." *Academy of Management Review* 20: 18–42.

16. B. J. Avolio. 2017. "The leadership development blueprint." *CLST Briefings*, vol. 1. Seattle: Center for Leadership and Strategic Thinking, University of Washington; B. J. Avolio.

2011. *Full range leadership development*. Thousand Oaks, CA: Sage; J. B. Avey, B. J. Avolio, C. D. Crossley, and F. Luthans. 2009. "Psychological ownership: Theoretical extensions, measurement and relation to work outcomes." *Journal of Organizational Behavior* 30: 173–191; and J. L. Pierce, T. Kostova, and K. T. Dirks. 2001. "Toward a theory of psychological ownership in organizations." *Academy of Management Review* 26: 298–310.

17. T. Reay, E. Goodrick, S. B. Waldorff, and A. Casebeer. 2017. "Getting leopards to change their spots: Co-creating a new professional identity." *Academy of Management Journal* 60: 1043–1079.

CHAPTER 2

1. T. Cosgrove. 2013. *The Cleveland Clinic way: Lessons in excellence from one of the world's leading healthcare organizations*. New York: McGraw-Hill.

2. Business Insider. "Elon Musk Uses This Ancient Critical-Thinking Strategy to Outsmart Everybody Else." Available at www.businessinsider.com/elon-musk-first-principles-2015-1.

3. "How Elon Musk Thinks: The First Principles Method." Available at http://99u.com/workbook/20482/how-elon-musk-thinks-the-first-principles-method.

4. Kurt Lewin. 1989. *Organizational development: Theory, practice, and research*, 3rd edition. Chicago: Irwin Press, page 87.

5. J. Kotter and H. Rathgeber. 2006. *Our iceberg is melting: Changing and succeeding under adverse conditions*. Boston, MA: Harvard Business Press.

6. D. Conner. 2012. *The real story of the burning platform*. Retrieved on August 15, 2012, from www.connerpartners.com/frameworks-and-processes/the-real-story-of-the-burning-platform.

7. C. Heath and D. Heath. 2010. *Switch: How to change things when change is hard*. Boston, MA: Crown Publishing Group.

8. M. A. Hogg and D. J. Terry. 2000. "Social identity and self-categorization processes in organizational contexts." *Academy of Management Review* 25(1): 121–140; and B. E. Ashforth. 1998. "Becoming: How does the process of identification unfold?" In D. A. Whetten and P. C. Godfrey (Eds.), *Identity in organizations: Building theory through conversations*, 213–222. Thousand Oaks, CA: Sage.

9. B. J. Avolio and F. Luthans. 2006. *High impact leader: Moments matter in authentic leadership development*. New York: McGraw-Hill; and B. J. Avolio. 2005. *Leadership development in balance: Made/Born*. Mahwah, NJ: Erlbaum & Associates.

10. E. Crowe and E. T. Higgins. 1997. "Regulatory focus and strategic inclinations: Promotion and prevention in decision-making." *Organizational Behavior and Human Decision Processes* 69: 117–132.

11. D. A. Gioia and J. B. Thomas. 1996. "Identity, image, and issue interpretation: Sensemaking during strategic change in academia." *Administrative Science Quarterly* 41: 370–403; and J. Ford and L. Ford. 1995. "The role of conversations in producing intentional change in organizations." *Academy of Management Review* 20: 541–570.

12. D. Ravasi and M. Schultz. 2006. "Responding to organizational identity threats: Exploring the role of organizational culture." *Academy of Management Journal* 49: 433–458.

13. A. Stuart and D. A. Whetten. 1985. "Organizational identity." *Research in Organizational Behavior* 7: 263–293.

14. B. E. Ashforth. 2001. Role transitions in organizational life: An identity-based perspective. Mahwah, NJ: Lawrence Erlbaum Associates; and B. E. Ashforth, S. H. Harrison, and K. G. Corley. 2008. "Identification in organizations: An examination of four fundamental questions." *Journal of Management* 34: 325–374.

15. N. Levy. 2016. "It's day one at Day One: Amazon opens second huge office building at new Seattle campus." Geekwire, November 7. Available at www.geekwire.com/2016/its -day-one-at-day-one-amazon-opens-second-huge-office-building-in-new-seattle-campus.

16. S. Albert and D. A. Whetton. 1985. "Organizational identity," in L. L. Cummings and B. M. Staw (Eds.), *Research in Organizational Behavior* 7: 263–293.

17. B. Burnes and P. Jackson, P. 2011. "Success and failure in organizational change: An exploration of the role of values." *Journal of Change Management* 11: 133–162.

18. M. B. Brewer and W. Gardner. 1996. "Who is this 'We'? Levels of collective identity and self representations." *Journal of Personality and Social Psychology* 71: 83.

19. Daphna Oyserman and Hazel Rose Markus. 1998. "Self as social representation." *The Psychology of the Social*: 107–125.

20. R. E. Johnson, C. Selenta, and R. G. Lord. 2006. "When organizational justice and the self-concept meet: Consequences for the organization and its members." *Organizational Behavior and Human Decision Processes* 99: 175–201.

21. K. E. Weick and R. E. Quinn 1999. "Organizational change and development." *Annual Review of Psychology* 50: 361–386; and K. G. Corley and D. A. Gioia. 2004. "Identity ambiguity and change in the wake of a corporate spin-off." *Administrative Science Quarterly* 49: 173–208.

22. K. G. Corley and D. A. Gioia. 2004. "Identity ambiguity and change in the wake of a corporate spin-off." *Administrative Science Quarterly* 49: 173–208.

23. G. E. Kriener, E. Hollensbe, M. L. Sheep, B. R. Smith, and N. Kataria. 2015. "Elasticity and the dialectic tensions of organizational identity: How can we hold together while we are pulling apart?" *Academy of Management Journal* 56: 981–1011.

24. "History: Special Forces Green Beret." Retrieved on February 5, 2016, from www .groups.sfahq.com/sf_heraldry/beret/history.htm.

25. M. Hammond, R. Clapp-Smith, and M. Palanski. 2017. "Beyond (just) the workplace: A theory of leader development across multiple domains." *Academy of Management Review* 42: 481–498.

26. G. E. Kriener, E. Hollensbe, M. L. Sheep, B. R. Smith, and N. Kataria. 2015. "Elasticity and the dialectic tensions of organizational identity: How can we hold together while we are pulling apart?" *Academy of Management Journal* 56: 981–1011.

27. R. S. Onorato and J. C. Turner. 2004. "Fluidity in the self-concept: The shift from personal to social identity." *European Journal of Social Psychology* 34: 257–278; M. H. Kuhn and T. S. McPartland. 1954. "An empirical investigation of self-attitudes." *American Sociological Review* 19: 68–76; and W. J. McGuire and C. V. McGuire. 1988. "Content and process in the experience of self." *Advances in Experimental Social Psychology* 21: 97–144.

28. M. B. Brewer and W. Gardner. 1996. "Who is this 'We'? Levels of collective identity and self-representations." *Journal of Personality and Social Psychology* 71: 83–93.

29. J. L. Pierce, T. Kostova, and K. T. Dirks. 2003. "The state of psychological ownership: Integrating and extending a century of research." *Review of General Psychology* 7: 84–107.

30. J. B. Avey, B. J. Avolio, C. D. Crossley, and F. Luthans. 2009. "Psychological ownership: Theoretical extensions, measurement and relation to work outcomes." *Journal of Organizational Behavior* 30: 173–191.

31. G. E. Kriener, E. Hollensbe, M. L. Sheep, B. R. Smith, and N. Kataria. 2015. "Elasticity and the dialectic tensions of organizational identity: How can we hold together while we are pulling apart?" *Academy of Management Journal* 56: 981–1011.

CHAPTER 3

1. S. L. Brown and K. M. Eisenhardt. 1997. "The art of continuous change: Linking complexity theory and time-paced evolution in relentlessly shifting organizations." *Administrative Science Quarterly* 42: 1–34; R. Greenwood and C. R. Hinings. 1996. "Understanding radical organizational change: Bringing together the old and the new institutionalism." *Academy of Management Review* 21: 1022–1054; and J. Kimberly and R. Miles. 1980. *The Organizational Life Cycle.* San Francisco: Jossey-Bass.

2. L. A. Isabella. 1990. "Evolving interpretations as a change unfolds: How managers construe key organizational events." *Academy of Management Journal* 33: 7–41.

3. M. L. Besharov. 2014. "The relational ecology of identification: How organizational identification emerges when individuals hold divergent values." *Academy of Management Journal* 57: 1485–1512.

4. The idea that a state such as excitement can scale in such a way that it has parallel forms in an individual, a team, a department, and an entire organization (that is, across micro-, meso-, and macrounits of analysis) is called isomorphism. K. J. Klein and S. W. J. Kozlowski. 2000. "From micro to meso: Critical steps in conceptualizing and conducting multilevel research." *Organizational Research Methods* 3: 211–236.

5. S. T. Fiske and S. E. Taylor. 1984. *Social cognition.* Reading, MA: Addison-Wesley; C. L. Guarana and M. Hernandez. 2016. "Identified ambivalence: When cognitive conflicts can help individuals overcome cognitive traps." *Journal of Applied Psychology* 101: 1013–1029; and D. Kahneman. 2011. *Thinking, fast and slow.* New York: Farrar, Straus and Giroux.

6. Robert S. Kaplan and D. P. Norton. 1992. "The balanced scorecard: Measures that drive performance." *Harvard Business Review* 70(1, January–February): 71–79.

7. D. M. Green and J. A. Swets. 1966. *Signal detection theory and psychophysics.* New York: Wiley.

8. A. Extance. 2016. "How DNA could store all of the world's data." *Nature* 537: 22–24.

9. M. A. Hitt, K. T. Haynes, and R. Serpa. 2010. "Strategic leadership for the 21st century." *Business Horizons* 53: 437–444.

10. J. A. Schumpeter. 2013. *Capitalism, socialism and democracy.* New York: Routledge.

11. D. Barton, D. Horbarth, and M. Kipping. 2016. *Re-imagining capitalism.* New York: Oxford University Press.

12. J. Battilana and T. Casciaro. 2012. "Overcoming resistance to organizational change: Strong ties and affective cooptation." *Management Science* 59: 819–836.

13. A. A. Armenakis and S. G. Harris. 2002. "Crafting a change message to create transformational readiness." *Journal of Organizational Change Management* 15: 169–183.

14. L. A. Isabella. 1990. "Evolving interpretations as a change unfolds: How managers construe key organizational events." *Academy of Management Journal* 33: 7–41.

15. T. Reay, E. Goodrick, S. B. Waldorff, and A. Casebeer. 2017. "Getting leopards to change their spots: Co-creating a new professional role identity." *Academy of Management Journal* 60: 1043–1070.

16. H. Ibarra and R. Barbulescu. 2016. "Identity as narrative: Prevalence, effectiveness, and consequences of narrative identity work in macro work role transitions." *Academy of Management Journal* 35: 135–154.

17. S. Kunish, J. M. Bartunek, and J. Mueller. 2017. "Time in strategic change research." *Academy of Management Annals* 11: 1005–1064.

CHAPTER 4

1. A. H. Van de Ven and M. S. Poole. 1995. "Explaining development and change in organizations." *Academy of Management Review* 20: 510–540.

2. K. D. Elsbach and R. M. Kramer. 1996. "Members' responses to organizational identity threats: Encountering and countering the business week rankings." *Administrative Science Quarterly* 41(3): 442–476.

3. J. M. Bartunek, J. Balogun, and B. Do. 2011. "Considering planned change anew: Stretching large group interventions strategically, emotionally and meaningfully." *The Academy of Management Annals* 5: 1–52; J. Bartunek, D. Rousseau, J. Rudolph, and J. DePalma. 2006. "On the receiving end: Sensemaking, emotion, and assessments of an organizational change initiated by others." *Journal of Applied Behavioral Science* 42: 182–206; and D. Gioia and K. Chittipeddi. 1991. "Sensemaking and sensegiving in strategic change initiation." *Strategic Management Journal* 12(6): 433–448.

4. P. Barr and A. Huff. 1997. "Seeing isn't believing: Understanding diversity in the timing of strategic response." *Journal of Management Studies* 34: 337–370.

5. Z. Carter. 2016. "The legal problem that could crash Uber." Available at www.huffington post.com/entry/legal-problem-could-crash-uber_us_5718d485e4b0479c59d714f6.

6. P. Mosendz. 2014. "Amazon has basically no competition among online booksellers." May 30. Available at www.theatlantic.com/business/archive/2014/05/amazon-has-basically -no-competition-among-online-booksellers/371917/.

7. M. Gladwell. 2000. *The tipping point: How little things can make a big difference.* Boston: Little, Brown, p. 12.

8. K. Weick. 1995. *Sensemaking in organizations.* Thousand Oaks, CA: Sage; K. Weick. 2001. *Making sense of the organization.* Hoboken, NJ: Wiley-Blackwell; and K. Weick and R. Quinn. 1999. "Organizational change and development." *Annual Review of Psychology* 50: 361–386.

9. S. Sonenshein. 2010. "We're changing—or are we? Untangling the role of progressive, regressive, and stability narratives during strategic change implementation." *Academy of Management Journal* 53: 477–512; and R. Lines, M. Selart, B. Espedal, and S. Johansen. 2005. "The production of trust during organizational change." *Journal of Change Management* 5: 221–245.

10. P. Dawson and D. Buchanan. 2005. "The way it really happened: Competing narratives in the political process of technological change." *Human Relations* 58: 845–865; J. Ford and L. Ford. 1995. "The role of conversations in producing intentional change in organizations." *Academy of Management Review* 20: 541–570; and J. Ford and L. Ford. 2008.

"Conversational profiles: A tool for altering the conversational patterns of change managers." *Journal of Applied Behavioral Science* 44: 445–467.

11. S. H. Wagner, C. P. Parker, and N. D. Christiansen. 2003. "Employees that think and act like owners: Effects of ownership beliefs and behaviors on organizational effectiveness." *Personnel Psychology* 56: 847–871.

12. J. G. March. 1991. "Exploration and exploitation in organizational learning." *Organization Science* 2: 71–87.

13. C. Argyris. 1993. *Knowledge for action: A guide to overcoming barriers to change.* San Francisco, CA: Jossey-Bass; and L. A. Isabella. 1990. "Evolving interpretations as a change unfolds: How managers construe key organizational events." *Academy of Management Journal* 33: 7–41.

14. N. DiFonzo and P. Bordia. 2007. "Trust and organizational rumor transmission." In N. DiFonzo and P. Bordia (Eds.), *Rumor psychology: Social and organizational approaches*: 185–204. Washington, DC: American Psychological Association.

15. B. J. Avolio and F. Luthans. 2006. *High impact leader: Moments matter in authentic leadership development.* New York: McGraw-Hill.

16. P. Ricoeur. 1988. *Time and narrative*, Vol. 3. Chicago: University of Chicago Press.

17. H. Ibarra and R. Barbulescu. 2016. "Identity as narrative: Prevalence, effectiveness, and consequences of narrative identity work in macro work role transitions." *Academy of Management Journal* 35: 135–154; and D. P. McAdams. 1999. "Personal narratives and the life story." In L. Pervin and O. John (Eds.), *Handbook of personality: Theory and research*, 2nd ed.: 478–500. New York: Guilford Press.

18. J. Howard-Grenville, M. L. Metzger, and A. D. Meyer. 2013. "Rekindling the flame: Processes of identity resurrection." *Academy of Management Journal* 56(1): 113–136.

CHAPTER 5

1. An example of a true field experiment is reported in D. Eden. 1985. "Team development: A true field experiment at three levels of rigor." *Journal of Applied Psychology* 70: 94–100.

2. *Wall Street Journal.* December 17, 2016, page A.

3. C. Bartel and R. Garud. 2009. "The role of narratives in sustaining organizational innovation." *Organization Science* 20(1): 107–117; B. Burnes and P. Jackson. 2011. "Success and failure in organizational change: An exploration of the role of values." *Journal of Change Management* 11: 133–162; and R. Daft and K. Weick. 1984. "Toward a model of organizations as interpretation systems." *Academy of Management Review* 9: 284–295.

4. R. Greenwood and C. Hinings. 1996. "Understanding radical organizational change: Bringing together the old and the new institutionalism." *Academy of Management Review* 21: 1022–1054; and M. Hammer and J. Champy. 1993. *Reengineering the corporation: A manifesto for business revolution.* New York: Harper Business.

5. C. S. Dweck. 2016. *Mindset: The new psychology of success.* New York: Penguin Random House.

6. J. Ford and L. Ford. 1995. "The role of conversations in producing intentional change in organizations." *Academy of Management Review* 20: 541–570; D. M. Berwick, D. R. Calkins, C. J. McCannon, and A. D. Hackbarth. 2006. "The 100,000 lives campaign." *JAMA: The Journal of the American Medical Association* 295(3): 324–327.

7. Y. Berson and B. Avolio. 2004. "Transformational leadership and the dissemination of organizational goals: A case study of a telecommunication firm." *Leadership Quarterly* 15: 625–646; W. Bommer, G. Rich, and R. Rubin. 2005. "Changing attitudes about change: Longitudinal effects of transformational leader behavior on employee cynicism about organizational change." *Journal of Organizational Behavior* 26(7): 733–753; B. Burnes, B. and R. By. 2012. "Leadership and change: The case for greater ethical clarity." *Journal of Business Ethics*, 108(2): 239–252; R. Daft and K. Weick. 1984. "Toward a model of organizations as interpretation systems." *Academy of Management Review* 9(2): 284–295; and R. Eisenbach, K. Watson, and R. Pillai. 1999. "Transformational leadership in the context of organizational change." *Journal of Organizational Change Management* 12: 80–88.

8. B. J. Avolio, C. Patterson, and B. Baker, B. 2015. *Alaska Airlines: Navigating Change*. London. Ontario, Canada: Ivey Publishing.

9. R. Kegan and L. L. Lahey. 2009. *Immunity to change: How to overcome it and unlock the potential in you*. Boston, MA: Harvard Business Publishing.

10. J. J. Pierce and I. Jussila. 2011. *Psychological ownership and the organizational context: Theory, research evidence, and application*. Northampton, MA: Edward Elgar Publishing.

11. B. J. Avolio. 2011. *Full range leadership development*, 2nd edition. Thousand Oaks, CA: Sage.

CHAPTER 6

1. Steven Mintz. "Avoiding the 'ethical slippery slope': How to build ethics into an organization." July 17, 2014. Available at www.workplaceethicsadvice.com/2014/07/avoiding -the-ethical-slippery-slope.html.

2. H. Martin. 2011, September 10. "10 years after 9/11, the airline industry is looking up." *Los Angeles Times*. Retrieved from http://articles.latimes.com/2011/sep/10/business /la-fi-911-cover-sept11-airlines-20110911.

3. "Why did Howard Schultz leave Starbucks, only to return eight years later?" March 30, 2015. *Investopedia*. Retrieved from www.investopedia.com/ask/answers/033015/why-did -howard-schultz-leave-starbucks-only-return-eight-years-later.asp.

4. "Starbucks to close all U.S. stores for training: Three-hour shutdown designed to educate, energize 135,000 workers." February 26, 2008. NBCNEWS.com. Retrieved from www.nbcnews.com/id/23351151/ns/business-us_business/t/starbucks-close-all-us-stores -training/#.WKCMm28rLM0.

5. R. W. Stewart (Ed.). 2005. "Rebuilding the army: Vietnam to Desert Storm." In *American military history. Volume II: The United States Army in a global era, 1917–2003*, 369. Washington, DC: Center of Military History, United States Army.

6. Ibid.: 370.

7. M. Egan. September 9, 2016. "5,300 Wells Fargo employees fired over 2 million phony accounts." CNNMoney. Retrieved from http://money.cnn.com/2016/09/08/investing/wells -fargo-created-phony-accounts-bank-fees/.

8. A. Zavyalovam, M. D. Pfarrer, R. K. Reger, and T. D. Hubbard. 2016. "Reputation as a benefit and burden? How stakeholders' organizational identification affects the role of reputation following a negative event." *Academy of Management Journal* 59: 253–276.

9. B. Burnes and P. Jackson. 2011. "Success and failure in organizational change: An exploration of the role of values." *Journal of Change Management* 11: 133–162; and E. Dent

and S. Goldberg. 1999. "Challenging resistance to change." *Journal of Applied Behavioral Science* 35(1): 25–41.

10. J. Aleccia. June 27, 2011. "Nurse's suicide highlights twin tragedies of medical errors." NBCNews. Retrieved from www.nbcnews.com/id/43529641/ns/health-health_care/t /nurses-suicide-highlights-twin-tragedies-medical-errors/#.WKClq28rLM0.

11. M. Hammer. 2004. "Deep change: How operational innovation can transform your company." *Harvard Business Review* 82: 84–93; M. Hammer and J. Champy. 1993. *Reengineering the corporation: A manifesto for business revolution.* New York: Harper Business; and B. Hedberg. 1981. "How organizations learn and unlearn." In P. C. Nystrom and W. H. Starbuck (Eds.), *Handbook of Organizational Design.* New York: Oxford University Press.

12. B. J. Avolio and F. Luthans. 2006. *High impact leader: Moments matter in authentic leadership development.* New York: McGraw-Hill.

13. R. Greenleaf. 2002. *Servant leadership: A journey into the nature of legitimate power and greatness,* 25th edition. New York: Paulist Press.

14. F. L. Luthans, B. J. Avolio, and C. Youseff. 2015. *Psychological capital and beyond.* Oxford, UK: Oxford University Press.

15. A. Edmonson. 1999. "Psychological safety and learning behaviors in work teams." *Administrative Science Quarterly* 44: 350–383.

16. B. J. Avolio. 2011. *Full range leadership development,* 2nd edition. Thousand Oaks, CA: Sage.

CHAPTER 7

1. J. B. Avey, B. J. Avolio, C. D. Crossley, and F. Luthans. 2009. "Psychological ownership: Theoretical extensions, measurement and relation to work outcomes." *Journal of Organizational Behavior* 30: 173–191.

2. B. E. Ashforth and M. Fred. 1989. "Social identity theory and the organization." *Academy of Management Review* 14: 20–39.

3. The Editor, December 9, 2008. Available at http://blog.martinig.ch/software -development/my-10-favorites-agile-project-management-articles/.

4. J. Kolko, 2015. "Design thinking comes of age." *Harvard Business Review*, September: 66–71.

5. B. Avolio. February 22, 2013, TEDx. Available at www.youtube.com/watch?v =9clFG5yBWEA.

6. J. V. Bittner and H. Heidemeier. 2013. "Competitive mindsets, creativity, and the role of regulatory focus." *Thinking Skills and Creativity* 9: 59–68; and A. H. Van de Ven and S, Poole. 1995. "Explaining development and change in organizations." *Academy of Management Review* 20: 510–540.

7. R. T. Keller. 2012. "Predicting the performance and innovativeness of scientists and engineers." *Journal of Applied Psychology* 97: 225–233.

8. N. Wasserman. 2012. *The founders dilemma.* Princeton, NJ: Princeton University Press.

9. B. J. Avolio and F. Luthans. 2006. *High impact leader: Moments matter in authentic leadership development.* New York: McGraw-Hill.

10. P. Tracey and N. Phillips. 2016. "Managing the consequences of organizational stigmatization: Identity work in a social enterprise." *Academy of Management Journal* 59: 740–765.

11. Ben Mutzabaugh. December 19, 2016. "'Frenemies' no more? Delta, Alaska Air to terminate partnership." *USA Today*.

12. S. W. J. Kozlowski and D. R. Ilgen. 2006. "Enhancing the effectiveness of work groups and teams." *Psychological Science in the Public Interest* 7: 77–124.

13. A. G. Tekleab, N. R. Quigley, and P. E. Tesluk. 2009. "A longitudinal study of team conflict, conflict management, cohesion and team effectiveness." *Group & Organization Management* 34: 170–205.

14. R. Van Dick, D. Van Knippenberg, S. Hägele, Y. Guillaume, and F. Brodbeck. 2008. "Group diversity and group identification: The moderating role of diversity beliefs." *Human Relations* 61: 1463–1492.

15. B. J. Avolio. 2011. *Full range leadership development*, 2nd edition. Thousand Oaks, CA: Sage.

16. W. L. Gardner, B. J. Avolio, and F. Walumbwa. 2006. *Authentic leadership theory and practice: Origins, effects and development.* Amsterdam: Elsevier JAI Press; B. J. Avolio and F. Luthans. 2006. *High impact leader: Moments matter in authentic leadership development.* New York: McGraw-Hill.

17. K. E. Weick. 1995. *Sensemaking in organizations.* Thousand Oaks, CA: Sage.

18. J. E. Dutton, J. M. Dukerich, and C. V. Harquail. 1994. "Organizational images and member identification." *Administrative Science Quarterly* 39: 239–263.

CHAPTER 8

1. M. Javidan. May 19, 2010. Available at https://hbr.org/2010/05/bringing-the-global-mindset-to.html; B. Buechal. Insights @ IMD 2014 No. 32. Available at www.imd.org/research/publications/upload/32-Global-minsets-27-01-2014.pdf; R. P. Weiss. 2015. "The global mindset leader: An interview with i4cp's Jay Jamrog." *Association for Talent Management.* Available at www.td.org/Publications/Blogs/Learning-Executive-Blog/2015/07/The-Global-Mindset-Leader-An-Interview-with-I4cps-Jay-Jamrog; E. Meyer. 2014. "Navigating the cultural minefield." *Harvard Business Review* May: 119–123; T. Khanna. 2014. "Cultural intelligence." *Harvard Business Review* September: 59–68; and S. L. Cohen. 2012. "Effective global leadership requires a global mindset." *Industrial and Commercial Training* Volume 42: 3–10.

CHAPTER 9

1. G. E. Kriener, E. Hollensbe, M. L. Sheep, B. R. Smith, and N. Kataria, N. 2015. "Elasticity and the dialectic tensions of organizational identity: How can we hold together while we are pulling apart?" *Academy of Management Journal* 56: 981–1011.

2. B. J. Avolio. 2005. *Leadership development in balance: Made/Born.* Mahwah, NJ: Erlbaum & Associates.

3. B. J. Avolio. 2017. *The leadership development blueprint.* Seattle: Center for Leadership and Strategic Thinking, University of Washington.

4. B. M. Bass and B. M. Bass. 2008. *The Bass handbook of leadership*, 3rd edition. New York: Free Press.

CHAPTER 10

1. B. J. Avolio and S. T. Hannah. 2008. "Developmental readiness: Accelerating leadership development." *Consulting Psychology Journal* 60: 331–347.

2. R. D. Arvey, Z. Zhang, B. J. Avolio, and R. Kruger. 2007. "Understanding the developmental and genetic determinants of leadership among females." *Journal of Applied Psychology* 9: 693–706.

3. Source documents for Development Readiness survey: S. B. Button, J. E. Mathieu, and D. M. Zajac. 1996. "Goal orientation in organizational research: A conceptual and empirical foundation." *Organizational Behavior and Human Decision Processes* 67: 26–48; J. D. Campbell, P. D. Trapnell, S. J. Heine, and I. M. Katz. 1996. "Self-concept clarity: Measurement, personality correlates, and cultural boundaries." *Journal of Personality and Social Psychology* 70: 141–156; K. Y, Chan and R. Drasgow. 2001. "Toward a theory of individual differences and leadership: Understanding the motive-to-lead." *Journal of Applied Psychology* 86: 481–498; Mark H. Davis. 1980. "A multi-dimensional approach to individual differences in empathy." *JSAS Catalog of Selected Documents in Psychology* 10: 85–104; J. J. Gross and O. P. John. 2003. "Individual differences in two emotion regulation processes: Implications for affect, relationships, and well-being." *Journal of Personality and Social Psychology* 85: 348–362; S. T. Hannah. 2006. "Agentic leadership efficacy: Test of a new construct and model for leadership development and performance." Lincoln: University of Nebraska-Lincoln. Dissertation Abstracts International; and G. Schraw, and R. S. Dennison. 1994. "Assessing meta-cognitive awareness." *Contemporary Educational Psychology* 19: 460–475.

4. S. T. Hannah, B. J. Avolio, F. Luthans, and P. D. Harms. 2008. "Leadership efficacy: Review and future directions." *The Leadership Quarterly* 19: 669–692; and S. T. Hannah, B. J. Avolio, F. O. Walumbwa, and A. Chan. 2012. "Leader self and means efficacy: A multi-component approach." *Organizational Behavior and Human Decision Processes* 118: 143–161.

5. J. B. Avey, B. J. Avolio, C. D. Crossley, and . Luthans. 2008. "Psychological ownership: Theoretical extensions, measurement and relation to work outcomes." *Journal of Organizational Behavior* 29: 1–19.

INDEX